# IMPERIAL MASQUERADE

# IMPERIAL MASQUERADE

## LEWIS H. LAPHAM

GROVE WEIDENFELD • NEW YORK

Published by Grove Weidenfeld
A division of Wheatland Corporation
841 Broadway
New York, NY 10003-4793

Published in Canada by General Publishing Company, Ltd.

Library of Congress Cataloging-in-Publication Data

Lapham, Lewis H.
    Imperial masquerade

    Collection of essays published 1980–1989.
    1. United States—Civilization—1970–
2. United States—Politics and government—1981–1989.
I. Title.
E169.12.L343      1990          973.927          89-16550
ISBN 1-55584-449-9

Manufactured in the United States of America

Printed on acid-free paper

Designed by Helene Berinsky

First Edition 1990

10  9  8  7  6  5  4  3  2  1

*For*
*Delphina, Winston, and Andrew*

# CONTENTS

# II  POLITICS & ECONOMICS

## III   STATES AND GOVERNMENTS

# PREFACE

**W**HEN CAESAR AUGUSTUS was dying at Nola in A.D. 14, he took comfort in the knowledge that he had ably performed his role as the first emperor of what he knew to be the gerrymandered stage play of the Roman Empire. To the courtiers nervously attending the ceremony of his death, he phrased his last words as a command: "I've played my part well. Dismiss me with applause."

President Ronald Reagan could have awarded himself the same review when he retired, in triumph and with a $7 million book deal, to California. For almost the whole of his eight years in the White House he had given a brilliant rendition of the American presidency, playing the part as if it were the romantic lead in a musical comedy—smiling at the cameras, tipping his cap, delighting the matinee crowd with red, white, and blue variations on the melody of "America the Beautiful." He exemplified the spirit of an age of mock-heroic empire, and he seemed to have such a good time on the stage of office that it was easy to forgive him not only his occasional lapses of memory but also the blundering venality of his friends.

It was clear from the beginning that Mr. Reagan wasn't interested in bad news. Neither were his audiences. In the campaign of 1980 Mr. Reagan wholeheartedly embraced the benign deism of an American business oligarchy that didn't wish to worry itself with tiresome questions about what was right and what was wrong, or what was true and what was false. His album of golden commonplaces conformed to the standards of moral and intellectual insignificance that were to become synonymous with the art and politics of the decade. By 1980 Mr. Reagan's countrymen no longer expected their politicians to argue a coherent system of thought, or to bring to office anything other than an amateur's amiable guesses about the enigmas of political economy and foreign affairs. His audiences understood that Mr. Reagan's political ideas, which were as chaotic as his economic theories, didn't matter as much as his instincts, his prejudices, and his sentiments. Here at last was an accommodating man at ease in the haze of gossip and the company of scoundrels, whose best hope for the nation he expressed in his promise that the United States would "above all" continue to be a country "where someone always could get rich." It was the only promise Mr. Reagan kept, at least for those of his countrymen who seized upon his revisions of the tax laws and regulatory codes as a heaven-sent chance to raid the Federal treasury.

Mr. Reagan presumably acquired his sympathy for the principles of moral and economic laissez-faire during his novitiate in Hollywood, where circumstances didn't permit the drawing of overly fine or un-American ethical distinctions. Make-believe armies came and went and so did screenwriters under option to the muse of cocaine; every year somebody one knew committed suicide or fraud, and the criminal syndicates took their customary percentage of the distribution deals. But such was the way of the world, and what was a fellow to do about it? It was also true that every year the Rose Bowl parade renewed the miracle of flower arrangement, and Jerry Lewis raised another $10 million for children afflicted with muscular dystrophy. If an actor knew what was good for his career, he did his best with whatever scripts were offered him and didn't ask boring questions about where the studio raised the production money or how the director amused himself on Sunday afternoons in Malibu.

The lesson implicit in so complacent an ethic worked to Mr. Reagan's advantage in Washington. He had no trouble accepting the rule of going along to get along, and he didn't ask boring questions about people who were old, sick, illiterate, or poor. Ignoring anything he didn't choose to see, Mr. Reagan brought to the presidency the excitements of new money, the comforts of a vacant conscience, and the opulent style of a wedding reception at the Beverly Hills Hotel.

As an existential proposition the Reagan administration presented itself as the triumph of an idea whose moment had already passed. The President declared his satisfaction with what Richard Hofstadter once called "a democracy of cupidity rather than a democracy in fraternity," and he proclaimed a utopia for people already rich enough to afford the club dues.

More than once during Mr. Reagan's terms in office I was struck by the thought that his administration meant to reenact the pageant of the 1960s, but this time with an older cast, a Republican chorus line, and a libretto composed by General Alexander Haig, Lieutenant Colonel Oliver North, and the late William Casey. It was the wish to regain the vigor of lost youth that imparted to Mr. Reagan's presidency the curious atmosphere of comic opera. Despite my best efforts to appreciate the theories of supply-side economics or the communist menace in Nicaragua, I was left with the impression that the country was being governed by a crowd of bond salesmen traipsing through the corridors of the State and Defense departments in costumes borrowed from a production of *The Merry Widow* or *The Pirates of Penzance*. The impression resisted my best efforts to take seriously the hundreds of thousands of pages of burbling praise published in *Time* and *Newsweek* under the rubrics of the conservative awakening. No matter how often I listened to one of Mr. Reagan's apologists (Pat Buchanan, say, or Don Regan) explain the grave questions of policy at risk in Detroit or the Persian Gulf, I couldn't help but remember that I was listening to people who formed their view of the world from their reading of Zane Grey, Tom Clancy, and Louis L'Amour. Most of them knew little or nothing of American history or constitutional law, and few of them could speak a foreign language or locate Czechoslovakia on the map. In between press conferences they helped themselves to the public money in the same way that cast members of a theatrical company playing summer stock in Westport, Connecticut, ravaged the buffet table on the governor's lawn.

Their ignorance did them no harm. Actors get paid to read the scripts, not write the dialogue, and Mr. Reagan and his companions had been hired to comfort their audiences with the good news that America was still—despite the need to borrow so much money from the Japanese—rich enough to do anything it pleased. For eight years the production received the unstinting praise of the media and an enthusiastic majority of the popular vote. Even so, I never could escape the suspicion that I was being asked to applaud the performance of an imperial masquerade. I had much the same feeling about the entertainments staged in New York by real-estate operators and Wall Street abritrageurs eager to buy a place in society, and I often found it hard to tell the difference between Caspar Weinberger's geopolitical theory, the realpolitik of Michael Milken, and Jay McInerney's minimalist despair. The *nouveau riche* sensibility presiding in Washington was reflected in the aesthetics of the art and the literary markets as well as in the sale of junk bonds. The gaudiness of Mr. Reagan's Fourth of July speeches matched the glitter of conspicuous consumption loose in the streets of New York and Los Angeles, and Mr. Reagan's staging of bombing raids over the Libyan coast found its patriotic analogue in Donald Trump's fireworks displays over the casinos at Atlantic City.

During the Reagan era I understood that it was proper to conceive the world as so much painted scenery, as light as canvas and as easily shifted as the corporations transferred between continents on the signing of a leveraged buyout deal. At the beginning of the decade Mr. Reagan described the Soviet Union as an evil empire; by the end of the decade he was walking arm in arm with Mikhail Gorbachev through the streets of Moscow. A similar feeling of weightlessness governed the workings of the economy and the arrangement of celebrity merchandise in the show windows of the media.

The essays and sketches collected in this book take as their common text the attitudes, suppositions, and habits of mind that sustained the spirit of an age. As has been said, it was an age of mock-heroic empire, an age defined by gesture and the play of images, by its moral emptiness and its delight in the wonder of money, and by what Augustus would have recognized as the eagerness of its wish for kings.

PART I

# ARTS AND LETTERS

# THE THEATER OF
# THE NEWS

*I really look with commiseration over the great body of
my fellow citizens who, reading newspapers, live and die
in the belief that they have known something of what has
been passing in the world in their time.*
                                        —Harry Truman

*I don't hold with high falutin' talk . . . I'm a
newspaperman. I tell stories.*
                                        —Derek Jameson, former editor,
                                        the *Daily Express* (London)

IN NEW YORK these days the lawyers advising book publishers on
libel matters ask for revisions in the fiction. The lawyers no longer
make much of a distinction between what is true, what might be
true, what a plaintiff will say is true. If the author of a lascivious
novel has portrayed an actress living in California, and if somebody
knows a woman who vaguely fits the description and can afford the
price of a lawsuit, maybe it is safer to change the character into a
man and move his story to Connecticut. With works of nonfiction the
lawyers take even more elaborate precautions. The anonymous
source of information becomes as adept as a secret agent at moving
his place of residence, acquiring a new occupation, revising his
nationality and date of birth.

Given the dubious composition of the stuff sold in the literary
markets as imitations of reality, the indignant denunciations of *The
Washington Post* in April seemed slightly forced. The *Post* had
received a Pulitzer Prize for a news story that proved to be a work of
fiction, and for a period of several days alarmed editorial writers in
newspapers around the country felt called upon to defend the honor

**3**

of the profession. Yes, it was true that the once glorious *Post* had defiled the holy places of journalism, and it was a terrible sight to behold, but let nobody think that such blasphemy had become habitual among the ladies and gentlemen of the fourth estate. No, no, said the collective editorial voice of the nation, we are good boys and girls; some of us are statesmen, and we never tell lies.

The offending story, a melodramatic account of an eight-year-old black child addicted to heroin, had been written by a young black reporter named Janet Cooke. It appeared on the front page of the *Post* in September of last year under the headline JIMMY'S WORLD. The boy was not further identified on the grounds that the reporter had promised to protect her sources of information. When the editors of the *Post* learned that Miss Cooke had received the Pulitzer Prize, they sent her notes of fond congratulation.

That was on Tuesday. Within twenty-four hours it was discovered that Miss Cooke had invented Jimmy. The boy was a composite figure, a fictional device pasted together out of Miss Cooke's notes in order to personify her impressions of drug addiction in the slum of southeast Washington. Her editors abruptly declared their praise inoperative. Benjamin Bradlee, the executive editor of the *Post*, characterized Miss Cooke as "a pathological liar" and compared her treachery to that of the infamous Richard Nixon.

The *Post* returned the prize, and on the Sunday after its disgrace the paper published an 18,000-word act of contrition written by its own ombudsman. The confession took up almost as much space as the news of the attempted assassination of a president, and the inflated self-importance of the writing (implying that the United States might relapse into barbarism because a newspaper had trifled with the facts) was characteristic of the "agony" suffered by the press as a whole. As might have been expected, it was *The New York Times* that achieved the most finely articulated tone of unctuousness. Every other reputable newspaper, said the *Times* (assuming without question its own comfortable place among the company of the elect), had sustained an affront to its dignity and loss of its credibility because "the fabricated event, the made-up quote, the fictitious source . . . debases communication, and democracy."

On the heathen side of the reaction, people bearing grudges

against the media expressed an ill-concealed delight in the *Post*'s humiliation. Mr. Nixon was rumored to have smiled when told of the sham in Washington. Commodores of yacht clubs were reported to be gleefully beating their hands on tables. Here was proof of everything they had been saying for years about the contemptible falsehoods circulated by the media in the name of conscience. How apt that the *Post* should have been cast as the villain of the piece. It was the *Post* that had hounded poor Mr. Nixon out of the White House; it was the *Post* that had been memorialized in a Hollywood romance starring Dustin Hoffman and Robert Redford; it was the *Post* that embodied all Spiro Agnew had meant to imply about the sanctimonious hypocrisy of the liberal eastern establishment. And now here was the *Post* passing off the counterfeit stuff of fiction as the coin of truth. God's will had been done, and to people envious or resentful of the media it was once again possible to believe that justice had not vanished from the earth.

Whether reading the high-minded explanations in the papers or listening to the sermons of corporate vice presidents once grievously wronged by a correspondent from *Newsweek*, I noticed that relatively few people took the trouble to wonder about the nature of the media. They wished to assign to the newspapers and television networks an almost magical omnipotence, and it didn't occur to them that much of the information they received in the course of a week or a year—in newsletters, stock market analysis, gossip, medical diagnosis, State Department announcements, scientific journals—sooner or later proved to be a figment of somebody's imagination.* Within a

---

* If the weekly best-seller lists can be taken as a measure of the current levels of credulity, the evidence suggests that people buy books for the same reasons that they turn to drugs or pornography—as a means of escape from anything so subversive as a new idea. The lists published in last Sunday's *New York Times* bespeak a retreat into the caves of superstition. The sixty titles listed in four categories (mass market and trade paperbacks, fiction and nonfiction) could be arranged more accurately under the following rubrics:

- Six advisories to the lovelorn
- Seven works of safe humor (mostly about cats)
- Five guides to the real world (one of them presented by Miss Piggy)
- Eleven romantic tales of crime and espionage
- Eight confessions in which the heroine discovers that her wishes have been granted by jinni variously disguised as Mafia capos, psychotherapists, or Arab princes
- Four collections of diets or recipes
- Seven chronicles of weird or monstrous families (among them John Irving's troupe in *The Hotel New Hampshire* and a Cro-Magnon family in the Stone Age).

few weeks of Miss Cooke's fall from grace, a columnist for the New York *Daily News* by the name of Michael Daly resigned his space because he had been accused of publishing a fraudulent report from Belfast. Mr. Daly apparently made use of quotations from a pseudonymous British gunner named "Christopher Spell" and then went on to pretend that he had been present when a British army patrol came under attack from Irish youths throwing gasoline bombs. Michael J. O'Neill, the editor of the paper, deplored the use of what were called "questionable journalistic practices." Mr. Daly said that he had employed those techniques in "three hundred columns over two years."

The confusion about the media seems widely distributed, and maybe people need to be reminded that the media tell stories. There is nothing reprehensible about telling stories. Some are more complicated than others. Gibbon told a story, and so did Einstein. Almost everything presented in the theater of the news constitutes a kind of story, and to some extent all the principal players, whether identified as Jimmy Carter, Billy Martin, or Jean Harris, appear as composite figures, their quotations fitted into a context suitable to the occasion, their images made up of fragments as easily transposed as the bits and pieces of a mosaic or a documentary film. Less than six weeks after Jean Harris had gone to prison for killing Dr. Herman Tarnower, NBC made a television movie of her trial, with Ellen Burstyn in the part of an imagined Jean Harris.

The distinctions between the degrees of fabrication have less to do with the chicanery of editors than with the desires of an audience that pays for what it wants to hear and stands willing to accept the conventions proper to its place and time. We are all engaged in the same enterprise, all of us caught up in the making of analogies and metaphors, all of us seeking evocations and representations of what we can recognize as appropriately human. Stories move from truths to facts, not the other way around, and the tellers of tales endeavor to convey the essence of a thing. Given the perspective of centuries and ten years to write a book, the historian finds it hard enough to discover the meaning of a single event. The journalist usually has a few hours to write and the perspective of last week. Why, then, expect the poor fellow to revise the history of the world? Journalists

have less in common with diplomats and soothsayers than they do
with vagabond poets.

Unfortunately for Mr. Daly and Miss Cooke, the literary conventions of the daily newspaper forbid the use of fictitious characters. It
is permissible to rely on the anonymous source, that is, an informant
who may or may not exist and who may or may not have said what the
reporter eventually attributes to him in the paper. If a reporter
telephones an acquaintance at the Defense Department and asks for
information about events in El Salvador or the State Department, the
acquaintance can elect to speak "off the record." Protected by an
invisible cloak, the acquaintance can then repeat as fact the gossip
overheard the day before yesterday about Secretary Haig's wish to
make himself emperor of all the Americas. The anonymous source
thus moves even further offstage, and what appears in the next day's
paper is a quotation of a quotation dressed up in the rubric of
authority.

It is also permissible in a daily newspaper to sustain those myths
that its audience wishes to believe. During the presidential campaign of 1976 the media wanted to believe that Jimmy Carter was a
romantic figure embodying the rural virtues of the imaginary South.
The media's belief reflected the wish of their audience. An influential
audience in 1976 felt that the country needed to be pardoned for the
sins committed in Vietnam and Washington. Who better to play the
part of the redeemer than an unknown evangelist from Plains, Georgia? The media thoughtfully left out of its accounts those aspects of
Mr. Carter's character that might have confused the image.

The conventional definitions of reality suffer little contradiction
because the media have neither the resources nor the desire to prove
them wrong. The connection between the use of drugs and the
committing of crimes, for instance, rests on a mythopoeic interpretation of the facts; so do the conceptions of realpolitik and
détente; so also do the explications of the Vietnam War, the justifica-
tions for profit and loss, the discussions of the grand abstraction
known as the Third World. Speaking through the personae of the
appropriate officials, a newspaper can lend its voice to the pieties of
the age. What it cannot do, at least not yet, is resort to such a crude
device as the fabrication of a composite figure.

Other instruments of the media have been playing on the device at least since the early 1960s, with varying degrees of success. So many of the books and magazine articles of the last twenty years have been shaped out of an alloy of fact and fiction that even the libel lawyers have trouble separating the truth into its component elements. *All the President's Men,* a book written in part by Robert Woodward, Miss Cooke's metropolitan editor, introduced the character of "Deep Throat," a source of information otherwise unidentified, to whom the authors assigned quotations inimical to the interests of President Nixon. It is possible that the *nom de presse* represented an individual well placed within the White House at the time of the drama in question; it is also possible that the name served as a disguise for several informants. Given the mythical requirements of the year in which the book was published, it didn't much matter whether "Deep Throat" had descended to earth in the body of a man. People believed that he existed, and that was sufficient to the purposes of the moment.

For many years a substantial number of people believed that Carlos Castaneda had discovered a sorcerer in the Mexican desert and that his name was Don Juan. In 1966 Truman Capote published *In Cold Blood,* a book that he described as a nonfiction novel because he had rearranged the objects of scene and character in such a way as to improve the interior decor of what he called reality. Gail Sheehy established her reputation as an investigative reporter by writing a magazine article about a prostitute and a pimp, both of them collages pasted together in much the same way that Janet Cooke made the pastiche of Jimmy. In David Halberstam's book *The Best and the Brightest,* few of the quotations from or about his cast of public men bear the weight of attribution. In 1977 Alex Haley won a Pulitzer Prize for *Roots,* a romance passing as history. In 1980 Norman Mailer won a Pulitzer Prize for *The Executioner's Song,* a supposedly factual account of Gary Gilmore's death, submitted to the prize committee as fiction.*

---

* For the purposes of example I have mentioned only a few of the more well-known books of the last generation. The list could be extended through a long series of titles—books about the Bermuda Triangle or the secrets of the Pyramids; David Rorvik's clone; novels of espionage; *The Spike,* by Arnaud de Borchgrave and Robert Moss; the romans à clef by Harold Robbins and Irving Wallace; books about faith healers and mystics of various powers and denominations.

None of these observations has anything to do with literary merit. They address the questions of technique. When I first went to work for the *San Francisco Examiner* in 1957, the oldest reporter in the city room occupied the desk next to mine, and I often marveled at the ease with which he wrote the accounts of routine catastrophe. In the drawer, with a bottle of bourbon and the manuscript of the epic poem he had been writing for twenty years, he kept a looseleaf notebook filled with stock versions of maybe fifty or sixty common newspaper texts. These were arranged in alphabetical order (fires, homicides, ship collisions, etc.) and then further divided into subcategories (fires—one-, two-, and three-alarm; warehouse; apartment building; etc.). The reporter had left blank spaces for the relevant names, deaths, numbers, and street addresses. As follows: "A——alarm fire swept through a——at——St. yesterday afternoon, killing——people and causing $——in property damage."

At the *Examiner* in the late 1950s the corps of correspondents understood that what appeared in the paper constituted a kind of stage play in which cops, politicians, Russians, war heroes, and ladies of doubtful virtue all played traditional roles. The reporters further understood that the most satisfying stories (about the mayor's sexual perversities or the park commissioner's deal with the governor) never made the paper. Nobody objected to these omissions because it was assumed that the newspaper language still could more or less accurately portray the world of events. The disjunction between reality and its evocation gave the reporters a sense of their importance of "being on the inside." In the absence of decent pay, the flattery compensated them for the work of writing pageants.

The conventions changed in the early 1960s, shortly after the election of John F. Kennedy and the disappearance of what used to be called the avant-garde. Even in the spring of 1961, by which time I had come to New York as a reporter for the *New York Herald Tribune*, it was possible to take substantial liberties with the facts. The editor of that paper assigned me to the rewrite desk, and for nights on end I would listen to the wavering voices of correspondents at the other end of a bad phone connection in Algeria or the Congo, taking down dictation and then revising their texts in a way that conformed to the editor's expectations of the world.

On one occasion the *Tribune*'s man in Moscow telephoned a dispatch about a meeting of the Soviet Academy of Sciences at which a few scientists had made a few inoffensive remarks about the uses of technology. My editor interpreted the dispatch to mean that First Secretary Nikita Khrushchev's initiatives toward détente had been defeated by the well-known militarists in the Politburo. He instructed me to seek guidance from a professor at Columbia University who knew enough about Russian affairs to explain why the meeting heralded the advent of World War III. (It is my distinct recollection that the professor was Zbigniew Brzezinski, but I cannot be sure of this, and I doubt whether Mr. Brzezinski would remember the conversation.) Once the professor understood what was wanted he supplied the missing explanation, and the story appeared on the front page of the next day's paper under a Moscow dateline.

I did the same with the news arriving over the phone from the paper's operatives in the metropolitan police bureaus, making notes about citizens found dead in cars or arrested for homicide. Almost always I was writing about people whom I had never seen, sometimes furnishing them with motives and characterizations at which I could only guess, arranging the acceptable abstractions of the day (Cold War, missile gap, new frontier) into the equations of social or political meaning. I find myself doing the same thing in the writing of this essay. Never having met Miss Cooke, and not having read her portrayal of Jimmy's World, I know only what I've read about her in the press, primarily the ombudsman's account in *The Washington Post*. Nor have I met Mr. Daly or read more than ten or twelve of his columns in the *Daily News*. On at least one level of meaning, I have only a formal or theoretical grasp of what I'm talking about; Miss Cooke and Mr. Daly appear to me as characters in a play of ideas. The same thing could be said of most of the news from Poland or the White House.

Thus abstraction doth make theologians of us all, and we exhaust ourselves in passionate arguments about things that few of us have ever seen. We talk about the Third World as if it were a real place rather than a convenient symbol, about the gears of the national economy as if they were as intelligible as the gears on a bicycle.

People become lifelong enemies because they disagree about the military strategy of the Soviet Union; on further investigation it generally turns out that neither antagonist speaks Russian or has been to Russia.

Within a year of President Kennedy's election the profession of journalism began to recruit apprentices from Harvard and Yale. Having enjoyed the privileges of both affluence and education, the new generation of journalists felt inhibited by the older conventions. They thought of themselves as "creative," as the possessors of "the truth" brought down from Cambridge in bound volumes, as novelists *manqués*, as the social equals of the politicians or popular celebrities about whom they were obliged to make romances. At the university they had been introduced to competing theories of reality, and they had heard rumors of discoveries in the sciences that called into question the structure of knowledge, reality, and matter. Apparently matter was a force that cohered, not a substance; physicists deduced the presence of subatomic particles, otherwise invisible, by tracking their passage through a bubble chamber. Einstein's notion of relativity did to Newton's mechanics what Cubism had done to Impressionism, and it was conceivable that a man's perception of the universe depended on the intensity of his belief in that perception. If the techniques of literary criticism could be applied to the canon of weapons in Robert McNamara's Pentagon, then maybe the devices of literary fiction could be applied to the data bases of the news.

What came to be called "the new journalism" made its gaudy debut in the magazines—in *New York, Esquire, Life*, and *The Saturday Evening Post*. The form was not, in the strict sense, new. *Time* magazine had been contriving an artificial reality for years; so had the makers of newsreels and Hollywood epics. But the form seemed new when contrasted with the stodginess of the 1950s and the old doctrine that journalism concerned itself only with facts.

The techniques of the new journalism had more in common with the making of documentary films than with the writing of novels. The writer seeks to make an image, not a work of art. He begins with an attitude of mind and a mass of random observations—notes on the weather, tones of voice, landscapes, fragments of conversation, bits and pieces of historical incident, descriptions of scene, impressions of character. These materials correspond to the filmmaker's unedited film or the raw information received every week by the newsmagazines. In order to impose a form on the chaos of his notes the writer decides on a premise and a point of view. He then can arrange the materials into a coherent design, as if he were fitting small stones into the pavement of a mosaic.*

It was, after all, a scientific age, supposedly capable of subtle measurement and highly technical analysis. Truth-tellers of all descriptions stood in anxious need of clothing their figures in the lineaments of reality. Otherwise, who would listen to them? Novelists and sociologists borrowed the forms of the empirical sciences, dressing up their stories in the costumes of "case histories," forcing the narrative into whatever language would carry with it the impression of truth. It was not enough to have grasped the essence of a thing; it was necessary to give it an age, a name, an address, a set of circumstances.

Janet Cooke apparently had a talent for the genre, but so also did Gail Sheehy, Norman Mailer, and Hunter Thompson. Before writing her account of Jimmy's World, Miss Cooke mentioned to her city editor that in traveling through southeast Washington she had been told of an eight-year-old boy addicted to heroin. "That's the story," said the city editor. "Go after it. It's a front-page story." Miss Cooke obliged. If she couldn't find the boy in question, she knew that such children had been reported to exist. She invented a plausible

---

* The similarity of the new journalism and the documentary film technique was made plain to me in the summer of 1974, when I was invited by NBC to consider the possibility of writing a film on the multinational oil companies. The price of oil had been going up, and the Arab states had combined into a cartel known as OPEC that apparently was making trouble. The network had collected, at huge expense, fifty or sixty hours of film on Armand Hammer, the chairman of Occidental Petroleum. The trouble was that the producers didn't know what the film meant. They had all these pictures—Armand Hammer in Los Angeles; Armand Hammer talking to Edwin Newman in a corporate jet somewhere over Poland; Armand Hammer at the Hermitage in Moscow; Armand Hammer with the Libyans; miscellaneous footage of oil tankers lying at anchor in New York harbor, refineries, the Persian Gulf, Arabs carrying hawks—but what in God's name was the story? Were the oil companies good or bad? Was Armand Hammer a scoundrel or the savior of Western civilization? What was the meaning of the Russian connection?

The producers had assembled the pieces of the puzzle, but without an image in mind, how were they going to put the pieces together into fifty-two minutes of coherent narrative? I didn't accept the offer, because I could foresee nothing but meetings.

speech for the child (plausible, at least, to the editors of the *Post*), and she described in detail the furniture of an imaginary house. Her account was not too dissimilar from the travel writing that used to appear in *National Geographic*. The explorer goes to darkest Africa and returns with an amalgam of scientific and anecdotal observation—photographs of the explorer standing with his wife and pet dik-dik, published in conjunction with reports about what the animal has been known to do or what the witch doctor might have said.

The uses of the new journalism escape the blame of critics and the resentment of prize committees if the author makes it clear to the reader that he has violated the sanctities of the facts. This can be done either with a brief digression into the first person singular, with a summary statement of method, or with a tone of voice sufficiently unique to defy classification as that of a disembodied narrator. In the hands of the less accomplished practitioners, the devices of the new journalism serve the purposes of evasion, and it becomes possible to present a reality of one's own invention as if it corresponded to an objective description of events. The newsmagazines do this every week.

Several years ago a writer employed by *Time* published in *Harper's Magazine* an essay written almost entirely in the omniscient third person. Toward the end of the last paragraph the author permitted himself a conclusion and went so far as to write the words *I think*. When he saw the galley proofs of the article he was horrified by his recklessness, and he changed the phrase to read "millions of people think."

Under the technical and epistemological pressures of the 1960s, the lines between fiction and fact became increasingly difficult to distinguish. The previously distinct genres of journalism, literature, and theater gradually fused into something known as media. The amalgam of forms resulted in a national theater of celebrity. If in 1965 the academic critics were beginning to notice that nobody was writing serious plays, the literary critics observed that the novelists had wandered off into the wilderness of self. Who could compete with the continuous performance on the stage of events? Network television presented a troupe of celebrities transported with the ease of a Shakespearean scene change to Dallas, Vietnam, Chicago, Vienna, Washington, and the Afghan frontier. The technical and lighting effects were astonishing, the verisimilitude of the characters so startling as to make them seem almost lifelike. By 1972 the tropes of the new journalism had become so commonplace that an anonymous writer for *The Economist*, a London weekly known for its rectitude, could begin his account of the American elections that year with the sentence, "It was raining in America on election day." The writer obviously didn't mean to say that it was raining everywhere in the United States. He wished to say something about the state of mind of the American people, and he used the rain as a metaphor to express his intimations of doubt and melancholy.

A similar sleight of hand governs the use of quotation from the secretary of state, the chairman of the Chase Manhattan Bank, or any of the other players in the national repertory company. The writer already has in mind the shape of the story, but he needs to give it a plausible authority or office of origin. He cannot possibly depict the matter at hand in all of its complexity, and so he asks a question that will carry along the plot in the direction of melodrama. Would the secretary say that the reports of Syrian troops east of Beirut mean war or peace? Is it true, Mr. Rockefeller, that your bank sustains the racist economy of South Africa?

The actors experienced in the theater of the news know what the prompters want to hear. People drawn into the play for a single performance, usually as minor or supporting characters when their businesses collapse or their children commit suicide, never know what to say. They make the mistake of trying to explain, at some length and in boring detail, and they wonder why the account in the papers the next morning bears so little resemblance to their understanding of the facts.

If the media succeed with their spectacles and grand simplifications, it is because their audiences define happiness as the state of being well and artfully deceived. People like to listen to stories, to believe what they're told, to imagine that the implacable forces of history speak to them with a human voice. Who can bear to live without myths? If people prefer to believe that drug addiction causes crime, that may be because they would rather not think that perfectly ordinary people commit crimes, people not too different from themselves, people living in the same neighborhoods and sending their children to the same schools.

The media thus play the part of the courtier, reassuring their patrons that the world conforms to the wish of the presiding majority. The media advertise everything and nothing. Yes, say the media, our generals know what they're doing (no, say the media, our generals are fools); the energy crisis was brought down on our innocent heads by the Arabs (the energy crisis is the fault of our profligacy and greed); Vietnam was a crusade (Vietnam was imperialism); homosexuality is a "lifestyle" (homosexuality is a disease); the Kennedys were demigods (the Kennedys were beasts); the state is invincible (the state has lost its nerve); yes, Virginia, there is a reality out there, and not only can it be accurately described but also it looks just the way you always wanted it to look.

By telling people what they assume they already know, the media reflect what society wants to think of itself. The images in the mirror compose the advertisement for reality. Janet Cooke's story received a Pulitzer Prize because it confirmed what the committee, most of whose members were both ambitious and white, wished to believe about people who were alienated and black. If blacks were lost to heroin at the age of eight, how could they mount a revolution? We are safe, my dear Trevor, for at least another generation.

Although notoriously inept at the art of disguise, the FBI agents dressed up to look like Arabs succeeded in their charade against the congressmen filmed in the ABSCAM screenings because the congressmen wanted to believe that a sheik was somebody in a robe who had nothing better to do than bestow $50,000 in cash on the princes of Christendom.

The simplicities of the media enjoy the further advantage of a much vaunted "communications revolution" that has had the paradoxical effect of lowering the norm of literacy. The immense increase of available information over the last generation has so fragmented the literate audience that instead of bringing people together the sophistication of the new technologies has forced them further apart and deprived them of the capacity to speak a common language. As recently as 1960 there was such a thing in the United

States as a fairly unified field of informed opinion. More or less the same people read more or less the same newspapers and magazines. They comprised an educated audience that was still small enough to talk to itself and that could agree, at least in rough outline, as to the country's history, character, and hope of the future.

After 1965 this single audience dispersed into a thousand audiences, each of them preoccupied with its own interests and realities, each of them speaking the jargon of a particular specialty or profession. The diaspora followed, in part, from the rise in the population after the Second World War and the subsequent multiplication of graduates of the nation's universities during the 1960s; in part, the diaspora reflected the wealth and dynamism of a society that could afford to pursue so many lines of random inquiry.

Who now can make sense of the surfeit of information? Even a middle-level executive at a middle-level brokerage firm receives five hundred household advisories a week (not to mention subscriptions to trade journals, the daily and financial press); dossiers of equivalent bulk circulate at every level of authority within the corridors of any American institution large enough to boast of its presence in the twentieth century. What, then, must be the data base provided for the officials holding the higher places in a bureaucracy the size of the State or Treasury Department? Who has the time to read what they have to read?

The more people know, the less they know. To the extent that society as a whole expands and complicates its acquisition of knowledge, so the individual members of society find less and less to say to one another on any level of meaning beyond the reach of Mike Wallace. They escape the burden of their anxieties by retreating into the magic shows of the national celebrity theater. The gaudiness of the television spectacle, which so obviously shifts the weight of personality against the subtlety of mind, imposes a kind of numb silence on people who might otherwise have had something useful to say.

In the autumn of 1977 I taught a seminar at Yale on the art of the press, and I noticed that of the eighteen students in the class five or six of them hoped to make careers in journalism; they were as ambitious as Janet Cooke, and their questions about Peter Zenger and the First Amendment served as preambles to requests for an introduction to a deputy editor at *The New York Times*. The other students in the class paid relatively little attention to the media. Their interest was that of an anthropologist or a student of comparative mythology. The media presented them with portraits of reality they thought inauthentic, a reality of a kind, but one without the dimension of insight or wisdom. Brought up with the wonders of the communications revolution, they somehow understood that the news had moved out of the newspapers. If, in the 1930s Bernard Baruch could speculate in the financial markets on the basis of what he read in the *Times*, by the late 1960s anybody who wanted seriously to follow events (whether in finance, foreign affairs, or the sciences) had to depend on more detailed sources of information.

Janet Cooke, like Michael Daly and the generation of correspondents raised on the principles of the new journalism, understood that the media had become a theater. Apparently she wanted to be a star, and the résumés she submitted both to the *Post* and then to the Pulitzer Prize committee read like the list of credits that producers receive from unemployed actors. I've never yet met an actor who, when trying out for a part, doesn't answer yes to every question asked. Can he sing? Like Sinatra. Can he dance? Like Astaire. Does he know languages? His mother was French. Thus, when applying for a job at the *Post*, Miss Cooke conferred on herself a degree from Vassar and a fluency in French and Spanish. Her advertisement to the Pulitzer Prize committee was further elaborated with a graduate degree from the University of Toledo, a year's study at the Sorbonne, and a fluency in Italian and Portuguese. It was this pathetic forgery of her life, not the fabrication of her story in the paper, that led to the discovery of her fraud.

If Miss Cooke had not won the Pulitzer Prize, perhaps the journalists who condemned her, both inside and outside of the *Post*, would not have been so harsh in their judgments. When Mr. Daly resigned from the *Daily News*, effectively pleading nolo contendere to the charge of having faked a dispatch from Belfast, nobody felt obliged to denounce him as a pathological liar and a disgrace to the profession. But the Pulitzer Prize is not something to be trifled with; like the Academy Award, it denotes grandeur. "Applause," remarked

Ambrose Bierce, "is the echo of a platitude," and even a brief study of the Pulitzer Prizes awarded over a period of years suggests that they sustain the passions of the moment. Thus William Styron receives a prize for *The Confessions of Nat Turner* in 1968, at just about the point in time when sentiment on behalf of civil rights had become thoroughly respectable; Frances FitzGerald wins a prize for *Fire in the Lake* in 1973, by which time it had become correct to bemoan the American presence in Vietnam; Herman Wouk wins a prize for *The Caine Mutiny* in 1952, when the country was far enough into the Cold War to think that naval officers showed virtue and maturity by obeying the orders of a demented captain.

If the prizes raise the politically expedient into the realm of authority and beauty, so also they maintain the pomp and majesty of a profession constantly in need of reassurance. The ladies and gentlemen of the fourth estate know that they have been living beyond their moral and intellectual means, and their desire to establish themselves as a social class reflects their anxiety about being discovered as bankrupts. The prizes might impress the groundlings on the public side of the curtain, but within the profession they shore up the confidence of the younger members of the troupe who might otherwise begin to question the validity of their claims to privilege. The continued credibility of the press, not to mention its hope of profit, rests on the popular belief that it deals in the currency of fact. If the reality of the press were seen to be as arbitrary as that of the government or the Mobil Oil Corporation, what would happen then? No wonder Miss Cooke was driven from the temple, followed by stones.

The custodians of the press undoubtedly have a point. As has been said, people like to believe in myths, and the extravagance of the libel awards recently bestowed on Carol Burnett and a former Miss Wyoming suggests that the audience has begun to grow restive. *The National Enquirer* published a silly gossip item about Miss Burnett in a Washington restaurant with Henry Kissinger. The gossip was false, as is most gossip published in even the most reputable of newspapers, but a jury in Los Angeles awarded Miss Burnett $1.3 million in punitive damages, a sum equivalent to half the *Enquirer*'s assets. The former Miss Wyoming claimed that a work of fiction published in *Penthouse* magazine (a story about an imaginary Miss Wyoming) caused her immeasurable suffering and embarrassment, and a jury in Cheyenne presented her with $12.5 million.

The disproportionate levy of punishment further suggests that people may expect too much of journalism. Not only do they expect it to be entertaining, they expect it to be true. It isn't so much that people insist on believing in the accuracy of the media (the *Enquirer,* after all, regularly announces cures for cancer and sightings of UFOs); the mistakes and distortions they will forgive if they can retain their faith in the underlying honesty of the enterprise. But once let them suspect that the difference between fact and fiction may be as random as a number drawn in a lottery, and their resentment will wreak an expensive vengeance. More than once I have heard the media described as "an army of occupation," and Congress has been besieged with bills offering redefinitions of the liberties granted under the First Amendment.

Once there was a religious theater in which God staged cataclysmic floods, plagues, and heavenly fires with the effortless aplomb of ABC's *Wide World of Sports.* Now that God has been pronounced dead, it is conceivable that people would like to transfer His powers and dominions to the media. What else do they have to put in His place? To a large extent the media have had the roles of judge and inquisitor thrust upon them because so many other institutions have proved themselves inadequate to the tasks of omniscience. The media disguise their lack of knowledge with the quality of knowingness, their weakness with the power to forge the metal of celebrity and transmute a political issue into a salable commodity.

If the individual can be flattered into believing that he is present at all important public occasions, he may also be tricked into believing that he has no story of his own. The man who substitutes what Saul Bellow once called the nonstory of the news for the line of his own narrative condemns himself to an unending contemplation of the images that crowd across the media's many mirrors, a man forever suspended in the revolving light show of names, issues, events, votes, hearings, treaties, wars, scandals, and final scores.

The resulting loss of identity leads to the familiar chronicle of confused conflict, which in turn can be reprocessed into tomorrow's broadcast or next year's best-selling murder.

The huge imago of the media expands in a vacuum, and before it engulfs all other forms of authority it might be useful to ask what is meant by the old proverb about truth making men free. If people seek knowledge in the hope that it will grant them freedom and power, and if the media can satisfy neither of those desires, maybe that is because the customers expect the media to include those favors in the price of admission. The truth unfortunately has to be discovered every day, by each individual working with the tools of his own thought, imagination, and patient study. If we are all engaged in the same endeavor, seeking the representations of the truly human, then probably we should not assign so much belief to the contrived mythologies of the media. In the same editorial in which it admonished *The Washington Post*, *The New York Times* expressed the complacent notion that "great publications magnify beyond measure the voice of any single writer." This is not quite accurate. The instruments of the media multiply or amplify a voice, serving much the same purpose as a loudspeaker in a ballpark or a prison. The amplification leaches the soul out of the voice, squeezing it into the institutional sound that pays the enormous costs of the big media. What magnifies a voice is its human character—its compassion, honesty, and moral intelligence.

HARPER'S MAGAZINE,
*July 1981*

# BELLES LETTRES

J UDGING BY THE note of suppressed panic in their voices, the book publishers in town have not been having an easy time of it. The recession discourages people from buying books priced at $15.95, no matter how splendid the reviews; the market for paperback reprints has gone the way of the market for California real estate, and the bookstores return as many books as they sell.

Two or three years ago the publishers liked to talk about the death of literature and the decay of culture. They have bequeathed these stately and elegiac themes to the universities; they talk instead about the techniques for survival in a business that has become as speculative as coffee futures. The shift in sensibility does terrible things to people accustomed to thinking of themselves as friends of the tax-exempt muse.

On Tuesday of last week poor Hastings had the look of a man no more than two days ahead of the police. His publishing house had been losing money for eighteen months, with the result that it had revised its literary ambitions and discontinued some of its more esoteric lines of goods. For twenty years Hastings had been content to edit works of poetry, belles lettres, and serious fiction. On suddenly being told to acquire manuscripts that stood a better than 3 to 1 chance of reaching the best-seller list, Hastings had fallen into a state of doubt that he previously had associated with French novelists.

"If I don't come up with something by Friday afternoon," he said, "I'll know what Beckett was trying to say in *Waiting for Godot*."

**21**

He had been studying the charts and making the rounds of the paperback displays in drugstores and airports. His investigations had inspired him to make a preliminary list of titles, but he wanted a second opinion before presenting them to his editorial board. He looked over both shoulders before taking a sheet of paper from his coat pocket and sliding it across the table concealed in a napkin. His typewritten list had been so heavily marked up with changes and crossings out that it looked like a first draft of a lyric by Dylan Thomas:

1. *The Priapus File*: Case histories of the twenty-five most depraved men and women known to the annals of history and psychoanalysis. Foreword by Irving Wallace or Thomas Hoving, editor of *Connoisseur*.

2. *The Third World Diet*: Exotic recipes with results proved by the experience of people in Poland, Zaire, Mexico, etc.

3. *Aladdin's Lamp*: The final secret in investing in the stock market by Henry Kaufman, Joseph Granville, or any other securities analyst believed to possess unearthly powers. Complete with 400 pages of graphs.

4. *Jane Fonda's Book of Pets, Jane Fonda's Book of Gardens, Jane Fonda's Book of Antique Cars*.

5. *My Funny Valentine*: The letters and diaries of Al Capone.

6. *Geopolitics Made Simple*: A portfolio of maps, together with a glossary of terms (détente, window of vulnerability, hegemony, etc.). Introduction by former President Richard M. Nixon.

7. *The Last Berwick*: Long novel set against the vivid pageantry of the history of the world. The author, preferably a woman, begins the chronicle of the Berwick family at the Battle of Troy.

8. *More for Me*: An anthology of tips about how and where to buy anything and everything. Entries arranged alphabetically by commodity (ascots, bread, chinoiserie, debutantes, etc.) with commentary by noted experts.

9. *Winning Nuclear War*: Military strategy by a prominent official in the Reagan administration.

10. *The 250-Minute Orgasm*: Ancient Hindu techniques discovered in the carving on the wall in Madras. Verified after five years of painstaking experiments by a board of medical authorities connected with the Beverly Hills Institute for Creative Human Relations. Illustrated.

While I was reading the list, Hastings stared at me with expressions of acute anxiety. I wished that I could have spared him the pain of criticism. "It's not a bad list, Hastings," I said, "and you are on the right track. But the conception is still too literary and you haven't got the feel for what is genuinely commercial. There's no Hollywood book; no life of Jesus, nothing about sports or the zodiac; no sensational murder; no guide to a happy and healthful divorce; not enough celebrities."

We continued the conversation for another hour or so, but Hastings couldn't fix his attention on what was being said. He drank a fourth and fifth bottle of Perrier water and began to talk about taking up a career as a trainer of performing elephants. He had always been fond of the circus, he said, and with an animal act you could tell where you stood with the crowd.

THE WASHINGTON POST,
*August 1982*

# THE AUDIBLE SILENCE

**T**WO WEEKS AGO yesterday, President Reagan issued an executive order stuffing the mouths of any and all public officials who, like Adam and Eve, have tasted of the knowledge of good and evil. In Reagan's Republican cosmology, the forbidden fruit takes the form of what the government denominates as "sensitive information." Let the poor sinner of a bureaucrat once glance at a classified document, and from that time forth, even unto retirement and death, he will require approval of the censors before he can write or say anything about the subjects—whether arms control treaties or White House tennis court schedules—to which he enjoyed access while resident in the Garden of Eden.

The order effectively stifles the vestigial echo of the free, open and informed debate on which the nation theoretically relies for the formulation of its wisdom and the conduct of its politics. If the hood of silence (not much different from the Mafia's code of *omerta*) falls on those people who presumably might know what they're talking about, then the level of conversation must, of necessity, sink even further into the mud of polemic.

Who will have anything to say except the ins and the outs, the police and the mob, the judge and the demagogue? What was intended as an experimental argument, capable of reasoned response to shifting circumstance, must degenerate into an exchange of insults. Words will be hammered into weapons, the suppleness of thought into the rigidity of slogans.

The presidential decree was bad enough, possibly as regressive an act as yet has been committed by an administration already remarkable for its squinting distrust of the human mind. What was even more depressing was the lack of objection.

As recently as nine years ago, amidst the waving of flags inspired by the Watergate bulletins and President Nixon's escape to California, the press would have pursued the implications of the new executive order with the diligence that it now brings to bear on the deals signed by Herschel Walker and Billy Martin. But except for a few ceremonial cries of alarm in the nominally liberal sectors of Congress and the media, Reagan's dictum seems to have been received as amiably as reports of yesterday's stock prices.

His attorney general has been busy for many months suppressing evidence about the workings of government, but as yet no organized opposition has made an effective protest against the dismantling of the Freedom of Information Act. Nor has anybody made too much of a fuss about the censorship imposed on films from Canada, books from Iran, and the dingy travelers from the socialist ghettos of the world.

In times of economic trouble, who can afford to invest precious assets in causes that don't pay? How much can a fellow earn from a defense of the First Amendment? What if the boss turns sullen when listening to idealistic claptrap?

Across the whole spectrum of public debate, the silence has become almost audible—not only in government (which now subjects to lie-detector tests any malefactors suspected of talking carelessly to the papers) but also the universities, the corporations, and the literary bazaars. Within all of these arenas the voices of dissent have become so soft and so circumspect as to hear comparison to the euphemisms deemed polite at the court of Louis XVI. The careerist intent upon his career learns to keep a respectably low profile and to say nothing that might offend the ear of wealth or power. Who knows to whom he will be beholden for his next meal, subsidy, opinion, or weekend at the Aspen Institute?

The premise of the American democracy assumes a raucous assembly of citizens unafraid to speak their minds. But with the loss of economic independence and the accompanying fear of social and technological change, too few people dare stray too far from the apron strings of Mother Bureaucracy. The majority seeks safety on a company payroll, all too eager to trade the uncertainties of freedom for the guarantee of an institutional credit card, an institutional pension, an institutional identity.

Last month in New Orleans the American Bar Association voted to bind its members to secrecy when instructing their clients in the crimes of fraud. The ABA approved this obligation to silence for what it called "ethical reasons."

Among university presidents the impulse toward outspoken expression has become so rare that Ernest L. Boyer, president of the Carnegie Foundation for the Advancement of Teaching, recently was moved to observe that he could think of only two or three prominent educators willing to violate the bounds of platitude. Most university presidents apparently spend so much time prostrating themselves in the presence of money or its surrogates that they learn to suppress any quotation that anybody with control of sums in excess of $50,000 might regard as dangerously seditious.

The prevailing silence testifies to the shrewdness of Reagan's judgment. He presents his edict to a constituency already cowed, and he provides the official classes with a useful excuse. Not that anybody would dream of making an unseemly noise, but on the off chance that someone might conceive of doing so, he can always explain that however much he would like to say a few words, it is, alas, against the rules.

THE WASHINGTON POST,
*August 1983*

# OLD RELICS IN
# NEW BOTTLES

O N THE NIGHT before the Turks sacked Constantinople in 1453, the Byzantine Emperor Constantine Palaeologus, accompanied by priests and a choir of the faithful, made a solemn embassy to the church of Saint Theodosia to pray to the martyr whose relics were believed to contain the powers that subsequent generations have learned to attribute to the hydrogen bomb. Having assigned the defense of his kingdom to the bones of a saint, the emperor died the next morning with those few of his followers who took the trouble to meet the Turks on the city walls. Most of the emperor's subjects chose to remain in one of the city's churches, trusting to the miracles of religion rather than to the force of their own courage and arms. When the Turks broke through the doors of Saint Sophia they found 10,000 people earnestly praying in a sanctuary sweet with the smell of incense and fear.

Something of this same credulous spirit informs the current attitude toward anything and everything that partakes of the aura of "high tech." Over the last ten or fifteen years the belief in the sovereign powers of various new technologies has taken so firm a hold of the public imagination that it has become the stuff of primitive religion. Let the school administrator announce that he has ordered computers for eight hundred illiterate sophomores, and lo, they have become educated. Let the stock salesman pronounce the holy words that rhyme with *onics* or *echnics*, and lo, the investor has entered into paradise.

The superstition shows up in the cultural as well as the commercial sectors of experience, endowing otherwise secular objects with sacred meanings once attributed to nymphs and stars and trees. In the fullness of time the new technologies undoubtedly will advance the hope of reason and support the nobler aspirations of mankind. For the time being, however, the worship of the higher technology serves the cause of barbarism. The placing of the deity in the machine makes it that much easier to discount the value of the merely human.

Maybe I have been keeping questionable company or reading the wrong news bulletins, but I cannot seem to avoid encounters with prophets of the new revelation. Last summer I had occasion to read Alvin Toffler's most recent tract, *Previews & Premises,* and I remember being surprised by the inertness of its prose. Not having read Toffler's best-selling spiels in *Future Shock* (1970) and *The Third Wave* (1980), I had assumed that he had something to say. His text, like those of his several imitators, runs somewhat as follows:

- Things change and time flies.

- The velocity of change is great and the old order (meaning big-time capitalism harnessed to the wheels of mass production) soon will give way to the mystical entity known as the "de-massified economy," in which infinitely diverse "cross-cultural communicators" will deal with one another through the medium of the computer.

- Unless people appreciate the unutterable significance of this event, Western civilization will come to a bad end. Savage mobs, predominantly black but also representative of "the poor and unemployed," will roam through well-lighted corporate office buildings, looting and burning and breaking up the infrastructure.

- Doom can be averted. Beyond the peril of anarchy lies the garden of technological Eden. Toffler conjures up the vision of kindly elves at work in far-off, modern California. Happy among avocados, the elves spin the golden threads of fiber optics and mine the jewels of microchips. Their fortunate assistants, no longer chained to the gun decks of industrial routine, do a different kind of work—work that is fun and healthy and clean and creative and safe.

Under the jurisdiction of a writer concerned with thought instead of incantation, the few and threadbare ideas promulgated in *Previews & Premises* could be set forth in ten pages generously illustrated with drawings of fairy tale beasts and castles. But Toffler isn't interested in thought. He wishes to present his customers with a mantra. To this end he constructs an unintelligible prose in which the words, almost all of them abstract, become magical objects. If the words could be understood, they would lose their value as moleskin.

What passes for the logic of the book bears resemblance to the systems analysis of those South Sea islanders who improvised religions (the so-called cargo cults) with the fragments of industrial society (motors, copper wire, aerosol cans, etc.) they had seen in the hands of Europeans. Toffler does something like this with the scientific and pseudoscientific words that he discovers in the popular press. He knows that out there in the ocean of incomprehensible events something very important is going on, that somewhere beyond the horizon a more evolved race of men (physicists, microbiologists, cyberneticians) sail to and fro in vessels of supernatural power and speed. Seeking to borrow their magic, Toffler assembles newspaper and magazine clippings, and from this collection of random sound he composes the chant that sells as a specific against despair. Reduced to its purest essence, Toffler's book becomes a high-speed, aluminum Om, the words running together into a single syllable pronounced, very quickly but with a murmuring intonation, "microchipunidimensionalmodularadhocraticdecisionalenvironmentcomputerprogramcreditcardspaceshuttleflextimecognitariatroboticsdiversitypositivefeedbackloop."

Being made of wishes, Toffler's magic contains as little intrinsic interest as the teeth and bones found in the bottom of a shaman's leather bag. But that, unhappily, is not the end of it. Toffler enjoys the patronage of governments, astonishes the ranks of managers gathered at business conventions, sells millions of books to the paperback trade. His success demonstrates the truth of Newton's third law, which posits for every action an equal and opposite reaction. In an age of anxiety, the forces bearing forward into the unknown future sponsor countervailing forces beating backward into the familiar past. The more complex and civilized the advance, the more simpleminded and barbarous the retreat.

No businessman these days dares to embark upon the journey of incorporation without first acquiring a computer so huge and so omniscient as to strike terror into the software of its enemies. The pornographers in Times Square set up massage parlors behind neon signs that promise "Compusex" or "Erotics Ltd." The magazines glitter with advertisements for copying machines that seem better looking and a good deal more competent than the people who serve them with sacrificial gifts of paper.

On Broadway the successful musicals depend on brightly polished dance numbers remarkable for their inanity and for what Arlene Croce called their "pitiless energy." The interest centers on the complexity of the lights and the speed of the set changes. The same can be said of the popular movies (cf. *Flashdance* or *The Right Stuff*), as well as of the television serials in which the protagonist turns out to be an automobile, a robot, or a special effect. Hardly anybody knows how to develop human character or construct a plausible narrative. The human actors invariably make a mess of things, and were it not for the goodness of a machine, the poor saps never would win safely through to the IBM commercial.

Probably it is in the hospitals and the building of weapons that the veneration of high tech results in the most obvious forms of dehumanization. Too often the medical technicians offer the first claim on their sympathies to the whims of their equipment. They bring patients to the intensive care units in much the same way that Aztecs brought maiden girls to the sacrificial altars. The nuclear strategists concede that their weapons no longer have a practical military use. The doctrine of mutual assured destruction, which has governed American missile theory for twenty years, assumes that the weapons have become so frightful that nobody would send them against a strategic or tactical objective. Like the bones of Saint Theodosia, the arsenal of deterrence stands as both symbol and embodiment of absolute power. What was human becomes divine. The Pentagon spends a great deal of its money buying high-tech weapons so delicate and fundamentally useless as to acquire the beauty of religious sculpture.

So pervasive is the superstition that the failures of the new technologies excite little criticism among the faithful. Explaining the death of two hundred and forty-one Americans in Beirut last October, a writer on terrorism at the Rand Corporation said that the military command had made the mistake of sending "just an off-the-shelf unit" to do the work properly left to a more specialized force component. As quoted in the newspapers, the gentleman might as easily have been talking about items on sale in a sex shop or an electronics store.

Only the impious make blasphemous remarks about the systems that don't work, the computer systems utterly devoid of meaning. It is the technique that counts—the seventy-four modes and the speed of transmission, the camera angle and the high gloss on the metal. When the technology fails, the believers keep their faith intact by assigning the fault to the messy sludge of human emotion that clogs up the workings of the Utopian machinery.

The obsession with technique arouses the dream of power. Sensitive to the desperate wish for demigods among the consumers of ready-made myths, the producers of *The Right Stuff* supply an ode to power in its romantic and Promethean form—as a pillar of fire on which it just might be possible to climb out of the well of death. It is a very noisy movie. Accompanied by loud explosions in stereophonic sound, rockets of various caliber rise ceremoniously from the earth in circles of flame. By the end of the movie the producers have managed to forge the persona of the American hero into an aluminum object impervious to re-entry speeds and the heat of the sun.

Toffler achieves an analogous purpose with intimations of a new social order. He tells his readers that soon they will belong to "the cognitariat," that they will have tiny but important parts to play in the retooling of the world's economic machinery, that they will discover "job enrichment" and be admitted, as shiny as new push buttons, into the sacred grove of "the decisional environment."

He doesn't describe this new order very clearly; if he made the mistake of writing in English, the great, good place somewhere south of San Jose might be confused with a communist work camp in the Siberian snow. Somehow the new order resembles the hierarchical society of the late Middle Ages. On the highest tiers of power the brain people—the priests of the new technology—will make all the necessary decisions. This they will do selflessly, of course, not because they covet the trivial privileges of office but because, by virtue of their education and intelligence, they belong to the company of the elect. Elsewhere in the society, arranged in descending levels of knowledge, people of lesser value and attainment will go freely about their innocent and creative ways—tossing salad, playing volleyball, singing folk songs; they too will be happy, because they will have learned to leave the troubling exercise of power to the bones of a saint.

HARPER'S MAGAZINE,
*March 1984*

# THE COUNTERFEIT
# MUSE

T HE QUESTION OF the national obligation to the arts promises to weigh heavily on the conversation this fall, and if early reports from the cultural frontiers are a fair indication of the rhetoric to come, the argument seems likely to resemble a theological dispute. Quite a number of people hold violent opinions on the subject, but relatively few can define what they mean by the word *art*. Art has somehow become sacred, as if it were an object or collection of objects that must be approached with a proper show of respect and a feeling of holy dread.

When the Reagan administration announced last March the decimation of the federal subsidies for the National Endowments for the Arts and the Humanities (in both cases a reduction of the annual appropriation from about $150 million to roughly $100 million), no cry of public indignation disturbed Congress or excited the passions of the popular press. Nobody carried placards through the streets. The silence confirmed what most people had known for many years but had been too polite to mention in supposedly literate company. Mr. Reagan conceded that the American government cannot stimulate the manufacture of high art, and his countrymen breathed a sigh of relief. No longer would they need to feign appreciation for sets of themes and variations performed by troupes of feminist mimes.

Most of the people who even bothered to notice the raid on the federal Parnassus did so with a detachment verging on indifference. Yes, it was too bad, and probably a disappointment to a cousin studying stage design in Winston-Salem, but for the country as a whole the subtraction of funds amounted to little more than accepting a tax loss on a romantic investment. Certainly the government had tried hard enough, but no matter how earnest its intentions or how munificent its expenditure of money and sentiment, the American people, so clever and inventive at so many other tasks, couldn't learn to weave the tapestries of culture.

But if this was the feeling of the unappreciative majority, for the suppliers of what has become the official sensibility the news from Washington signified the victory of the philistines. Loud and vociferous in their lament, they mourned the pillaging of the holy places. By Memorial Day the lobbies representing the rituals of artistic endeavor had begun to rally support in the more refined quarters of the media. Celebrities appeared on public television, raffling off their memorabilia and imploring the audience to win this one for Beethoven; arts councils and opera companies sent envoys to the larger corporations, among them Exxon and Citibank, appealing to the civic-mindedness of Mammon; authors of pornographic novels convened in solemn assembly and muttered sadly about the rape of the muse.

By the end of the summer so many worthy organizations were holding so many conferences that it was possible to suspect them of trying to distribute their funds before the new budgets took effect. At one of these conferences several weeks ago I heard a man say that art in the United States might enjoy its long-awaited renaissance if only it could get the government off its back. He risked this observation in what he thought was secular company in the merchant city of New York, but his remark produced the shock of blasphemy in the midst of a synod of bishops.

"Good Lord," said a woman in a hat, "you can't seriously mean that . . . surely . . . I mean . . . the arts."

Her dismay was seconded by the other people in the room, almost all of them curators of museums, foundation hierarchs of various ranks, directors of regional dance theaters, or critics beholden to *The New York Times*.

Not only did the man mean what he said, but he had the effrontery to suggest that the government should dismantle the entire apparatus of what he called its ignorant and condescending patronage. "The cultural subsidy," he said, "is a coin tossed to a beggar. The government gives money to art as it would give a tip to a blind man. So do the corporations and foundations. They hope that art will take its pittance and go away."

The door closed on his antic opinions before he had a chance to disgrace himself further, and the assembled friends of the arts resumed their placid vilification of materialism. Listening to them talk, I noticed that the discussion of cultural subsidies tends to confuse artistic and political patronage, and that by and large the speakers neglect to make a number of useful distinctions. As follows:

I

*The distinction between artistic and political patronage.*

Despite the praiseworthiness of its ambition, the American democracy in the late twentieth century doesn't know how to play the part of a Medici prince living at the zenith of the Renaissance. Various individuals might still aspire to the role, but the committees and institutions assigned to elevate the public taste look clumsy and overdressed in the aristocratic costumes of the fifteenth century.

Undoubtedly this is a sad comment on the progress of industrialism, which could probably be developed into a philippic against mass education, the dehumanization of literary criticism, and the hydrogen bomb. Given the surfeit of clichés on the theme already in circulation, I'm sure that Robert Brustein or Joseph Papp could mount an experimental revival that also portrayed what the program notes would inevitably describe as the "loss of human value." The NEA or one of the oil companies probably could be persuaded to underwrite the production.

The fact remains that the rulers of the American state, most of them lawyers and businessmen, don't look to the arts to answer questions they consider important. The most expensive debates in any age resolve themselves into the question, Why do I have to die?

As recently as the nineteenth century the question could be addressed by artists and clergymen. The events of the twentieth century have referred the question to the politicians, who have access to the final weapons, and to the scientists, who perhaps will discover the secret of immortality. The most beautiful images are those that sustain the illusion of immortality. If the fifteenth century discovered the face of God on the Sistine ceiling, the twentieth century looks for the same reassurance on the smooth surfaces of an ICBM.

Long ago, in the 1960s, it was thought that a nation acquiring economic and military eminence in the world should display the cultural appointments suitable to its wealth and station. Other empires had done so, most noticeably Periclean Athens, the Venetian Republic, France during the reign of Louis XIV. Surely the United States could arrange something equally impressive. Was not America richer than any other nation known to history? Were not its weapons more terrible, its virtues more numerous? How, then, could its painting not be more luminous, its literature more profound, its music more sublime?

The questions have ended in comedy. The United States cast itself in the role of Shakespeare's Henry V, but discovered twenty years later, somewhat to its embarrassment, that it had been playing Molière's Bourgeois Gentilhomme. Since their creation by Congress the National Endowments have invested nearly $1 billion in the hope of art, but the result has been as disappointing as a speculation in Brazilian railroad bonds. American letters have deteriorated to the point where their most celebrated practitioners, among them Norman Mailer and Tom Wolfe, discover in their own personae their most memorable characters. American drama doesn't exist. In the arts of sculpture, musical composition, and poetry the country lacks craftsmen of the first rank. The landscape has been encumbered with a public architecture of unsurpassed mediocrity, and American painting addresses itself to the illustration of aesthetic theory. The cultural impresarios can put a high gloss on foreign goods, but the more honest among them know they have lived their entire lives in a period as barren of accomplishment in the creative arts as it has been prolific of discovery in the sciences.

The failure of speculation in the arts need not be interpreted as a fall from grace. At various points in time various peoples choose to invest their energy and imagination in literature, poetry, music, painting, drama, and architecture. Throughout most of its history the United States has pursued other interests. John Adams associated the arts with "despotism and superstition" and hoped that they could be discouraged in the new republic. "To America," said Benjamin Franklin, setting the direction of the American grain for the next two hundred years, "one schoolmaster is worth a dozen poets, and the invention of a machine or the improvement of an implement is of more importance than a masterpiece of Raphael."

Americans have a talent for brilliant performance and interpretation; they have made sophisticated arts of jazz music, of journalism and the movies, of history and criticism and commercial advertising; they build monumental cultural centers that stand like the forlorn fortresses of the Maginot Line, empty of meaning, perpetually on watch against the invasion that has already passed by. The Nobel Prizes awarded every year to American chemists and biologists, to men unwinding the double helix and dissolving the mysteries of the stars, suggest that the great play of the American mind takes place in the theater of the sciences. The National Science Foundation continues to receive an annual stipend of \$1 billion (a grant commensurate with the national sense of priority), and it is probable that three or four hundred years hence, when only the antiquarians will remember any lines from the American poetry written in the last thirty years, schoolchildren will be taught to quote from the canon of American equations.

If the federal cultural subsidies have been notable for their failure to inspire passionate argument in the realm of aesthetics, they have been equally notable for their success in the arena of politics. What the subsidies could not call forth in the shape of poems or plays they have summoned up, in bewildering abundance, in the shape of studies, grants, lobbies, regional offices, stationery, exhibitions, gossip columns, directives, programs, colloquia, and opening nights. The national genius for money and tables of organization has managed to domesticate the terrifying intuitions of high art into something with which a man can feel safe.

Daniel Terra, a Chicago businessman employed as the government's "ambassador at large for cultural affairs," explained to the newspapers in July that he had spent thirteen months campaigning with his friend Ronald Reagan, who often told him that "his favorite subject for relaxation was the arts." Mr. Terra went on: "Because I had the interest in the arts, he kind of sought me out at eleven or twelve at night when you could take your shoes off and say, 'The hell with the campaign, let's talk about something that's fun.' "

Under a democratic system of government the dispensation of patronage devolves upon a body of earnest citizens—whether constituted as a congressional committee or a board of directors—who conceive of their obligation as a public trust. Even assuming that they possessed an aesthetic judgment of their own, they could not afford the luxury of indulging it. They bear a responsibility to the taxpayers or the stockholders, to the appearance of racial harmony, to the preferences of the chairman's wife, to the vagaries of the tax laws, and to the pretensions of the city or state in which they do their principal business.

How, for example, could it have been possible for the National Endowment for the Humanities or the Ford Foundation to confer patronage on Ezra Pound? Pound is arguably the greatest American poet of the twentieth century, but what board of trustees could have defended, at least in public, the man's abominable politics? Who could have explained the fellow's anti-Semitism to Senator Claiborne Pell? What would *The Washington Post* have said about spending the public money on a fascist and an avowed enemy of the United States in time of war?

The elected or appointed Maecenas learns to think not of art but of a line of goods known as "the arts." It is an important distinction because "the arts" (at least as perceived by congressmen, corporate vice presidents, and the authors of federal guidelines) allow for a bureaucratic shape and a political identity. Art remains too much within the province of the individual, an unpredictable entity that cannot be relied upon to correctly process the forms. *

---

* For the relevance of this distinction I'm indebted to Ronald Berman, a critic and historian who for seven years served as chairman of the National Endowment for the Humanities and who, in 1980, published an article in *Commentary* on the language of federal patronage.

"The arts" comprise any and all activity believed to be "creative" in nature. Thus defined, the arts have almost as many uses as religion—as a specific against crime, boredom, and drug addiction; as a palliative to send to slums, hospitals, and depressed coal-mining towns; as any hobby, craft, or innocent amusement that keeps people off the streets. Art is what enough people say is art, especially if they have the votes in Washington. Given the easiness of the democratic approach to Parnassus, more than a million people in the United States last year listed their occupation as "artist."

Having classified "the arts" as a form of political patronage, the makers of soap and laws can distribute their largesse under the familiar rules. They reward their friends and punish their enemies, arrange rites of passage (e.g., a year on a Guggenheim Fellowship in Paris) for the deserving children of the *haute bourgeoisie*, provide temporary employment for an alcoholic brother-in-law down on his luck, award construction contracts to builders with a long-standing interest in Thucydides. As blameless in its purpose as the ASPCA, more fun to talk about than cancer or heart disease, as American as mother and the flag, the cultural subsidy enjoys an advantage over other forms of patronage because nobody would be so impious as to argue against it. "The arts," Richard Nixon once said, his voice trembling with integrity (and his golfing companions cut in for a percentage), "provide the intangible but essential qualities of grace, beauty, and spiritual fulfillment." Albert Speer or the Mobil Corporation couldn't have said it better.

The Maecenases go among their constituents bearing gifts, their passage accompanied by the sweet but unheard melody of self-applause, and if it so happens that their progresses take them among the more affluent and fortunate of their neighbors (i.e., those worthy citizens likely to serve as ornaments on a state or municipal arts council), well, that is a testament to the success of democracy and the wonder of the creative spirit.

## II

*The distinction between the patron and the quartermaster.*

If the words *patron of the arts* carry an aristocratic connotation (implying that the patron in question possesses more than a passing acquaintance with the arts to which he contributes his money, his presence, or his voice), then the United States could not escape the embarrassment of making invidious distinctions in a society supposedly egalitarian. The patron might harbor something so subversive as an independent taste, and this would play havoc with the rules for distributing the annual incentives and rewards. Fortunately for the Republic, if not for the arts, the United States construes its obligation in this sphere as a moral or political activity, not as an existential necessity.

The disbursement of cultural subsidies thus falls to the same lawyers, politicians, and corporate managers who direct the country's more urgent affairs, for the most part people who take pride in the depth of their feeling rather than the acuity of their judgment. It is easy enough to imagine George Bush handing Claes Oldenburg a check for $50,000 and congratulating him, with a boyish grin, for his perfectly wonderful paintings of soup cans.

As has been noticed by innumerable poets in residence at the nation's more expensive universities, the rulers of a middle-class democracy bear a conspicuously small resemblance to the princes of the Italian Renaissance. If they haven't got the wit to commission portraits from Piero della Francesca, neither do they have a talent for poisoning their sisters. Frederick the Great was enough of a musician to compose concerti for the flute and set old Bach a theme for a Ricercare in three parts. Louis XIV was an accomplished dancer as well as a close student of Molière's theater. In the absence of television and the Sunday *New York Times*, both kings had the leisure and inclination to practice an art. So also did the Elizabethan grandees who employed Shakespeare and could themselves write sonnets, or the wives and daughters at the Habsburg court who could play the music of Haydn and Mozart.

Until the early years of the twentieth century the excitements of high art had not yet passed into the safekeeping of pedants and museums. The vast collection of things (paintings, metaphysical conceits, poems, porcelains, and musical compositions) that we name "the Western cultural tradition" still belonged within the sphere of active daily life. Art was part of the furniture, and otherwise unexceptional people could read Voltaire and Goethe without benefit of footnotes. Their number might have been relatively small, but by and large they were the same people who carried on the business of state.

The times changed, and so did the educational requirements. In the United States, citizens of mark now offer their ignorance of culture as proof of their devotion to the more serious matters of money and politics.

Gazing wistfully out to sea, past the Impressionist view of horses purchased in exchange for a lifelong preoccupation with corporate intrigue and maneuver, the magnate permits himself the indulgence of a minor regret. "Ah, my friend," he says. "If only I'd had the time to read Proust . . ." The remark drifts away beneath the roar of the helicopter settling on the lawn behind the tennis court, and the magnate hurries away to a meeting of unutterable significance.

The more sophisticated donors to museums disguise their philistinism in the rags of humility. They are simple men, they say, who know that something is good when it inspires in them a warmth of feeling. The substitution of sentiment for judgment or reason allows them a complex pleasure that combines a feeling of awe (for the mysterious objects arrayed under the rubrics of high art and big money) and a gratifying condescension toward the poor wretch of an artist who has wasted his life in the making of toys, an attitude comparable to that of the senior generals at the Pentagon who patronize the intellectuals who have supplied them with the miracle of atomic weapons.

The manufacture of art in the United States comes under the heading of a frivolous or domestic pursuit—an occupation similar to weaving baskets or making jam. An artist belongs to the same category of incompetence as women, children, and homosexuals;

one might even say that Americans conceive of art as something made by children and sold to women through the medium of homosexuals. The arrival of an artist dressed in a business suit, his hair neatly trimmed and his conversation sparkling with references to the bond market, invariably arouses suspicion among his patrons. They prefer to see their clients in more romantic costumes, and it comforts them to think of artists as demented figures—people who cut off their ears, scream at radical meetings, and walk their pet lobsters at the end of a leash.

Knowing that the "people who count" must "do something for the arts," in much the same way that they must send their children to school and appease their wives with a charge account at Bergdorf's, the democratic patrons apply to the cultural authorities for the best advice that money can buy. Left to their own devices, they might commission works from artists whom they read or genuinely admire (Irving Stone, for example, or Victor Borge), but these artists so rarely hold the proper credentials that the mere mention of their names may prompt ridicule.

Molière's comedy *Le Bourgeois Gentilhomme* follows from his hero's dependence on the suite of dancing, fencing, and speech masters who invest him with the costumes of a nobleman. The same relation between anxious master and supercilious servant produces equally comic effects among the democratic patrons of the arts who depend on a suite of critics, scholars, curators, archivists, custodians, impresarios, and promoters to provide them with the furnishings of culture. Pity the poor patron, squinting at the tiny circles on the wall, suspicious of the jargon with which his most recent major-domo demands $100,000 for wrapping the Grand Canyon in a blanket. He nods and squirms and bleakly smiles, never knowing whether he has commissioned a masterpiece or been gulled by a knave.

On the other side of the bargain, the cultural servant also plays a comic part. He must affect a haughty manner, but not so haughty that he offends against the canons of the common man. He can afford to take only so many liberties with his institutional masters (corporate boards or directors of congressional committees), and he must be careful not to disturb the equilibrium of the presiding fashion. It doesn't matter whether the fashion happens to have a classical or nihilist surface. A bureaucracy, by definition, administers the established order of objects or reputations. Its habit of dependence, together with its nervous cast of mind, inclines the cultural bureaucracy to bestow its awards on the already arrived, on the eminently acclaimed, on those artists and authors who come bearing certificates of approval and letters of recommendation from the Ford Foundation or *The New York Times*.

Perhaps this is why, as George Steiner observed some months ago in his essay "The Archives of Eden," the American cultural enterprise reflects such a conservative bias. Never in the history of the world have so many people trooped through so many museums or been provided with so many classical texts, reproductions, musical performances, libraries, concordances, and adult education programs. Almost every hamlet in the country boasts a dance group, an atheneum, and an orchestra.

All this coming and going undoubtedly constitutes an immense social good and accords with the meliorist precepts characteristic of the United States since the eighteenth century. If the expansion of knowledge and the advancement of learning benefit the individual as well as the Republic as a whole, who can quarrel with the display of culture so generously strewn around the countryside and so assiduously collected in air-conditioned vaults?

The question addresses the purpose of the national cultural subsidy in both its public and private aspects. If patrons intend to provide what their brochures sometimes describe as "life-enhancing experience" for large numbers of people who otherwise might not have a chance to see Picasso's paintings or a fourteenth-century Chinese bronze, even the surliest critic would be hard put to find fault. But if it is the intention of the donors to encourage the making of American art and thought, then the dominion of bureaucratic taste tends to smother—albeit with affection—the movement of the spirit. Unparalleled in its dedication to the past and to the preservation of the European collection, the cultural bureaucracy remains, perhaps correctly, suspicious of people with anything new to say.

Steiner offers as a metaphor the Stradivarii on display in the Coolidge Room of the Library of Congress:

*They hang lustrous, each millimeter restored, analyzed, recorded. They hang safe from the vandalism of the Red Brigades, from the avarice or cynical indifference of dying Cremona ... Americans come to gaze at them in pride; Europeans in awed envy or gratitude. The instruments are made immortal. And stone dead.*

Something of this same lifelessness infuses the opera performed at Lincoln Center, the monographs published under the auspices of the NEH or the NEA, the public affairs programming on PBS, and the proceedings of the Aspen Institute. No matter how brilliant the performance, how polished and technically correct the surface of the prose, the work itself seems to have been arranged with the busy tidiness of the notions counter in a well-kept department store.

### III

*The distinction between the passive and the active voice.*

*Superman II* opened in 1,408 theaters across the country during June of this year, and within three days had earned over $14 million. *Raiders of the Lost Ark,* another of the summer's epic tales, earned $50 million during the first twenty-six days of its release.

If Americans can spend such princely sums on opéra bouffe, why is it implausible to hope that they might spend even a fraction of that amount on works in more difficult genres? It certainly isn't a question of money. The Reagan administration contemplated reducing the federal cultural subsidy from $338 million to $167 million, the appropriation divided almost equally between the NEA and the NEH. In the order of American magnitudes, even the larger sum amounts to about an hour's worth of the year's gross national product. The television networks spend a million dollars to broadcast the Super Bowl game, and in the space of a week the great advertising agencies probably commission television commercials worth, in aggregate, as much as the entire budget of the New York State Council for the Arts.

Last summer in Rhode Island I watched a production crew make a thirty-second film of a new car; the shooting cost $96,000, needed three days' worth of the light at sunrise and sunset, twenty vehicles, and a cast of sea gulls. The cost of the time on network television was expected to come to another $200,000.

Given the number of wealthy and eccentric citizens in our country, many of whom have amassed riches infinitely greater than those of even the most covetous Renaissance pope, why do so few of them feel moved to commission works of art? Perhaps they don't care to, but if this is true, on what grounds comes the complaint that the government (or the foundation or the corporation) refuses to provide people with what they will not provide themselves?

Art cannot exist without a passionate and discriminating audience, but despite the numbers of people shuffling past King Tut's gold, the evidence suggests that the United States has not yet developed such an audience.

Over the last generation a few thousand pianists have no doubt become competent enough to get all the way through *The Well-Tempered Clavier*; many more thousands of poets, potters, weavers, and students of creative writing have enjoyed innumerable hours of communion with the muse of their choice. Nobody could begrudge them their pleasure or accomplishment, and maybe this is the entire and proper purpose of the cultural subsidy.

But what else is there to show for so much earnest endeavor? How many people read the literature of other languages or study the models of English prose set by Swift and the King James Bible? Who can tell the difference between a cello sonata performed by Rostropovich and the same music played by a second-year student at Juilliard? What six people can agree on a definition of art, or even care enough about the subject to get into an argument? Who has enough confidence in his own judgment to raise an articulate defense against the gang of critics promoting this week's masterpiece?

By and large, the audience remains as passive as it was before the advent of Mr. Herbert Schmertz and Senator Pell, an audience astonished by celebrity and opulent spectacle, eager to consume whatever the merchants in New York and Washington distribute under the designer labels of culture. It is an audience that associates freedom with power, not with thought, an audience restlessly in search of diversion rather than balance of mind. The buyers pressing through the doors of the New York auction galleries have come to seize the insignia of power and success. Because there are more millionaires in Kansas than there are paintings by Degas or Cézanne, the market bids up the price of almost any painter with a foreign name. The buyers have made their mark in the world, and they want it known that they, too, have won through to virtue and that they possess the outward and visible signs of an inward and spiritual grace. The old painting on the wall corresponds to a marker buoy floating over the wreck of a Spanish treasure galleon.

The appreciation of high art requires not only thought but also some technical understanding of what's being done, but Americans tend to bring this kind of informed judgment to their fondness for cars, handicrafts, and computer systems—for objects that move and do things, as opposed to those that merely sit there and wait to be understood. The American spirit has a Faustian rather than an Apollonian bent, and it is typical of the national curiosity that it is much more interested in what Van Gogh's crazed hand did to his ear than in what his incomparable eye saw in the sunlight of Arles.

HARPER'S MAGAZINE,
*September 1981*

# THE ARMED
# TEDDY BEAR

---

I

N THE EARLY spring of 1961 several million Hindus in northern India knew that the world was coming to a sudden end. Their astrologers noticed an impending conjunction of planets (principally Mars and Saturn, as I remember the diagrams), and from this observation they calculated a precise date and time for the long-awaited catastrophe. Immense crowds gathered on the shores of the Ganges, scattering flowers on the sacred water.

For reasons that seemed to me as obscure then as they do now, the New York newspapers delighted in this prophecy of alien doom. About a week before the fatal alignment, all the papers in town began to publish front-page stories that resembled the counting down of the last ten seconds of a football game by 53,000 triumphant fans. The city editor of the *New York Herald Tribune* appointed me to what he called the Doomsday Desk, and for seven days and seven nights I revised the dispatches from Srinagar and points south, studied star maps, and stayed closely in touch with the movements of obscure sects in California.

After three days of headlines the Doomsday Desk began to receive inquiries from citizens who wished to know if they should sell their property and move to Florida. An eight-year-old girl on West Seventy-fifth Street, frightened and crying, wondered what would happen to the dog she had been given on her birthday. Earlier that morning she had called *The New York Times* to ask if it was true that the world was coming to an end. Presumably under the impression that he was making a joke, the editor assigned to answer the question had said, "Yes, little girl, at two o'clock tomorrow afternoon, on the rowboat pond in Central Park."

Fortunately the girl had a friend, age twelve and more sophisticated, who understood that different newspapers provide different answers to the same question. The friend persuaded her to call the *Tribune*, and I explained to the younger girl that no, the world wasn't coming to an end, that her dog was safe, and that the man at the *Times* probably thought he was talking to his sister, who pulled his hair and wrecked his toys.

Having had roughly twenty-three years to reflect on the two answers to the little girl's question, it occurs to me that between them they all but exhaust the emotional repertoire of both journalism and pulp fiction. The gentleman at the *Times* succinctly enunciated the apocalyptic theme repeated with so much effect in the commercial literature of the last two decades. Were it set to music and scored for woodwinds, it could serve as the opening motif in the symphonies of despair composed by the preachers of nuclear war, environmental ruin, and whatever other phenomenon, natural or unnatural, can be made into a synthetic conjunction of Saturn and Mars.

The comforting answer belongs within the optimistic tradition of self-help; it is the stock-in-trade of Walt Disney and the editorial page, of the professional bearers of good news who assure their clients that yes, Virginia, there is both a Santa Claus and a Democratic party.

Surprisingly enough, it is this sunnier realm of progressive well-being, a place fit for Pollyanna or Rebecca of Sunnybrook Farm, that gives rise to the espionage novel, or, as it is known in the trade, the thriller. The principals traffic in cynicism and betrayal, but the lesson to be drawn from their exemplary efforts is meant to assure the reader that the apparent irrationality of events yields to comfortable explanation. Excepting only the historical romances, no genre of popular writing over the course of the last generation has enjoyed so constant a success. As given form by Ian Fleming, Eric Ambler, John le Carré, Frederick Forsyth, Trevanian, and Robert Ludlum, the thriller probably has become the principal source of popular instruction in the otherwise impenetrable mystery of foreign affairs. The success of the genre has coincided with a period in which the public discussion of guerrilla war has been all but unanimous in its censure of political murder. The paradox implies at least the semblance of a division in the mind of the reader, who apparently derives as much pleasure from signing peace petitions as he does from taking vicarious part in the exploits of James Bond. By day he denounces the cruelty of realpolitik; by night he consorts with it as if with a demon lover.

Like their grand progenitors in nineteenth-century England, Russia, and France (and unlike the contemporary authors of art novels, who work only in the precious enamel of metaphor), the writers of pulp fiction depict their characters on the canvas of the real world.

Their stories can begin anywhere—with a killing on the deck of a Russian steamer in the Black Sea; with a deal in a London art gallery; with the sale of a Radcliffe girl to an agent of the Saudi Arabian slave trade. Over the next few hundred pages other scenes, equally baffling at first sight, rely for their effect on descriptions of a Czechoslovakian airliner or a Bulgarian passport office. All the characters eventually meet at an appointed time and place (a rendezvous no less unlikely than the conjunction of Saturn and Mars), and with any luck our side triumphs over their side, and once again Western civilization is saved from death by communism or bubonic plague. By offering to explain how the world really and truly works, the espionage novel, no matter how frequent the killing or how urbane the moral relativism of its leading lady, retains the character of a bedtime story.

Every year the lullaby becomes more implausible. Twenty years ago it was still possible to present a hero flawed with the marks of self-doubt or middle age. Even if the writers drew their figures with the nursery school crayons of fourth-grade cliché, it was still conceivable that moral virtue or intellectual courage might have some bearing on the story.

The human likeness is no longer expected or sufficient. As the media magnify the perceived threat on the frontiers, so also it comes to be believed that maybe the world is a more savage place than previously had been imagined in suburban Michigan. The restless children find it hard to go to sleep unless they have been told that chrome-plated gargoyles stand watch on the lawn behind the tennis court. Le Carré, in *The Little Drummer Girl*, invents at least five characters who might as well have been manufactured by McDonnell Douglas or Boeing. Ludlum and Trevanian imagine similarly mechanical beings, enlarging their godlike powers to encompass the sexual as well as the martial arts.

Addressing what they correctly discern as their readers' desperate wish, the writers of thrillers supply the supreme illusion of absolute control. Yes, they say, the world can be made to come to heel, to obey the commands of the enraged or frightened self. The fantasy conveniently assumes the absence of conscience and presents the modern hero as the embodiment of instinct regained. The truly fortunate man achieves the status of a nation-state or a wolf, to which, as both the Afghans and the Nicaraguans know (and as Little Red Riding Hood also knew), all things are permitted.

HARPER'S MAGAZINE,
*September 1985*

# WEIMAR REVISITED

O N A PLANE to Washington two weeks ago I ran across
R——, an urbane and genial theatrical agent whom I hadn't seen in
several years but with whom I sometimes exchanged correspondence about one or another of the inane book reviews that decorate
the New York literary press. R—— left Germany in the 1930s, but
he had known Thomas Mann and Alban Berg as well as the theater
crowd around Bertolt Brecht in Berlin. We got to talking about the
brilliant but oddly sterile character of American letters. Both of us
could name a good many writers who had polished the surface of
their prose to a sheen compatible with the marble floors of the atrium
of Trump Tower. But why was it that so few of these writers published
books that either of us cared to read? Somewhere south of Baltimore
I asked R—— why no American author in the last twenty years had
written what could be construed as a preeminent novel or play. Many
of them had written good books, but none to measure against the
best work of Dos Passos, Lewis, Fitzgerald, Eliot, O'Neill, or
Pound.

"Everybody is still in the Weimar Republic," he said. "If there is
such a thing as an American avant-garde, it is to be found in the
precincts of crime."

The remark had the balance of an epigram, but it prompted me to
think of publishers instead of writers. To walk into a bookstore these
days is to step backward in time. Behind the cashier's desk, between the celebrity posters and the astrological charts, the Sierra

**51**

Club calendars show the year to be 1985. The merchandise is displayed in poses as decorative as the arrangement of blouses and scarves in an opulent boutique. Given enough time between trains, the reader can find the newest collections of erotica, the latest histories of jewelry or costume design, cookbooks, luxurious editions of Proust or Whitman, art books, anthologies of college humor and eighteenth-century pornography, the confessions of this week's movie star, diet and exercise books, the season's geopolitical tract, manuals guaranteed to impart the secrets of the orgasm and the stock market.

Surrounded by so much expensive paper it is possible to imagine, at least for as long as it takes to read the titles of the books, that the Sierra Club has got its dates right, that yes, this is the ninth decade of the twentieth century in a nation so advanced that the exuberance of its literary genius deserves comparison with the force of its scientific discovery. The impression soon fades. Most of the supposedly new books turn out to be what the movie people call remakes, variations on the themes of the Weimar Republic in orchestrations by the Iowa School of Creative Writing.

The publishers do what they can to compensate for the absence of a new idea with innumerable works of intelligent history and criticism. The trade and university presses furnish encyclopedias, dictionaries, chronologies, and revised translations of classical texts. The abundance of fact available to the reader surpasses anything that could have been imagined by Aristotle or Shakespeare.

But a society comes to know itself not so much by the accumulation of data (no matter how arcane or handsomely boxed) as by the argument with death that is its literature. It is in the specifically literary forms—the novel, the drama, the moral essay, the poem—that the current silence becomes embarrassingly audible.

Every morning I read in the papers that I live in what the editorial writers like to call "an era of rapid and unprecedented change." The phrase presumably means something when referred to the nonliterary sphere of influence. Over the last quarter of a century the United States has let loose so many genies out of so many laboratory bottles that the government's army of clerks cannot keep track of all the people following the courses of electrons, experimenting with the properties of hydrogen, observing the permutations of cells. The nation's research vessels voyage into distant seas and the farther reaches of space, sending back messages from the Mindanao Deep and the other side of Saturn. Freebooting lawyers, at work behind the lines of both the public and private sectors of privilege, revise the balance of the laws with the recklessness of high-energy physicists flinging particles together to achieve temperatures of 40 million degrees. Swindlers and merchant bankers arrange the transportation of money through five currencies and seven tiers of taxation. In Africa, forty-nine nations have come into being since World War II, most of them in births as violent as those of stars. The Chinese have staged two cultural revolutions. The Arabs found and lost Aladdin's lamp. The Japanese abducted the automobile industry from the American seraglio.

But in the little room of American letters, the conversation remains as it was in the last years of the Eisenhower administration. When I first came to New York in January 1960 I counted among the authors already well established not only Norman Mailer and Saul Bellow but also Philip Roth, William Styron, Arthur Miller, Tennessee Williams, John Updike, Truman Capote, Mary McCarthy, V. S. Naipaul, John Cheever, Lillian Hellman, Gore Vidal, and Robert Penn Warren. Kurt Vonnegut, Edward Albee, and Joseph Heller joined the company in 1962, and that, by and large, was that.

A few members of the troupe have died, but with surprisingly few additions (I think of Thomas Pynchon and Ken Kesey), the same writers who first entered the limelight in the 1950s continue to occupy the center of the literary stage. They do so despite the proliferation of the publishing industry (49,545 new titles in 1983 as opposed to the 15,012 in 1960) as well as their own reluctance to develop or amend the text of a sensibility imported from Weimar and taught to two generations of American university students. They sit there still, perennial guests on an old talk show, exchanging pleasantries about the ugliness of "mass culture," wishing they understood law or finance or astronomy, thundering against the foul corruptions of the establishment, asking or answering the questions posed by Einstein, Darwin, Picasso, Marx, or Freud. The same questions, of course, were current in Berlin when R—— was still young enough to believe the promises heard at 4 a.m. in a waiter's Gypsy violin.

Historical parallels can be as dubious as any other juxtaposition of images, but if I compare the change of the intellectual light between 1825 and 1885 with the corresponding change between 1925 and 1985, I notice (or at least I think I notice) a pronounced fluctuation in the first interval and, in the second, an equally pronounced immobility. What was once the bright vanguard of a literary generation resembles the carcass of the Pleistocene mammoth found fifty years ago in the Siberian snow. The Ice Age descended so abruptly on the animal that it froze to death with a flower in its mouth.

In 1825 John Quincy Adams was inaugurated President of the United States, and in Europe the sensibility of the age was reflected in Constable's paintings and Beethoven's music, in the writings of Goethe, Balzac, and John Stuart Mill. The Americans talked about James Fenimore Cooper and Washington Irving. By 1885, the play of the mind took place against the backdrops of Wagner's opera and Nietzsche's metaphysics. The voices in the prompter's box were those of Tolstoy, Flaubert, Ibsen, Maupassant, and Henry James.

The sixty years between 1925 and 1985 haven't brought about as dramatic a shift of scenery. The latter-day modernists lack the range and expression of their forebears, but they continue to follow the chalk lines marked on the stage by Kafka and Joyce.

Elsewhere on the intellectual front the forces of cultural regression ally themselves with a military establishment brilliantly equipped to meet the emergencies of 1943, with the economists who have yet to think of a rejoinder to Keynes, with the grand simplifications of Jerry Falwell, and with a Republican administration that might as well be working for Herbert Hoover.

Newton's third law of motion holds that every action engenders an equal and opposite reaction, and perhaps this accounts for the rigidity of contemporary American thought. The more alarming the threat or rate of change, the more insistent the denial of change. If the scientific and technological factions begin to take on the aspect of bearded radicals, then the literary factions can be forgiven the wish to make time come to a comforting stop. The expensive writers make no attempt to shift the angles of perception between the familiar and the unfamiliar, to provoke the reader to say, in the moment of startled transformation, "I had not known this; this is how it must be." The reader already has anxieties enough, and so the literary guilds seek to calm and soothe him, persuading him to nod and doze and mumble to himself, "Yes, this is what I have always known."

HARPER'S MAGAZINE,
*February 1985*

# PARADISE REGAINED

THE RECENT NEWS from the international frontiers has been mostly bad, and were it not for the television commercials, even a cheerful and quiet-minded citizen might conclude that the tide of events was running in a direction inhospitable to the American Dream.

For many days the broadcasters have been talking about Soviet aircraft shooting down a Korean airliner en route to the Orient from New York, about American troops being killed in Lebanon, about leftist guerrillas sacking a city in El Salvador, about the chance of a larger war in Chad. They read grim bulletins, show ominous maps, consult with alarmed military and diplomatic authorities.

Fortunately, they never get more than a few minutes into their tales of unrest before they pause for a word of hope from the sponsor. It is the juxtaposition between these two advertisements for reality that lends to the evening news the aura of absurdity so prized by the Dadaist poets.

The portrait of the ideal American place seen in the television commercial has remained constant ever since the Eisenhower administration. Elsewhere in the world, people have suffered the effects of violent and subversive change. New generations of weapons and computer technologies have come and gone; the American automobile industry has been exported to Japan; since 1945 the nations of the earth have fought at least a hundred and forty wars. But in the never-never land of the American television commercial, almost nothing has changed. The conversation is largely as it was thirty years ago; so are the people, and so are the commodities and social values offered for sale.

No matter what the product being advertised, no matter what the slogan or camera angle, the geography of the illusion remains constant. If the landscape and principal characteristics of the American Eden were to be reduced to the rubrics of a gazetteer, the travel agents' brochure would read as follows:

*Location:* Indefinite, but part of the real instead of the mythical world. Within reach of the scheduled airlines.

*Metaphysical Type:* Classical and Arcadian rather than Christian. Attainable by anybody with the minimum economy fare. No requirements having to do with virtue, moral worth, good works, etc.

*Climate:* Tropical on the seacoast; temperate inland.

*Time of Day:* Either dawn or sunset. The sun low and red on the horizon. The landscape suffused in a flattering half-light.

*Land Area:* About the size of North Carolina or Belgium.

*Population:* Less than 100,000. No large cities. No overcrowding.

*Topography:* A pleasant coastline similar to the French Riviera; picturesque fishing villages, and harbors deep enough to accommodate large yachts. Behind the sea a landscape recognizable as that of the American historical past; the frontier, Marlboro Country, charming New England towns.

*Roads:* Superhighways and shaded country lanes. No traffic lights, heavy traffic, or speed limits. Nobody ever gets killed in an accident.

*Purgatory:* None. All transformations instantaneous, within minutes of swallowing the tablet or spraying the wax or applying the cream.

*Faith:* Limited to the empirical; what a person can see, taste, feel, or smell.

*Time:* Meaningless.

*Children:* Confined to a woodland glade in which they are forever playing ball, riding bicycles, and catching frogs. They never intrude.

*Wishes:* All granted. Whatever anybody wants is good for you.

*Waiters, Chauffeurs, and Gas Station Attendants:* Delighted to be waiters, chauffeurs, and gas station attendants.

*Architecture:* Suburban American. Everybody's house the same size and construction.

*Churches:* Irrelevant.

*Merchants:* Never grasping or suspicious.

*Plumbing and Household Appliances:* Forever being improved upon.

*Appearance of the Inhabitants:* Beautiful, young, anonymous, and predominantly white. Nobody is ugly, old, crippled, or poor. To acquire any of these characteristics, or to become in any way unlikable or unhappy, will result in being denounced or driven out.

*Art:* None. To make it presupposes pain, which is a reason for expulsion.

*Love:* None. For the same reason.

*Marriage:* A subject for light opera or science fiction.

*Popular Amusements:* Similar to those at a well-run European or Florida resort. At the gambling table the winners are allowed to keep what they win; the losers get their chips back.

*Polite Conversation:* Comparable to that among strangers on the first night of a Caribbean cruise.

*Serious Conversation:* The same.

*Freedom:* Total permissiveness; liberty understood in a pagan rather than a Christian sense. The license of a sailor on shore leave.

*The History of Western Civilization:* An amusing bedtime story. Nobody can ever quite remember what happened exactly, but it doesn't make any difference.

THE WASHINGTON POST,
*September 1983*

# POWDERED ROSES

*He [the Comte de Cagliostro] has discovered that drugs
against life are infinitely more desired even than drugs
against death.*

—William Bolitho
*Twelve Against the Gods*

SOME WEEKS AGO *Newsweek* published selected fragments of
*Ferraro: My Story,* the former candidate's memoir of her lost vice
presidential campaign. The newspaper advertisements coinciding
with the magazine's appearance on newsstands promised "never-
revealed conversations with Fritz Mondale, her husband, and her
closest advisors." As was to be expected of a magazine that touted
its publication of the counterfeit Hitler diaries as one of the leading
cultural events of the twentieth century, the revelations proved to be
impressively empty. A random transcript of conversations overheard
on a Greyhound bus might have yielded discoveries of a higher
order.

Like most politicians who write self-serving memoirs, Ferraro
blames as many other people as possible for her own failures.
Mondale condescended to her; the sexists (mostly Republicans or
insensitive newspaper reporters) didn't take her seriously as a
woman; Archbishop John O'Connor misrepresented her attitude
toward abortion; bigots hated her because she was Italian; and her
husband, the otherwise wonderful, supportive, and long-suffering
John Zaccaro, forgot to tell her that he had been doing business with
criminals. *Newsweek* published an abridged text of roughly 12,000
words, but over the full length of the book I'm sure that Ferraro
manages to nominate at least twenty additional individuals or historical accidents to her catalogue of recrimination.

The most grotesque aspect of the memoir is its tone. The writing attests to a mind complacently devoid of wisdom, skepticism, or humor. *Ferraro: My Story* is propaganda, the story not of a person but of a product, its voice that of an advertisement for a hair spray or a brokerage house. The once and future candidate has become a commodity in need of an image and a market share.

Ferraro never doubts that if fortune had been kind, she would have become an exemplary Vice President: "There wasn't anything I couldn't do—and do well—if I put my mind to it." Nor does she feel abashed by the prospect of becoming President: "If, God forbid, Walter Mondale were to die on inauguration day, then I certainly would be in a tough situation. But if I had six months to absorb all the details . . . ? I felt confident that I could lead the country."

Six months? To absorb all the details?

Even at the end, after she and Mondale have lost the election by a humiliating margin, Ferraro has found "many personal satisfactions along the way"; she thinks she "strengthened [her] marriage" and takes "undeniable pride in making history." Her jaunty egoism makes of the campaign the equivalent of a course in macramé or aerobic dancing. She is incapable of discovering even the tiniest flaw in her perfection, and it never occurs to her that the voters in their hundreds of thousands might have failed to find her plausible because they saw her as a hack politician married to a real estate operator under criminal investigation.

The question remains as to why people can bear to read celebrity memoirs written in the manner of Ferraro's extended press release. The genre has become the staple of contemporary literature, attracting the talents not only of politicians but also of car salesmen, television actresses, and retired brothel keepers. The last few years have brought forth works of self-adoration from sources as various as Joan Collins, Jimmy Carter, Ed Koch, Lee Iacocca, Estée Lauder, and John DeLorean.

I used to think it possible to ascribe the enthusiasm for such books to the illiteracy of an audience that didn't know the difference between honest and dishonest writing. Perhaps if people could be encouraged to read the reflections of Harold Macmillan or François Mitterrand, maybe they also might learn to read Montaigne, Grant,

Clemenceau, even Jefferson or Lincoln. Maybe then they would come to sense the humility and self-doubt characteristic of politicians who know how fragile are the illusions on which their power rests, and know also how heavy is the burden the exercise of that power places on a suffering world. It is one thing for Henry Kissinger to tell after-dinner stories about his dialogue in Paris with the charming little gentlemen from Hanoi; it is another thing if the author also can remember that while the waiters were changing the wineglasses a boy of eighteen, sitting in the mud six kilometers east of Saigon, was holding his intestines in his hands.

Given the currency of books like those by Ferraro and Iacocca, it's foolish to assume that the readers don't know what they have bought. Like the audiences for prime-time television and Broadway musicals, the audience for political romance presumably takes comfort in the denial of intellect and feeling. Who could bear the thought of being governed by human beings, by people as confused and imperfect as oneself? If a politician confessed to an honest doubt or emotion, how would it be possible to grant him the authority of a god? Better to remain numb, to applaud mediocrity with a feeling of relief because nobody onstage has raised any troubling questions, to buy books for the same reasons that one buys cocaine or tickets to *A Chorus Line*—as anesthetics against the fear of death or the unpatriotic suggestion that maybe all stories don't have happy endings.

The Comte de Cagliostro (a.k.a. the Pupil Adored of the Sage Althotas, the Son of the Last King of Trebizond, the Unfortunate Child of Nature) made the same profitable discovery in the later episodes of his career as a magician. Christened Giuseppe Balsamo at Palermo in 1743, the same year that Diderot completed the *Encyclopédie*, Cagliostro by the age of twenty-nine was touring Europe in a japanned black coach, attended by six armed servants in black livery and accompanied by a woman of incomparable beauty and silence whom he sometimes introduced as his wife, Seraphina, at other times as a sibyl in one of the Egyptian mysteries or the Grand Mistress of the Fixed Idea.

Bolitho makes the point that the Age of Reason was also an age that believed in fairy tales. Rousseau's Social Contract was a kind of fairy tale, and so were the stories in the *Cabinet des Fées*, with which Marie Antoinette consoled herself while waiting her turn under the guillotine. It was tiresome to know too much about mankind, to have reduced the chaos of superstition to the classical lines of rational thought, to understand too thoroughly the mechanics of cause and effect. The surfeit of science engendered a feeling of disgust. The Enlightenment cherished a longing for the dark.

Like any other successful mountebank or doctor of souls (in the twentieth century, as in the sixteenth or the third), Cagliostro found his audience among the impoverished rich—that is, among people who, having received most or all of the presents in the world's gift, still think themselves cheated of the ineffable. The cities of eighteenth-century Europe maintained in sufficient luxury a satisfactory number of Italian counts, French marquises, German baronesses, and miscellaneous masked ladies of fashion troubled by the vapors of ennui. Like the repertory company seen in contemporary gossip columns, they had been to all the parties and wondered why it wasn't possible to escape into a happier domain (presumably as exclusive as Walter Annenberg's estate in Palm Springs) where even their least articulate wishes might promptly be granted and where death came only for the poor.

Upon gaining the confidence of the nobility resident in Paris or Berlin (an educated clientele, subtle and fantastic, but, in Bolitho's phrase, "as critical as the paying audience at the first night of an opera"), Cagliostro revealed the preliminary tricks of his trade. He could change hemp into silk or make roses out of powder. Occasionally he called forth materializations of the devil; sometimes he presented a mandragore, a small woodland creature born of "the voluptuous but ambiguous tears of a hanged man." In his luggage he carried a sylph, six inches high, "of the most perfect beauty and life"; for an additional fee he could fabricate, "by rare distillation," homunculi who answered questions and lived in bottles, "carefully sealed because they were quarrelsome."

By these and other devices Cagliostro made believers of the ladies and gentlemen whom he converted to the expensive worship of one or another of his illusory selves. During the earlier phases of his career he took a craftsman's pride in the ingenuity of his effects.

But as he became more successful and more cynical, he understood that the magic wasn't necessary. The customers didn't require transport to other worlds; instead of looking for a way out of the cosmos, they were looking for first-class accommodations at a luxury hotel. The sum of their desire was as simple as the addition in a child's first book of arithmetic, and the difficult therapeutics of *Weltschmerz* could be resolved by guarantees of long life, perfect health, sexual prowess, and easy riches.

The magician released the mandragore and devoted himself to the love-philtering and gold-making trades. In the black japanned coach he wandered across Europe touting cures for gout and impotence, recommending diets, teaching the secrets of alchemy, and, on occasion, selling the carnal manifestations of the Grand Mistress of the Fixed Idea. During the last fifty years of the *ancien régime*, Cagliostro made the passage from medieval necromancer to modern publisher. The prostitution of his talent coincided with the breaking up of a coherent moral apparatus that allowed for the possibility of an agreed-upon definition of art as well as the practice of magic. The French Revolution let loose the genies of Romanticism (not unlike the quarrelsome homunculi once confined to bottles), which by the end of the nineteenth century had changed even the greatest artists into music hall entertainers.

If the Inquisition hadn't caught up with him in Rome, or if he hadn't failed in his last search for the elixir of eternal youth, Cagliostro undoubtedly would have found work in New York as a promoter of literary sensations. I can imagine him summoning materializations of Elvis Presley or trading the paperback rights for *The Setpoint Diet*. I like to think of him on his way to the Frankfurt book fair, carrying in his luggage a sylph in the shape of Geraldine Ferraro, an object "of the most perfect beauty and life" capable of being transformed, "by rare distillation," into Pepsi-Cola.

HARPER'S MAGAZINE,
*December 1985*

# LA DIFFÉRENCE

WHEN I MET Grierson for lunch the other day at the Italian Pavilion, he was, as usual, in the throes of a cause. Earlier that morning he had signed a petition recommending the admission of women to the Century Association, and he was impressed by the loveliness of his hero's pose on the ramparts of justice.

"This isn't Victorian England," he said. "When will people understand that women cannot be discriminated against?"

Having known Grierson for many years, I was surprised that he didn't also say that some of his best friends were women, that he had grown up in the same neighborhoods with them, and that they were amazingly good dancers. During the middle 1960s Grierson often mentioned the gentleness of the North Vietnamese, whom he regarded as an endangered species as sorely in need of East Hampton lawn parties as the blue whale. Now that he had come to the rescue of women, he wished to invest them with a moral beauty as carefully groomed as his own.

"You might find this hard to believe," he said, "but there are still a lot of people out there who don't know that men and women share the same feelings, think the same thoughts, speak the same language, and live the same lives."

Because I counted myself among the dwindling number of such people, I didn't find it at all hard to believe. Since the age of thirty it never has occurred to me to doubt that men and women inhabit reciprocal hemispheres of thought, feeling, and language. Except under duress, and then only with a good deal of shouting, the two genders seldom come close to living the same lives; nor do they look like one another, speak in the same tones of voice, write the same prose, value the same passions, or plot the courses of their destinies against the same coordinates of space and time.

Grierson went on with his sermon for the better part of an hour, but rather than argue with him, which would have been as futile as arguing with a Marxist or a twice-born Christian, I passed the time wondering how it came to be that a man of forty-five could confuse the drama of human sexuality—sometimes tragic, sometimes comic, always subtle and often beautiful—with a script written for afternoon television. To Grierson, the difference between the genders consisted in styles of dress. Apparently he thought of human nature as a kind of nursery school clay in which he could model tiny and fantastic images copied from the intellectual fashion magazines.

His naïveté was earnest and well-meant. In other years and other rooms, I had listened to his touching confessions of faith in Consciousness III, the economic theory of zero growth, and the redeeming purity of Jimmy Carter's politics.

But why did he think he could still afford the luxury of ignoring biological fact as well as the lesson, however poorly learned, of his own experience? To my certain knowledge, he had read at least four novels written by women, and his losses in the divorce courts had stripped him not only of his holdings in General Motors but also of his house in Nantucket.

Coming to the crux of his argument, he was saying something about how the admission of women wouldn't change the character of the establishment and how certain women of his acquaintance took offense (properly, he thought) at being excluded from their chance at the big-time literary and financial deals.

Both statements reflected Grierson's considerable talent for denying any reality of which he disapproved or which had failed to receive departmental recognition at Harvard. As late as 1981 he still believed that the world's supply of oil wouldn't last through the summer vacation.

Obviously the admission of women to the Century Association (or to any other club, school, gymnasium, caucus, or men's room) would change the character of the place. A women's choir has a different sound than a men's chorus. Join them together, and the harmony of voices makes still a third music. Within the hemispheres of their own sex, men and women speak to one another in ways different from the way in which they speak for publication. This is not to say that one way of speaking is better than the others, merely that they are different. I often have thought that among themselves women communicate in the manner of dolphins, precisely measuring their relative positions in the social sea by means of sonar-like signals inaudible to the ears of men, but this is another subject and not one that I would care to press at a dance sponsored by the American Civil Liberties Union.

Nature divides the whole of its creation into opposing forces (proton and electron, positive and negative, matter and antimatter, masculine and feminine) in order that their dynamic symmetries might decode and organize the unlicked chaos. The clarity of gender makes possible the human dialectic. Let the lines of balanced tension go slack and the structure dissolve into the ooze of androgyny and narcissism.

As for the proposition that the loss of access to the Century Club cheats women of their inalienable right of avarice, this also is a canard. A woman might as well say that she had been denied her constitutional privileges because she wasn't elected governor of New Jersey or made a god-person in the Mafia. Of the property still in the possession of private individuals, roughly 60 percent rests in the safekeeping of women. The daughters of affluence outnumber the sons, and heiresses live longer than their husbands or brothers. The deals done in the nation's secret trysting places (bedroom, kitchen, powder room, dinner table, spa) have a far more direct bearing on the redistribution of the national wealth than all the acts of Congress.

Watching him taste the wine that he pronounced "companionable," it occurred to me that Grierson was either rich enough or frightened enough to imagine that he could substitute words for things. Like so many of his comrades trooping along behind the skirts of the women's movement, he found abstractions so much easier to deal with than facts; so much more refined and so much less likely to make an emotional mess. He could afford to believe that the important differences between the genders were "socially fostered" because he could afford the cost of his opinion.

By denying the reality of women, Grierson granted himself an exemption from the war between the sexes. He didn't have to confront his wife, his mistress, or his own feminine impulses; he didn't have to raise his voice or try to impose what little was left of his well-bred will. If things didn't turn out as advertised in the syllabus circulated by the New School for Social Research, certainly it wouldn't be Grierson's fault. He could assign the blame for his inadequacy and fear to the unseen, impersonal and anonymous forces hidden under the blankets of "culturalization."

The pornographers exploit the same lie. They also deny the reality of women; they also think of women as little lumps of modeling clay subject to the shaping tools of commercial or sentimental abstraction. The possibilities implicit in this line of observation struck me as too subversive for Grierson's delicate politics, and I was grateful when he began to speak of oysters. About oysters and Victorian England, Grierson is never wrong.

THE NEW YORK TIMES,
*March 1983*

# CORPORATE
# PROTOCOLS

*Without the aid of prejudice and custom, I should not be
able to find my way across the room.*

—William Hazlitt

AT LEAST TWICE a year one or another of the nation's leading
pollsters announces yet again that American institutions have
achieved a new low in the public esteem. The percentages of trust—
in business and government as well as in the media, the courts, and
the medical professions—continue to fall as steadily as a winter
rain. Every after-dinner speaker says something about "the loss of
leadership" and bemoans the lack of respect for property and
persons of consequence. The attorney general looses the agents of
the Justice Department like a pack of hounds on the scent of any
free or careless expression, and the mayor of New York, amplifying
the fear of an AIDS epidemic, recommends chastity as a government policy. The remnant of the intelligentsia (for the most part,
comfortably employed as fuglemen of the ideological right) pub-
lishes a ceaseless spate of sermons against the voluptuousness of the
popular culture. The nation's editorial writers give voice to the
alarm that Claude Manceron, speaking of Louis XVI's foreign minister, ascribed to "the born conservative's fear of anything that
moves."

Alas, nothing seems to do much good. No matter how stern the
adjectives or how repressive the laws, not enough people out there
in the streets have the common courtesy to kneel in the presence
of their betters. As a remedy against this disturbing trend I think
the civil authorities might give some thought to the success of the

**68**

military services. Against the trend of the past ten years only the military has improved its standing in the popular mind. It's hard to know why. Certainly the nation's armies and navies haven't distinguished themselves in battle. The Marines couldn't hold a position in Beirut; the space shuttles have ceased to operate; the fleet in the Persian Gulf has trouble telling the difference between its enemies and its friends. Nor has the nation's officer class presented an impressive show of character. During the Iran-*contra* hearings a tawdry parade of military witnesses has entertained Congress with tales of dishonesty, ignorance, and schoolboy zeal. Listening to them tell their stories of how they tried to rescue the free world from the chains of communism, I think of vaudeville clowns hitting one another over the head with rubber bats. In Iran they dressed up as parachutists and thought to win the Ayatollah Khomeini to their cause by offering him a Bible and a cake. In Switzerland they deposited $10 million in the wrong bank account. In Nicaragua they hired drunken aircraft mechanics and dropped munitions in the wrong jungles.

And yet, despite these reversals, the military services continue to enjoy the admiration of the media and to receive, against all reason, lavish monetary gifts from a somnolent but still ambulatory Congress.

Maybe it's because of the uniforms. The armed forces may not be very effective in the conduct of the nation's wars, but they know how to stage a wedding or deploy a band. They present the spectacle of a handsomely illustrated class system, and it is their gift for pageantry that the civil authorities might do well to imitate. The public has been waiting impatiently for something along these lines ever since it first saw, during the Kennedy administration, what things could be like if only presidents had the wit to play the role of princes. President Reagan understands the sentiment well enough to know that he must dress himself up in the airs and graces of a citizen monarch. It isn't a very literate performance, but then neither is the television audience a very literate public. Having been formed by the ethos of Hollywood, Reagan offers a miniseries rendition of Kennedy's Camelot, comic farce instead of sentimental grand opera, an imitation of Napoleon III instead of Napoleon I.

The lack of trust measured in the opinion polls reflects a feeling of dissatisfaction not with the competence of American institutions— the general state of incompetence being taken for granted by everybody over the age of twelve who doesn't write newspaper editorials—but with their seediness and lack of pomp. A restoration of the nation's feeling for hierarchy might promote a revivification of its morals. The authorities should place less of their faith in the police and more of their hope in tailors.

Before setting up a class system, of course, it would be necessary to amend the reputation of the word *elitist*. In the alphabet of opprobrium, this epithet clearly stands well above the lesser and preliminary insults expressed in the terms *fascist, racist, communist,* and *sexist pig.* To denounce a fellow citizen as an elitist is to give the cut direct, to pronounce the all-American anathema and the final excommunication from the assembly of the ideologically pure in spirit.

The pejorative use of so vague a word as this always has seemed to me both humorous and perverse. I don't think I've ever met an American who didn't consider himself a member of an elite, if only an elite of one. As long ago as 1866 William Dean Howells observed that "inequality is as dear to the American heart as liberty itself."

The orthodox theory of democracy holds that all citizens possess equal rights and opportunities, that they succeed or fail according to their individual merits, that nobody is better than anybody else. The doctrine is patently false, and most Americans spend most of their lives trying to join one of the several hundred thousand elites disguised as clubs, associations, residential neighborhoods, and social registers. When everything is more or less the same, and when everybody can compete on the same footing for the same inventories of reward, then the slightest variation of result produces a sickness of heart.

Never has the world seen a nation so preoccupied with the buying and selling of the emblems of elitism. The sale of luxury goods in the nation's better department stores rests on an appeal to snobbery that would do credit to a British duke. The advertisements for cosmetics and real estate glitter with the promises of admission to the lost Eden. Let the customer buy the white shoes, and she will walk on marble terraces at Newport and Palm Beach; let the customer drive an elite car, drink an elite cognac, eat elite food in elite restaurants, travel on elite airplanes to elite resorts on elite oceans, and he will find himself transformed from egalitarian frog into celebrity prince.

In colonial America it was customary to arrange the order of dancing in accordance with the net worth of the young ladies present in the ballroom. The principal guest, usually a British peer or naval officer, danced first with the richest girl, then with the next richest girl, and so forth through the protocol of wealth. Were such customs to be revived in New York, Los Angeles, and Washington, I can imagine the presiding oligarchs reserving the right to wear rich and luxurious colors—purple, vermillion, emerald green—as well as the more costly silks and furs. The servants in the important fiscal households—the Mobil Corporation, say, or *The Washington Post*—might be permitted to wear liveries trimmed in gold.

To the extent that the world has become subject to the rule of images, the people who succeed in business, government, and the media display an aptitude for the arts of the seventeenth-century courtier. They know how to laugh at the chairman's jokes, how to charm the ambassadors from CBS and *Time*, how to sit on ornamental commissions and stay awake at international conferences, how to speak the several languages of euphemism in which the larger and more subtle organizations conduct the business of larceny and fraud.

Within most large institutions these days the most urgent questions center on the refinements of etiquette—who gets the office with the view of the river, who rides in the chairman's limousine or travels on the company airplane, who goes to Barbados for the annual meeting and finds his name on the list of recipients for important memoranda. Recognizing these distinctions as essential to the preservation of the theories of "democracy" and the "free market," the society ought to encourage its ambitious young men and women to study dancing and small talk instead of accounting or mechanical drawing.

As has been remarked by a generation of public relations counsel, the titles "Mr. President" and "Mr. Chairman" sound entirely too common. They lack resonance and could as easily be applied to a clerk in charge of a small-town savings and loan association. Corporations holding assets in excess of $1 billion ought to be permitted to endow their senior management with sonorous titles similar to those bestowed on country clubs (say, Balmoral, River Oaks, Fairlawn). The title couldn't pass from parent to child, but it would carry the irrevocable right to inscribe a coat of arms on one's stationery, cuff links, and tennis racquet.

In a country blessed with so many elitists, the badges of rank would make it easier to know when and toward whom to show proper respect, and to distinguish—at long last—the true custodians of the national conscience from the impostors. Outfitted in a velvet hat or ermine robe, Edwin Meese might find it easier to revise the nation's laws. Let Dan Rather carry a falcon on his wrist, and his audience might think that he was telling the truth.

HARPER'S MAGAZINE,
*August 1987*

# A MAN AND HIS PIG

**T**OWARD THE END of last month I received an urgent telephone call from a correspondent on the frontiers of the higher technology who said that I had better begin thinking about pigs. Soon, he said, it would be possible to grow a pig replicating the DNA of anybody rich enough to order such a pig, and once the technique was safely in place, I could forget most of what I had learned about the consolations of literature and philosophy. He didn't yet have the details of all the relevant genetic engineering, and he didn't expect custom-tailored pigs to appear in time for the Neiman-Marcus Christmas catalogue, but the new day was dawning a lot sooner than most people supposed, and he wanted to be sure that I was conversant with the latest trends.

At first I didn't appreciate the significance of the news, and I said something polite about the wonders that never cease. With the air of impatience characteristic of him when speaking to the literary sector, my correspondent explained that very private pigs would serve as banks, or stores, for organ transplants. If the owner of a pig had a sudden need for a heart or a kidney, he wouldn't have to buy the item on the spot market. Nor would he have to worry about the availability, location, species, or racial composition of a prospective donor. He merely would bring his own pig to the hospital, and the surgeons would perform the metamorphosis.

"Think of pigs as wine cellars," the correspondent said, "and maybe you will understand their place in the new scheme of things."

He was in a hurry, and he hung up before I had the chance to ask further questions, but after brooding on the matter for some hours I thought that I could grasp at least a few of the preliminary implications. Certainly the manufacture of handmade pigs was consistent with the spirit of an age devoted to the beauty of money. For the kind of people who already own most everything worth owning—for President Reagan's friends in Beverly Hills and the newly minted plutocracy that glitters in the show windows of the national media— what toy or bauble could match the priceless *objet d'art* of a surrogate self?

My correspondent didn't mention a probable price for a pig made in one's own image, but I'm sure that it wouldn't come cheap. The possession of such a pig obviously would become a status symbol of the first rank, and I expect that the animals sold to the carriage trade would cost at least as much as a Rolls-Royce or beachfront property in Malibu. Anybody wishing to present an affluent countenance to the world would be obliged to buy a pig for every member of the household—for the servants and secretaries as well as for the children. Some people would keep a pig at both their town and country residences, and celebrities as precious as Joan Collins or as nervous as General Alexander Haig might keep herds of twenty to thirty pigs. The larger corporations might offer custom-made pigs— together with the limousines, the stock options, and the club memberships—as another perquisite to secure the loyalty of the executive classes.

Contrary to the common belief, pigs are remarkably clean and orderly animals. They could be trained to behave graciously in the nation's better restaurants, thus accustoming themselves to a taste not only for truffles but also for Dom Pérignon and béchamel sauce. If a man needs a new stomach in a hurry, it's helpful if the stomach in transit already knows what's what.

Within a matter of a very few months (i.e., once people began to acquire more respectful attitudes toward pigs), I assume that designers like Galanos and Giorgio Armani would introduce lines of porcine couture. On the East Side of Manhattan, as well as in the finer suburbs, I can imagine gentleman farmers opening schools for pigs. Not a rigorous curriculum, of course, nothing as elaborate as

the dressage taught to thoroughbred horses, but a few airs and
graces, some tips on good grooming, and a few phrases of rudimentary French.

As pigs became more familiar as companions to the rich and
famous, they might begin to attend charity balls and theater benefits. I can envision collections of well-known people posing with
their pigs for photographs in the fashion magazines—Katharine
Graham and her pig at Nantucket, Donald Trump and his pig at
Palm Beach, Norman Mailer and his pig pondering a metaphor in
the writer's study.

Celebrities too busy to attend all the occasions to which they're
invited might choose to send their pigs. The substitution could not
be construed as an insult, because the pigs—being extraordinarily
expensive and well dressed—could be seen as ornamental figures of
a stature (and sometimes subtlety of mind) equivalent to that of their
patrons. Senators could send their pigs to routine committee meetings, and President Reagan might send one or more of his pigs to
state funerals in lieu of Vice President Bush.

People constantly worrying about medical emergencies probably
wouldn't want to leave home without their pigs. Individuals suffering only mild degrees of stress might get in the habit of leading their
pigs around on leashes, as if they were poodles or Yorkshire terriers.
People displaying advanced symptoms of anxiety might choose to sit
for hours on a sofa or a park bench, clutching their pigs as if they
were the best of all possible teddy bears, content to look upon the
world with the beatific smile of people who know they have been
saved.

I'm sure the airlines would allow first-class passengers to travel to
Europe or California in the company of their pigs, and I like to
imagine the sight of the pairs of differently shaped heads when seen
from the rear of the cabin.

For people living in Dallas or Los Angeles, it probably wouldn't
be too hard to make space for a pig in a backyard or garage; in Long
Island and Connecticut, the gentry presumably would keep herds of
pigs on their estates, and this would tend to sponsor the revival
of the picturesque forms of environmentalism favored by Marie

Antoinette and the Sierra Club. The nation's leading architects, among them Philip Johnson and I. M. Pei, could be commissioned to design fanciful pigpens distinguished by postmodern allusions to nineteenth-century barnyards.

But in New York, the keeping of swine would be a more difficult business, and so I expect that the owners of expensive apartments would pay a good deal more attention to the hiring of a swineherd than to the hiring of a doorman or managing agent. Pens could be constructed in the basement, but somebody would have to see to it that the pigs were comfortable, well fed, and safe from disease. The jewelers in town could be relied upon to devise name tags, in gold or lapis lazuli, that would prevent the appalling possibility of mistaken identity. If a resident grandee had to be rushed to the hospital in the middle of the night, and if it so happened that the heart of one of Dan Rather's pigs was placed in the body of Howard Cosell, I'm afraid that even Raoul Felder would be hard pressed to work out an equitable settlement.

With regard to the negative effects of the new technology, I could think of relatively few obvious losses. The dealers in bacon and pork sausage might suffer a decline in sales, and footballs would have to be made of something other than pigskin. The technology couldn't be exported to Moslem countries, and certain unscrupulous butchers trading in specialty meats might have to be restrained from buying up the herds originally collected by celebrities recently deceased. Without strict dietary laws I can imagine the impresarios of a *nouvelle cuisine* charging $2,000 for *choucroute de Barbara Walters* or potted McEnroe.

But mostly I could think only of the benign genius of modern science. Traffic in the cities could be expected to move more gently (in deference to the number of pigs roaming the streets for their afternoon stroll), and I assume that the municipal authorities would provide large meadows for people wishing to romp and play with their pigs.

Best of all, terrorists might learn to seize important pigs as proxy hostages. A crowd of affluent pigs would be a lot easier to manage than the passengers on a cruise ship. If the demands for ransom weren't promptly met, the terrorists could roast the imperialist swine and know that they had eaten the marrow of their enemies and sucked the bones of fortune.

HARPER'S MAGAZINE,
*June 1986*

# SON ET LUMIÈRE

SOME WEEKS AGO at the Museum of Natural History, in a gathering of celebrities as impressive in its bulk as the stuffed elephants and Styrofoam whales, the president of Columbia Records introduced Michael Jackson as "the greatest artist of all time." Not the greatest recording artist of all time, not the greatest rock singer or break dancer of all time, but, simply and unequivocally, the greatest artist.

Although accustomed to the spiel of ringmasters and the promises of racetrack touts, I couldn't help wondering what it was that the gentleman from Columbia Records meant by the word *artist*.

At first I thought he merely wished to say that Jackson was extremely rich. This form of politeness is now so prevalent in New York and Los Angeles that if a performer of any description earns an income that can be counted in "megabucks" he or she becomes, as if by royal proclamation, an artist. The title is another of the honors that come with the Mercedes, the house in Beverly Hills, the appearances on the Carson show. The patents of aesthetic nobility coincide with one's rank in the best-seller lists or the Nielsen ratings. The more megabucks, the more profound the distillation of truth.

But why then "the greatest artist of all time"? Why not merely "a sublime artist" or "one of the greatest artists of all time"? Surely the gentleman from Columbia Records had taken note of the sums paid to Bob Dylan and Barbra Streisand, and surely they were equally

deserving of flattering comparison to da Vinci, Bach, and Shakespeare.

If not money, then perhaps celebrity. Jackson promotes in his
admirers a wealth of feeling that can be coined into the sale of junk
merchandise, and he approaches the ideal of immortality once set
forth by an editor of the *National Enquirer.* When asked to imagine
the greatest newspaper story of all time the editor thought for a
moment, and then, his voice rising in an excited rush of words as the
inspiration seized him, he said, "Elvis . . . Elvis comes back from
the dead, and he's got all these great stories about other dead
celebrities—what they've been doing, who they've been seeing,
what they think about *Dynasty,* how they've been getting along with
God."

But even this line of argument didn't quite explain the record
executive's hyperbole. Eventually I remembered what Paul Johnson, the British historian, had said about Adolf Hitler. In his book,
*Modern Times,* Johnson portrayed Hitler as the first modern rock
star, the first totalitarian statesman to conceive of himself as an
artist. As early as 1919 the surrealists in Paris demanded a government of artists, but, as is customary among intellectuals, they badly
misjudged the form that such a government was likely to assume.

Like Mao and Ronald Reagan (or any other politician dependent
on the mass media), Hitler understood that the staging of a leader is
more important than what a leader has to say. He set the scenes of
his speeches as artfully as the producers of rock videos arrange the
visual accompaniments for songs. Recognizing that in Germany
politics was music, especially music drama, Hitler derived his
effects from the study of Wagnerian opera, which also is the precur-
sor of MTV.

In the same way that MTV makes use of images reflecting average
American tastes (automobiles, neon lights, hillbillies, wheat fields,
guitars), Hitler relied on the devotion of his audience to images
expressing average German tastes—castles, misty forests, blond
titans, peasant villages, the Rhine. At Nuremberg he experimented
with searchlights and the amplifications of sound that were the first,
modern forms of *son et lumière,* later adapted to the technique of
lighting a disco. Hitler's talent for political costume resulted in the

Nazi uniforms and insignia that remain, in Johnson's phrase, "the standard of excellence in totalitarian sumptuary."

It is the standard to which rock musicians, particularly those attempting a synthesis of elegance and sadism, still aspire. A correspondent called from New Haven last week to report having seen a Yale student wearing a T-shirt that said, "Adolf Hitler—The European Tour—1938–1945."

The lines of connection between totalitarian art forms suggested what the president of Columbia Records might have had in mind when billing Michael Jackson as "the greatest artist of all time." Like so many of his peers in the entertainment as well as the weapons business, he identified art with power. Not with thought or wisdom, not even with skill and ingenuity, but with force and the surrender of self.

In *Mein Kampf* Hitler observed that the object of all propaganda was "an encroachment upon man's freedom of will" and to this end, he resolved to whip up and excite . . . the instinctive." The television impresarios look for the same effect, and by art they mean, more often than not, the frenzied, Dionysian burst of feeling that draws a crowd, elects a president, burns the Reichstag, or sells 30 million copies of *Thriller*.

THE WASHINGTON POST,
*March 1984*

# CITIZEN GOETZ

*The longing to be primitive is a disease of culture; it is archaism in morals. To be so preoccupied with vitality is a symptom of anemia.*

—George Santayana

EVERY NOW AND then the fantastic wishes seen in the movies bear so striking a resemblance to the dreams of power loose in the streets that it seems as if they had been produced in the same studio, with the same lighting effects and the same delight in barbarism. One of these baleful conjunctions occurred during the first week of the new year, when the discovery of Bernhard Goetz, known variously as the Death Wish gunman or the Subway Shane, coincided with the box office success of *Beverly Hills Cop*, an anarchic comedy starring Eddie Murphy.

Goetz made his entrance onto the stage of the news in the role of an honest and God-fearing citizen too long made to suffer the cruel indifference of the state. Some years earlier he had been assaulted by three black youths who attempted to rob him in the subway. The police failed to deal with the incident in a manner of which Goetz approved. Not only did they fail to punish his tormentors but they also subjected him to the indignity of callow and prolonged questioning. Bearing in mind his injury and humiliation, Goetz bought a gun.

A few days before Christmas he was again molested in the subway, this time by four black youths who made threatening gestures and asked him for $5. Goetz promptly shot each of them in turn, apologized to one or two other passengers for any inconvenience he might have caused, and calmly left the train. Nobody knew where he went, and for the next several days agents of the *New York Post*, like the Trojan women grieving for the lost Hector, searched the city for a glimpse of their "anonymous vigilante."

A week later in New Hampshire Goetz surrendered to the police and was returned, mostly in triumph, to New York. The *Post* welcomed him as a hero. So did a depressing number of his fellow townsmen. They took up a public subscription to pay Goetz's bail, posted handbills praising him for "a job well done," wrote letters to editors commending him for his good citizenship and resolve. Joan Rivers sent best wishes from California, and George Clark, chairman of the New York State Republican party, pledged $1,000 to Goetz's defense fund.

"Here at last," so ran the tenor of the newspaper encomiums, "stands a man who knows that the courts cannot be trusted, that the police don't care a dime for justice, that the law is a joke."

*Beverly Hills Cop*, which has been playing to sellout crowds since early December, makes precisely the same points. Eddie Murphy appears as a Detroit police detective whose best friend, a small-time thug, makes the foolish mistake of stealing $50,000 from big-time thugs. The friend gets murdered for his impertinence, and Murphy decides to present the bill of retribution. The big-time thugs happen to live in Beverly Hills, and so Murphy takes a leave of absence and goes to California as a self-appointed government. Contemptuous of the local police and with no authority other than his own grievance, Murphy conducts an antic investigation, gathers enough evidence against the big-time thugs to assure himself of their guilt, and summarily executes them for their crimes against his finer feelings.

Throughout the movie Murphy takes every occasion to ridicule the puppets of the white establishment (all fops, wimps, and sodomites) and prey upon their fear of blacks. He advances behind a shield of insolent jive probably not too dissimilar from the manner of the black youths whom Goetz found so frightening and offensive on the subway train. The movie audiences respond with laughter and the loud stomping of feet.

"Here at last," so runs the tenor of their applause, "stands a man who knows that the courts cannot be trusted, that the police don't care a dime for justice, that the law is a joke."

These sentiments express the fondest passions of the American soul. Despite our obligatory mumbling about "a government of laws," few of us take much pleasure in the tiresome chore of justice. Given a choice in the matter, how many of us wouldn't prefer the romance of crime? A society that presumes a norm of violence and celebrates aggression, whether in the subway, on the football field, or in the conduct of its business, cannot help making celebrities of the people who would destroy it. The best-selling entertainments require the presence of a grand predator—the Godfather, Xaviera Hollander, James Bond, a great white shark—anybody or anything that takes what it wants and shows an appropriate contempt for an abstraction as bloodless and chicken-hearted as the due process of law.

*Newsweek* made Eddie Murphy's comic genius the subject of its first cover story of 1985. In support of their admiring adjectives, the magazine's critics offered the conclusive proof that *Beverly Hills Cop* had grossed $64 million in the first three weeks of its release. Fittingly enough, in the same issue of the magazine George Will, the reactionary columnist and author of a treatise on government enti- tled *Statecraft as Soulcraft*, congratulated Citizen Goetz for his "healthy anger." On a good day Will can supply the reason for shooting just about anybody, but on behalf of Goetz he got to say that without the pleasures of revenge life wouldn't be worth living. He compared the courageous Goetz to Clint Eastwood's inspirational characterization of "Dirty Harry" and somehow managed to cite Shakespeare as an authority who recommended the medicinal uses of "virtuous vengeance."

Like the radical apologists for the 1960s counterculture, who justified their disregard for the law by reason of their allegiance to what they called "the higher consciousness," Will presents himself as a civilized friend of anarchy. He assumes that he can make distinctions between the forms of terrorism as if he were a connois- seur choosing between bottles of wine.

Apparently it never occurs to Will that another heroic citizen, unsympathetic to his politics but blessed with a "healthy anger" equal to that of Bernhard Goetz, might take it into his head to eliminate Caspar Weinberger. At his first press conference the

"Pentagon vigilante" could say that he acted in self-defense, that Weinberger's militaristic policies were frightening and offensive and demanded of him a good deal more than $5. Hugs and kisses presumably would arrive by telegram from California, if not from Joan Rivers then possibly from Jane Fonda; a committee in favor of disarmament undoubtedly would post the hero's bail and nominate him for the Nobel Peace Prize.

That's the trouble with dreams of power. The dreamers come to imagine that the laws of men should embody the law of God. By their delight in bloodletting they confess their own anemia, and they forget that terrorism is a proof not of virility but of impotence.

HARPER'S MAGAZINE,
*March 1985*

# SHOOTING STARS

*The trees in whose dim shadow*
*The ghastly priest doth reign,*
*The priest who slew the slayer,*
*And shall himself be slain.*

>—Thomas Babington Macaulay.
>Quoted by Sir George Frazer as the
>epigraph to *The Golden Bough.*

WHEN HE OPENED fire on President Reagan in a Washington street last March, John W. Hinckley, Jr., posed the question as to how the United States can protect itself against one of its most cherished dreams. The question has been put before, as recently as last Christmas in New York by Mark Chapman when he killed John Lennon; almost certainly the question will be asked again, probably sooner rather than later, by somebody else with the price of a secondhand gun and the yearning to enter, however briefly, the sacred grove of celebrity.

The cherished dream might once have been Jean-Jacques Rousseau's, a romantic panorama of man as noble savage at play in the meadows of paradise, of man set free from the constraints of laws and schools and institutions, free to constitute himself as his own government, free to declare himself a god.*

Although easily corrupted and almost always misconstrued, the dream had a considerable influence on the making of American democracy; transposed into definitions of "individualism" as var-

---

* Or to define himself by any other name that might come into his head. Edward M. Richardson, the would-be assassin arrested in New York on April 7 while on his way to Washington to complete what he called "Hinckley's reality," styled himself "Interrogator, People's Court."

ious as the individuals capable of "doing their own thing," Rousseau's dream came to be accepted as a dogma of the American faith. Thomas Jefferson preached the virtues of a genial anarchy, explaining that "government is either needless or an evil, and that with enough liberty, everything will go well." Things went well enough as long as the individuals elected at birth to the highest offices in heaven and earth could buy or seize the space in which to stake out the boundaries of Eden. Thoreau established a new Jerusalem on the shores of Walden Pond, and Joseph Smith discovered the golden tablets of the Book of Mormon in a field at Palmyra, New York; Melville found Satan swimming in the Great South Sea, and for the apprentice prophets bankrupted in the panic of 1837 the western frontier offered not only an escape from their debts but also the hope of a congregation, a tabernacle, and a choir. Before the century was over the anarchy had become less genial and the savages less noble. The Union victory in the Civil War denied the Confederacy its slaveholding interpretation of Rousseau, and the capitalist incorporators of railroads preyed upon their customers with a systematic ferocity that would have offended the sensibility of a Neolithic hunting band.

To the ideal of a primitive association of gods and heroes, the Americans from the beginning opposed the countervailing ideal of a civil government conducted by mere mortals. This older, Roman idea of a republic recommended itself not only to Jefferson in his more Federalist moments but also to Washington, Jay, Hamilton, Adams, and everybody else in Philadelphia in the summer of 1787 who held the "natural man" in fairly low esteem. The authors of the Constitution put their faith in the vices rather than the virtues of their fellow citizens. On the assumption that if left to their innocent devices most men would prove themselves as merciless as wolves, the founders designed a mechanism that balanced interest against interest, class against class, faction against faction.

The history of the American dialectic could be written as the ceaseless struggle between these two contrary ideas of government. The Romantic dream of Eden aligns itself with barbarism and the past, the classical hope of the republic with civilization and the future. Since the fire at Hiroshima the argument has shifted in favor of primitivism, magic, and Rousseau. The pagan gods enjoyed a restoration comparable to that of the Republican party in last November's election. More terrible and omnipotent than in the dear, sweet days before the death of Christ, the old idols discover that their powers of creation and destruction have been much augmented. Not only can they make life in the labyrinths of genetic engineering, they can also annihilate cities.

Against the pressure of events the republican idea of government raised up the resourcefulness, courage, and self-discipline of the free citizen. No man was thought to be indispensable. Given the instruments of law, and the institutions governing the use of those laws, otherwise ordinary men were deemed capable of conducting the business of the state. Joseph Alsop expressed the republican sentiment accurately, if somewhat condescendingly, when he described President Nixon as "a workable plumbing fixture."

So mundane an approach to politics has gone out of fashion. Once the pressure of events comes to be seen as so immense and so bewildering as to defy the comprehension of men, government becomes confused with religion. People begin to say, as they did prior to the appointment of Alexander Haig as secretary of state, that in the whole of the United States only three men could be relied on to bear the burden of so august an office. The identity of the state comes to be embodied in a small repertory company of magic individuals, all of them dressed by the media in the wardrobe of immortality. Authority vested in institutions succumbs to authority vested in persons, and the republican idea of a magistracy gives way to a star system. On the great stage of the national political theater a succession of miraculous mandarins recites speeches to the moon and the stars.

The effect is much magnified by the ubiquity of the media and by the media's delight in melodrama, a word coined by Rousseau. By granting primacy to names over things, the media sustain the illusion of a hierarchy of greater and lesser celebrity. So habitual has become the popular adoration of these images that people find it easy enough to imagine celebrities enthroned in a broadcasting studio on Mount Olympus, conversing with one another in an eternal talk show.

A week after President Reagan was shot, Abbie Hoffman, the once-upon-a-time Yippie and media hero of the 1960s, was sentenced to a year in prison for selling three pounds of cocaine. Under the laws governing Mr. Hoffman's arrest and conviction the sentence was mandatory, but to Mr. Hoffman's friends and fellow celebrities the thought of Mr. Hoffman actually going to prison did violence to everything they knew about the orderly arrangement of the universe. It was monstrous, a perversion of nature, a blasphemy so unspeakable as to constitute an offense against the divine right of kings. They wrote letters to the court explaining that Mr. Hoffman was a celebrity and therefore exempt from the niggling constraints of a temporal jurisdiction. *

Being themselves players in the magical theater, most of Mr. Hoffman's companions understood that their public personae were likely to attract not only the homage of applause but also the compliment of gunfire. Quite a few of them employ bodyguards. Simplicity begets simplicity, and individualism begets counterindividualism.

The affinity of interest between William F. Buckley, Jr., and Abbie Hoffman—Mr. Buckley offered to carry Mr. Hoffman's cause to the pages of the *National Review*—suggests a resemblance between the Republican Risorgimento and the old countercultural revolution of the Woodstock generation. The manner of dress has changed, and so has the age of the malcontents, but the mighty spirit of Rousseau still beckons the wagons westward, the apparition

---

* The names of the four hundred or so people, of various degrees of charismatic intensity, who wrote letters on Mr. Hoffman's behalf, revived the memory of the blessed 1960s. Norman Mailer wrote a letter, and so did William F. Buckley, Jr., and the Right Reverend Paul Moore, Jr.; so did Allen Ginsberg, Benjamin Spock, Jon Voight, Bert Schneider, Jerry Rubin, and Bob Rafelson. The Hoffman Defense Committee claimed that it also had received testimonials from, among others: Ramsey Clark, Noam Chomsky, Peter Yarrow, Ed Asner, Studs Terkel, Joseph Papp, Shana Alexander, Ed Doctorow, William Burroughs, Joyce Carol Oates, Joseph Heller, Paul Newman, Ralph Nader, Larry Rivers, Ossie Davis, Joan Hackett, Donald Sutherland, Jason Epstein, Jane Fonda, and Woody Allen. Mr. Ginsberg, the poet, took Rousseau's line when he said, "My own view is that government must . . . act and judge and discriminate its Law with good nature." Mr. Rafelson, the movie director, said, "I pride myself on my intuition about people. Abbie is real." Bishop Moore said, "I feel he has undergone enough punishment . . . Many outstanding entertainment people have been arrested on charges surrounding cocaine, but as far as I know none has gone to jail."

these days revealing itself as the avatar of John Wayne instead of Jack Kerouac.

Like any other troupe of actors, the celebrities of the moment find it difficult to agree on any definition of law that might take precedence over the supremacy of individual wish, and so they prefer to base their authority on the rule of love. The blurring of the distinction between love and power has a diminishing effect on the people excluded from the sacred grove and for whom the fates have neglected to provide even a supporting role. In order to fuel the engines of publicity the media suck so much love and adulation out of the atmosphere that unknown men must gasp for breath. They feel themselves made small, and they question the worth, even the fact, of their existence. If the bloated persona of the chairman of the Federal Reserve Board takes up so much space in the public mind, who can feel respect for the president of the local bank? Once the audience is accustomed to making obeisance to the images of Nobel Prize laureates, how can it honor the advice of the local physician? At any one time the ecology of the media can bear the weight of only so much celebrity, and as the grotesque personae of the divinities made for the mass market require ever more energy to sustain them, what is left for the weaker species on the dark side of the camera?

Rousseau himself was acutely conscious of the subjugating power of fame. His writings allude constantly to his desire to complete other people's lives, to walk into a room and seize the instant and universal approbation of everyone present, to focus on himself all eyes, all praise, all attention, all sexual feeling. No doubt Henry Kissinger would understand what he meant. So would Abbie Hoffman. So would the literary critics who take pleasure in murdering one another's books.

Plutarch tells the story of Aristides of Athens, a statesman admired as a lawgiver but nevertheless banished from the city because he had become too popular. When the vote was taken, Aristides helped an illiterate countryman mark his shell for ostracism, and while he was doing so he asked the countryman why he wished to banish Aristides. The countryman, not knowing to whom he was speaking, said he was sick of hearing Aristides praised as "the Just."

A few days before going to Washington with the notion of shooting Mr. Reagan, Mr. Hinckley wrote a letter to an actress he had never met, saying, "If you don't love me, I'm going to kill the president." Mr. Hinckley had seen the actress, Jodie Foster, in *Taxi Driver*, in which the deranged protagonist attempts to assassinate a United States senator because one of the senator's legislative aides has disdained to notice, much less requite, his love. Mr. Reagan so obviously enjoyed the love of so many more people than even knew of Mr. Hinckley's existence that Mr. Hinckley apparently regarded the President as his principal rival for the affections of one of the girls in the chorus.

It is conceivable that nobody summoned the energy to attempt the killing of President Nixon or President Carter because neither of those gentlemen attracted an aura of devotion. Both Mr. Nixon and Mr. Carter demonstrated an emotional inadequacy so palpable as to quiet the provinces of the id. But Mr. Reagan seemed to be having such a good time; a smiling man, laughing at prerecorded Hollywood jokes, feeding on jelly beans, and all the while cheerfully withdrawing food stamps from the poor and chatting amiably to the press about his arsenal of hideous weapons. Who can bear the sight of a man so comfortable in the role of a grim and vengeful god? Like the other public men attacked by assassins in the last twenty years (John and Robert Kennedy, Malcolm X, Martin Luther King, Gerald Ford, and John Lennon), Mr. Reagan presented himself as a bringer of bad news who wanted to be loved for his trouble.

If it is possible to believe that the world can be redeemed by the sudden advent of a god from a machine, then if things don't work out quite the way the audience had hoped, maybe the mistake can be corrected by an equally abrupt departure. If the god cannot be made to listen or to feel the pain of noncelebrities murmuring in the shadows beyond the circle of magical light, perhaps he can be touched by other means. Unlike the rule of law, which derives its force from its impersonality, the rule of love can be overturned as easily as can a Nielsen rating.

Although it is impossible to know what Mr. Hinckley had in mind while he waited for President Reagan to come out of the Washington Hilton Hotel, it is probably safe to assume that he had watched a lot of television and had accepted the symbolism of the political theater as a literal rendering of the world. He owned a television set, a guitar, and a gun. These were his only possessions.

Every important event he'd ever seen, he'd seen on television. Wandering from hotel room to hotel room, unnoticed by the management, he may have come to think of himself, in Justice Holmes's phrase, as "a puny anonym." Maybe he would have been content with an appearance on the Johnny Carson show. Maybe he wished to abrogate his treaty with the United States. Whatever his reasons, they would have made sense to Rousseau.*

The media, of course, portrayed Mr. Hinckley as a near lunatic who in no way could be said to represent anything fundamental to the homespun steadiness of the American character or the wholesomeness of the American experience. The official denial has become obligatory in the aftermath of all assassinations or attempted assassinations that cannot be ascribed to a political plot. If it sounds less and less convincing, perhaps that is because it has been too often repeated. Once they had pronounced Mr. Hinckley a uniquely alienated young man, the promoters of correct opinion went on to ask the customary questions about what might be wrong with the country. Will the violence never cease? What is the matter with those people out there who keep showing up with cheap guns and third-rate film scripts? Nobody could find convincing answers for these questions. *The New York Times* admitted to a feeling of "raging helplessness." Max Lerner blamed the Secret Service (apparently for failing to impose martial law throughout the District of Columbia), the laxity of the gun laws, and Mr. Hinckley's parents (for not employing detectives to follow their son on his appointed rounds). Other columnists mentioned the rising levels of crime in the United

* They also would have made sense to John Wilkes Booth, the actor who assassinated President Abraham Lincoln. On several occasions before Mr. Lincoln's murder, Booth talked compulsively about pulling down the Colossus of Rhodes. He was once quoted as saying, "You have read about the Seven Wonders of the World? Well, we'll take the Statue of Rhodes, for example. Suppose that statue was now standing, and I by some means should overthrow it . . . My name would descend to posterity and never be forgotten."

On the Thursday before the Monday that he was shot, President Reagan attended a "command performance" at Ford's Theatre in Washington, the same theater in which President Lincoln was shot. The event was televised; Mr. Reagan made a theatrical show of applauding the star turns performed by a succession of singers, comedians, and magicians distinguished principally by their celebrity.

States (up 13 percent in 1980), the pervasiveness of the presidential symbol, and the porousness of a political system that allows the head of state to walk around in a shopping center without a sullen escort of lictors.

All these observations having been duly noted on the record, the authorities took pains to warn against the drawing of overwrought generalizations about the illness of American society. They didn't want anybody to get the wrong impression. Yes, it was true that the President of the United States had been shot down in broad daylight almost within sight of the White House, and, yes, it was also true that the secretary of state had yielded to a pardonable seizure of megalomania, but American society wasn't sick, and it was irresponsible of anybody to say so. The President recovered bravely from his wound, and within a few days the worried questions had died away to a distant mutter in the periodicals. The impresarios of the media circus encouraged everybody to go back to what they were doing before the program had been so tastelessly interrupted by a commercial for the assassin as celebrity.

Even so, assassination remains the leading cause of death among serving American presidents (four out of eight), and the United States seems likely to remain a dangerous place for public figures who inspire in too many people a fever of love and admiration. Unless enough of us can learn to ignore the pandering of the media, or to discount it with appropriate mockery, it is likely that the noble aspects of Rousseau's dream will continue to deteriorate into brutal fantasy. The tyranny of weakness imposed by Mr. Hinckley, Mr. Oswald, Mr. Sirhan, Mr. Bremer, and Mr. Chapman cannot be allowed to result in the remembrance of their names. If, as Andy Warhol foretold, the media will make everybody famous for fifteen minutes, what is to prevent a boy growing up with the ambition not of becoming the President but of killing the President? The latter ambition certainly is easier to achieve; easier, less expensive, and more consistent with the educational requirements set forth in the federal guidelines.

HARPER'S MAGAZINE,
*June 1981*

# SHOW BUSINESS

$\mathbf{A}$N ITEM IN the press last week briefly acknowledged the collapse of the negotiations between the White House and "Miami Vice." Vice President George Bush apparently had wished to appear on the show, but only if he could play a part flattering to his dignity. He agreed to the money ($2,500) and the working conditions (no stunts, no nude scenes), but the deal foundered on the question of image. The Vice President's speech-writers concluded that there was no cameo role in all of network television appropriate to their client's stature as the last best hope of the Republican party.

Mr. Bush's willingness to audition, for second billing behind Don Johnson and Philip Michael Thomas, testifies both to the scrawniness of his self-esteem and the magnitude of the ratings for the nation's leading allegory of good and evil. "Miami Vice" delivers a large audience (roughly 39 million) distinguished by its relatively high quotients of literacy and income. In short, precisely the kind of people who, if they have nothing more exciting to do that day, might remember to vote in the next presidential election.

"Miami Vice" makes a market in expensive media images, and a number of celebrities adept at self-advertisement—among them G. Gordon Liddy, Little Richard, Ted Nugent, and Miles Davis—have dropped by the set in recent months to make guest appearances. Why the Vice President thought it might be fun to follow these gentlemen into so lurid a light I cannot say. Nor do I care to speculate. Maybe Mr. Bush was tired of walking into crowded rooms and discovering that nobody knew his name.

What interests me is the discussion that must have preceded the White House decision to withdraw. How many story conferences took place between the writers for Mr. Bush and the writers for "Miami Vice"? Not having been present at the meetings, I can only guess at three of the characters that must have seemed, at least for twenty minutes, likely to satisfy both the political and dramatic specifications:

1. Mr. Bush plays himself, the Vice President of the United States, who happens to be passing through Miami at a moment convenient to the script. At long last, Tubbs and Crockett have captured "Mr. Big," the well-dressed drug dealer worth $670 million who always eludes arrest by putting in a fix with the cynical bureaucrats in Washington.

The two detectives force their way into Mr. Bush's hotel suite, and after some playful roughhousing with the Vice President's Secret Service thugs, they tell a tale of unspeakable crime. Mr. Bush is visibly moved. Aroused by righteous indignation, he nullifies the Washington connection that guaranteed Mr. Big's safe conduct to Peru. Mr. Bush uses the occasion to deliver an eloquent speech about the moral beauty of the Reagan administration. For the first time on network television Lieutenant Castillo weeps.

2. Mr. Bush plays the high school football coach, now retired, who taught Sonny Crockett how to move to his left. The coach lives on a houseboat in the Everglades, revered by all who know him as the wisest man in Dade County. Like King Arthur's magician, Merlin, the coach quotes Aristotle and talks to birds and rabbits.

The episode turns on Crockett's falling-out with Tubbs. The two friends have been tricked into believing themselves enemies. Just before the second commercial break, it is conceivable that one could set up the killing of the other. Crockett drives into the swamp to speak to the coach. Leading his favorite quarterback through a series of Socratic dialogues, the coach explains the meaning of the universe. All of the Vice President's lines come from the Oxford Book of Quotations.

3. Mr. Bush reads the voice-overs for God. The plot follows the story of a Colombian woman—deeply religious but very beautiful—who seeks to rescue her brother from a gang of communist drug smugglers. Burdened with gambling debts, the brother has no choice but to accompany a shipment of cocaine from Cartagena to Miami.

His sister stows away on the ship, praying constantly for the salvation of the boy's soul and asking God if she should bribe the principal villain (played by Gary Hart or by an actor who looks an awful lot like Gary Hart) with the gift of her flesh. God speaks to her three times—appearing in the form of a cloud, a flamingo, and a motorboat. "No," he says, "do not sign treaties with Satan or the friends of Fidel Castro."

In less anxious times any or all of these parts would have been deemed fit for an aspiring politician. Teddy Roosevelt certainly could have been persuaded to ride a horse in the Orange Bowl, and Ronald Reagan appeared in a good many less flattering disguises when he was learning the rudiments of American foreign policy on the back lot of a Hollywood movie studio.

It's too bad that Mr. Bush's agents didn't let him take the gig in Miami, and maybe it's time to work the scam the other way—booking the talent into Washington. If the State Department could sign Crockett and Tubbs to a cameo role in Libya, I'm sure that it wouldn't be too long before Colonel Qaddafi quit trafficking in terrorism.

THE SUN, *Baltimore,*
*January 1986*

# CAUTIONARY TALES

*Realism is a corruption of reality.*

—Wallace Stevens

T HINGS HAVEN'T BEEN easy lately for the manufacturers of network television news. The available audience, distracted and easily bored, has divided into almost as many subspecies as appear in a botanist's classification of plants. Other products on the market—cable, MTV, independent syndications, soap opera, videotext, game shows, movies, detective dramas—further dilute the attention of the relatively small number of people who can still tell the difference between George Shultz and Stacy Keach. Like their peers in the steel and automobile industries, the corporate news managers confront the sorrows of a lost monopoly. General Motors divests itself of 29,000 workers in the Midlands, and the television networks wonder if it's really necessary to send 2,000 semiliterate journalists to Iceland to gather twelve minutes of unintelligible news. The pervasive mood of suspicion and alarm results in mass firings, which in turn result in states of paralysis throughout the news divisions, which result in threatened ratings, which result in more firings. At CBS News during the past eighteen months the steady sound of desks being emptied of paper has settled into a rhythm as monotonous as the mowing of autumn wheat. Although not so well publicized, the decimations at the other networks keep pace with the measurements of decline.

Not surprisingly, the sense of impending doom instills terror within the ranks of the journalistic bureaucracies. Their collective fear finds expression in memoranda. For the past few years network executives have been studying "action plans" with the desperate hope of bankrupts looking at treasure maps. One of these documents was sent to me last month by an agent behind corporate lines. His careerist instincts prompted him to delete all references to specific programs or individuals. Judging from the textual evidence I would guess the memorandum to be the work of a junior impresario familiar with the vocabulary of film images but conveniently ignorant of politics or art or literature. He apparently was addressing his remarks to an older producer in whom he had encountered, on at least two or three prior occasions, distressing signs of timidity.

The memorandum begins with a short preamble complaining about news executives who, "instead of recognizing themselves as trainers of performing bears, prefer to think of themselves as government officials." It then goes on to offer thirty-one criticisms and suggestions, all of them indicative of a sensibility impatient with words of more than one syllable. The paragraphs quoted below can be taken as representative:

3. THE NAME OF THE SHOW. Can't we think of another word for "news"? Every time I hear the word, I think of medicine or homework—stuff that's supposed to be good for you but always turns out to be a lot worse than you thought. Mention news to anyone under the age of thirty and he thinks of a Spencer Tracy movie that he once saw on late-night television.

5. THE CREDITS. These need to look a good deal more like the credits on "Dynasty" or "The A-Team." At the top of the program, we could show film of our people getting off an airplane in Beirut, entering the White House, arm wrestling with Sly Stallone. Something with a little movement in it, for God's sake; something to hold the audience through the first commercial.

8. THE MUSIC. Obviously we need a decent sound track. I've said a lot about this in other notes, Harry, and I don't want to repeat myself about matching the week's hit tunes with the images presented on the broadcast. At the very least, we should associate each of our principal newscasters with their own musical theme—salsa for the Hispanics, jazz for the blacks, Mozart for the diplomatic analysts, Johnny Cash for the old ballplayers. If we could get any serious development money from the corporation, we could commission Springsteen to write a network song.

9. CLOTHES. In New York or Los Angeles—maybe even in Omaha—you can walk six blocks in any direction from any major intersection and see some really interesting clothes. Why do our people look like they're going to funerals? Check out the photographs in *Vogue*, Harry; look at the scene on MTV. If I've said it once, I've said it a hundred times: Hire Ralph Lauren to dress the women as well as the sets.

10. PROPS. Everybody on the show ought to bring to the set one distinctive object or mannerism. For example:

a. *A funny hat*
b. *A genuinely weird hairstyle*
c. *A foolish pet (aardvark, duck, raccoon, lobster, etc.)*
d. *A lisp.*

14. RACE BAITING. Desirable under any pretext. Ted Koppel used the technique to good effect on "Nightline" when he pitted the Rev. Jesse Jackson against the Rev. Jerry Falwell in what was nominally a discussion of South African apartheid. The two preachers nearly came to blows, which, as you well know, Harry, is very, very good television.

If we must do debates about social issues (a practice I don't recommend), at least we should book guests who detest one another, preferably for social, racial, or sexual reasons. The audience is sick of hearing professors agree on points so abstract as to have lost the name of meaning.

16. POLITICS. Another word as boring as news. Politics interests people who don't know how to make money or love. Not our kind of audience—not the upscale buyers of big-ticket items that impress our friends at the ad agencies. Maybe we should require all politicians to come on the show dressed in costume—Mario Cuomo as a Venetian gondolier, say, or Gary Hart as a Franciscan monk.

23. SPECIAL CORRESPONDENTS. Another topic that I've mentioned in other memoranda. You and I both know that the definition of news is as arbitrary as one of President Reagan's improvisations in the theme park of American history. Everything is news, and nothing is news. It depends on the circumstances and the available footage.

We should feel no embarrassment about imposing our own categories. It's about time we learned to ignore Washington and pay some attention to sex and astrology. With this strategy in mind, I suggest we hire at least three special correspondents, each of them responsible for five-minute segments at least once a week:

a. *The sexual correspondent*—an attractive blond woman in leather or silk reporting from locations as various as a singles bar in Kansas City, the von Bülow trial, or an orgy in Beverly Hills. (When we sign her to a contract, remember to retain 50 percent of book rights.)

b. *The medical correspondent*—an earnest young man in white who travels around the country in the manner of Charles Kuralt, looking into emergency rooms, touring cancer wards, doing live broadcasts of experimental operations in which the patient's life trembles (as precariously as a Nielsen point, Harry) in the balance.

c. *The criminal correspondent*—preferably a senior figure in the Mafia or a retired New York City judge. In any event, somebody with the air of an expensively manicured lizard, the sort of guy likely to know George Steinbrenner, Frank Sinatra, and Richard Nixon. Imagine an urbane and cynical gentleman, smoking a cigar, providing languid commentary on the day's most promising murder, drug bust, or Wall Street swindle.

31. CONSPICUOUS CONSUMPTION. This is what it's all about, and we ought to figure out something comparable to the newspaper lotteries. At least once in every show we ought to see somebody (celebrity or common citizen) eat $4,000 worth of caviar in ninety seconds; alternatively, we could watch somebody like Joan Collins buy, also in ninety seconds, $14,000 worth of perfume, lingerie, or fur.

Set the audience an example, Harry. Remember that we have a responsibility to educate as well as entertain. Give people an ideal toward which they can aspire; tell them a cautionary tale.

HARPER'S MAGAZINE,
*January 1987*

# WALL PAINTING

*The artistic temperament is a disease that afflicts amateurs.*

—G. K. Chesterton

IN NEW YORK last spring Christie's sold at auction, for $26,400, an idea for a drawing. Not the drawing itself. Nothing so crass as an object or a design on paper, but the right to render the drawing in a space eight feet square. The buyer of the work in question, *Ten Thousand Lines Ten Inches Long, Covering the Wall Evenly*, received a sales receipt and a set of instructions not unlike the page in a first-grade coloring book inviting a child to connect the dots. The buyer retained the right to choose the texture and placement of the wall—stucco, fiberboard, facing south, in the library—but it was strongly recommended that he hire (at his own considerable expense) the artist's own draftsmen to draw the lines in their proper width and sequence. Under the terms of the sale, the buyer further agreed to wash the drawing off the wall if and when he decided to sell it to another collector or donate it to a museum. The subsequent owner would be entitled to proof of erasure.

The artist, Sol LeWitt, expounded the thesis of conceptual art as long ago as 1969: "Ideas can be works of art—they are in a chain of development that may eventually find some form. All ideas need not be physical."

The observation is neither new nor profound. An unkind critic might go so far as to say that it was both fatuous and banal, on a par with the discovery that sailors have been known to die by drowning. But the unkind critic would miss the point and fail to appreciate LeWitt as a prophet. Within the span of a single generation LeWitt's

**100**

minimalist aesthetic has come to define the character of postmodernist politics, sex, literature, and war.

For many years now the more refined literary fictions have relied on the techniques of omission. The authors tastefully leave out of their narratives all the emotion and most of the drama. In the manner of Samuel Beckett or Ann Beattie, they supply 10,000 lines of oblique irony with which the reader is expected to construct his or her own story on a blank page. Sometimes the authors furnish a few lines of dialogue, but in language so abstract that the words can mean anything the reader wishes them to mean. The effect bears comparison to a conversation partially overheard at a distance of four hundred feet through the rifts in a strong wind.

What else is the presidency of Ronald Reagan if not a work of conceptual art? Like LeWitt, the President has a talent for promoting what isn't there. All his speeches, all his tinseled sentiments, all his homilies and tiny sermons might as well be entitled *Ten Thousand Words Five Letters Long, Covering the Silence Evenly.* He invites his audience to hear what they choose to hear, to connect the dots and make their own drawings of America the Beautiful.

Throughout the spring and summer the Iran-*contra* committees listened to daily reports of a National Security Council gone sick with paranoid delusions of Oriental grandeur, but none of the testimony damaged Reagan's reputation as a man of benign and democratic intent. Various unkind critics wondered why so much evidence produced so small a result. Their confusion followed from their failure to understand the minimalist aesthetic.

What was important about the hearing was what wasn't said and who wasn't there. If the politicians were careful not to ask impolite questions (about Israel's percentage in the deal, or the character of the assassins and arms dealers with whom the United States allied itself in two hemispheres), the witnesses were equally careful to describe the White House and the Departments of State and Defense as large empty spaces in which nobody of importance was ever present. All of the witnesses had heard rumors about the drawing in progress (*Ten Thousand Memoranda Ten Paragraphs Long, Covering the Failure Evenly*), but none of them had ever seen it rendered on a government wall. Certainly the President hadn't seen it, and neither had Secretaries Weinberger and Shultz. The only man that every-body was sure had seen it—William Casey, former director of the CIA—was dead.

What is telephone sex if not a display of conceptual art? The Puritan bias of the American mind, much exaggerated by the fear of AIDS, has chased the nation's sexual expression into the realms of the abstract. The back pages of the better pornographic magazines glow with advertisements for "live phone fantasy," "mind images," "telefantasies," "sensuous, exotic, live phone playmates!" In return for a draftman's fee (all major credit cards accepted), Lori or Cherry Blossom or Evita agree to describe any number of erotic acts ("150 Portrayals; Safe and Private!") that might be entitled *Ten Thousand Whispers One Syllable Long, Covering the Night Evenly.* To render the promises in physical form might prove too expensive, too incon-venient, too dangerous.

The curators of the nation's foreign policy haven't yet learned to manage their affairs as efficiently as Lori or Evita, but certainly they think of their wars and stratagems as works of conceptual art. The current naval expedition into the Persian Gulf might well be entitled *Ten Thousand Radar Signals Ten Seconds Long, Covering the Map Evenly.* The Reagan administration apparently wishes to make an avant-garde statement about America's place and stature in the world. To what end, or at what cost, nobody can say. Our geopoliti-cians don't know what the United States stands to win or lose in the event of a war with Iran, Iraq, or any other enemy as yet unan-nounced, but clearly the excitements of the moment demand some-thing impressive in "a chain of development that may eventually find some form." Understood as objects as crass as a collection of ungainly ships in warm water, our fleet has little or no chance of victory within the confines of what amounts to an Iranian lake. Understood as minimalist art, as an idea of power rather than a fact of power, our navy is invincible. We supply the military schematics and expect our enemies to fill in the blanks with their own trembling and fear.

LeWitt's drawing was one of the first works of conceptual art to be sold at auction, but I expect the prices to move steadily higher. The trend is so well established that the leading Democratic candidate for the 1988 presidential nomination exists as a set of instructions for a series of yet unconnected dots. Mario Cuomo retains his value in the opinion polls precisely because he hasn't declared his candidacy, because the political consultants (i.e., the analogues of LeWitt's draftsmen and the girls on "Lori's Hotline") haven't drawn his 10,000 lines on the walls of the media.

If the trend continues to follow the ascent of the stock market and the price of New York real estate, maybe the public will learn to occupy impalpable states of theory and possibility. Give people enough practice with the aesthetic, and maybe they will be persuaded to omit the tiresome chore of having to live their lives. Museums like to collect conceptual art because it takes up so little space in the basement. Rapacious landlords and ambitious politicians like to collect conceptual lives because they make so few demands and such little noise.

HARPER'S MAGAZINE,
*October 1987*

# SKYWRITING

*The moment Kafka attracts more attention than Joseph K.,
Kafka's posthumous death begins.*
                                                          —Milan Kundera

O NE OF THESE days I expect to see the author of a new book
parachute into New York harbor trailing clouds of blue smoke and
playing "Summertime" on the harmonica. If the book promises big
and best-selling news—of war or peace or the death of
conscience—I can imagine the author coming ashore at Battery
Park, resplendent in military uniform and welcomed by Lee Iacocca
and a line of cabaret dancers.

It's no easy trick to drum up interest in something so easily
misplaced as a book, and the writers who still nurture the hope of
readers have been known to try almost anything to attract the
attention of a camera. In a newspaper last week I noticed that a
consultant charges authors $500 an hour for lessons in the tech-
niques of self-promotion. Even if an author can write as well as
Herman Melville or Edith Wharton, literary talent counts for nothing unless he or she also knows how to sell the book on radio and
television. Some of the less delicate publishing houses now ask to
see not only a manuscript but also a videotape of the author telling
jokes and cautionary tales.

Under the rules of contemporary society, nobody, not even God,
can afford to offend the media. It is all very well to be rich or
talented or beautiful or brave, but unless one is known to be rich
or talented or beautiful or brave, one cannot be a celebrity, and if
one isn't a celebrity, one might as well be dead.

The nobility in seventeenth-century France felt the same way
about the brilliantly lit society at Versailles. No matter how magnifi-

cent their country estates or how numerous their horses and servants, they believed themselves invisible unless they could make a show at court. But before they could appear at court, they had to know how to walk and curtsy and speak an artificial language that would fall pleasingly on the ear of a duke.

In our own society—a society increasingly obsessed with the flutter of images—the ladies and gentlemen of the media serve as courtiers in the king's palace. Unless one knows how to conduct oneself in their august presence, even the richest of businessmen or the wisest of authors must vanish into the pits of anonymity and ridicule.

Two years ago, by virtue of a coincidence as implausible as it was unexpected, I found myself at what is known as a "media training session" for the chairman of a very large and very greedy insurance company. The gentleman had been invited to an interview on network television, and he was worried about the presentation of his image.

He had reason to be anxious. Insurance companies of late haven't been receiving the best of press notices, and for the modest sum of $10,000 the company in question had hired public relations counsel to give the chairman a one-day lesson in studio etiquette. He arrived promptly at 9 A.M., uneasy and nondescript despite the expensive tailoring of what was obviously a new suit. He was accompanied by seven assistants—the vice president in charge of political affairs, two secretaries, a speechwriter, a statistician, a consultant, and a valet. About the same number of people represented the public relations firm.

Everybody shook hands with everybody else, and the company arranged itself around a long and highly polished table. Somebody named Bernie came briskly to the business at hand. He introduced a troupe of "communications specialists" who would play the part of the television journalists, and then, speaking to the chairman, he said: "What you have to bear in mind is the simplicity of the medium and the stupidity of the hosts. Never answer their questions. Never be seen to think."

The chairman nodded complacently, delighted to hear Bernie confirm his dearest prejudices. Bernie made a few more observations—about dictating the terms of the interview and keeping one's fingers out of one's nose—and everybody moved into an adjoining studio for the first performance. The chairman settled himself into a chair opposite the surrogate host, an aggressively affable young man named Mort, and waited confidently for the first question.

His self-assurance didn't last thirty seconds. Mort smiled a greasy smile and said: "Perhaps you can tell us, Mr. Chairman, why your company gouges people with the viciousness of a Mafia loan shark?"

The chairman's mouth opened and closed like the mouth of a netted fish. Mort accepted his silence as a concession of guilt and went unctuously on to the next question: "I can't say I blame you, Mr. Chairman, but maybe you can tell us why your company robbed its own stockholders of $500 million last month to prevent the merger with E. F. Hutton?"

By an obviously heroic effort, as if struggling with giant snakes, the chairman achieved the victory of speech. It wasn't coherent speech, of course, and none of it resembled the notes on the index cards in the chairman's coat pocket—wonderfully succinct little statements about his company's benevolent service to the American people. Gasping with rage, he managed to say—not very distinctly, but distinctly enough to be heard by 25 million people in the viewing audience: "You're a dirty, lying son of a bitch."

Bernie stopped the camera. In a voice almost as breezy as Mort's, he said: "Yes, well, I can see we have a lot of work to do."

The rest of the day wasn't easy. Mort was sent away, replaced by a woman who wasn't quite so rude. The valet trimmed the chairman's hair; the speechwriter typed the prepared statement in capital letters; the secretary reminded the chairman that he was one of the richest men in the world.

By five that afternoon, the chairman was capable of getting through five minutes in front of the camera without committing a theatrical equivalent of suicide. His retainers helped him out the door, mopping his forehead, steadying his shoulders, murmuring reassurance in his ears. Watching him depart, Mort said: "Believe it or not, he was better than most."

And then, after the door had closed: "It's a wonderful world. Fifty years ago I could have been teaching debutantes to dance."

I assume that the consultant to the literary notables offers more or less the same instruction—maxims about the simplicity of the medium and the need for short sentences, tips and hints about the pitch of one's voice, the color of one's dress, the reduction of a thought to its least common denominator.

Reading the newspaper report of the season's newest authors smiling anxiously into their hired cameras, I thought, sadly, of circus dogs dressed up in funny little costumes, rolling through barrels and balancing clocks on their heads. Something of the same melancholy feeling overcomes me when I see a decent writer talking to Johnny Carson.

Not that writers have much choice in the matter, at least not in America. The native audience for literature never has been large or easily found, and apparently it was never enough for a writer simply to write. The public has always preferred sensations, and it tolerates authors only if they can be seen as freaks and wonders—the sort of people who make scenes in restaurants, supply the newspapers with salacious gossip, discover miraculous cures and new religions.

The work of self-dramatization is as much a proof of the writer's art as the composition of dialogue and the invention of plot. Even in the best of times the successful American writers have adopted the gaudy disguises that admit them to the stage of the national music hall. Walt Whitman and Ezra Pound appeared as mad prophets, Henry James as the aesthete in exile, Mark Twain as a clown, Emerson and Jonathan Schell as preachers, Tom Wolfe as a dandy, Norman Mailer as a Caliban or *enfant terrible* who periodically revises the hideousness of his mask to reflect the conventional fear and trembling of the prosperous middle class. In the early 1960s, soon after stabbing his second wife, Mailer wrote, "If you can use a knife, there is still some love left." Twenty years later Mailer sponsored the literary career of Jack Henry Abbott, a self-confessed murderer and psychopath. The boredom of his audience required more violent stimuli, and when Abbott killed a waiter a few days after the publication of his jailhouse memoir, *In the Belly of the Beast*, Mailer told a press conference, "Culture is worth a little risk."

Confronted with the literary success bestowed on the memoirs of wealthy real estate operators and notorious madams, the author who would be king stages his most elaborate productions in the theaters of the self. It is the life, not the book, that becomes the object of art. The choice works against the writing of literature, but not many American writers have the patience or the fortitude to stay out of the publicity mills.

Foreign writers—perhaps because they can rely on the presence of an interested and educated audience—find it easier to accept the blessing of obscurity. I think of John le Carré and Milan Kundera, both of whom define the press interview as a synonym for a hanging. But with few exceptions (among them J. D. Salinger, Thomas Pynchon, and Evan Connell) the American writer is drawn, moth-like, into the klieg light. It is impossible not to admire his reckless-ness, no matter how farfetched his prose or how grotesque his gestures and costumes.

To appreciate the achievement of American writers it is necessary to bear in mind the odds against their enterprise. The republic of American letters is invariably in a state of anarchy. Without a canon of common texts or cultural references, without standards, lacking even one critic whose judgment pretends to the weight of authority, barely literate and always receptive to a bribe, the administration of the nation's literary affairs falls naturally into the hands of touts and thieves. The American public doesn't look to the arts—whether painting or drama or literature—for answers to questions that it considers important. It is an opening night crowd, astonished by celebrity and opulent spectacle, willing to applaud whatever the merchants in New York and Los Angeles distribute under the labels of culture.

The writer is always playing against the house, and it's no wonder that he acquires the habits of mind congenial to the political left. It isn't that most American writers care for socialism or believe in the theories of a Utopian future. As often as not they despise socialists and prefer the dream of the Arcadian past.

What aligns them with the predicament of the left is the sense of operating behind enemy lines. Books have so little to do with the business of America that the author imagines himself traveling on a forged passport in a foreign country. He trades in metaphors, but everywhere he goes he discovers people who would rather deal in monuments, who delight not in the play of thought but in the displays of power. The vivid lights of the cities, the Babylonian architecture of the gilded office towers, the rain forests planted in the atria of the chrome-plated hotels—all proclaim the energetic faith of a people in thrall to the miracles of commerce.

Even if he has been outfitted with a trick smile and a new hat, the author cannot help defining himself as a guerrilla in the mountain wilderness of a lost cause, a romantic figure plotting sudden descents on the prosperous sensibility of the seacoast resorts. Possibly this is why so many American writers have distinguished themselves in the shorter forms of literary expression—I think of Bierce's aphorisms, Hemingway's short stories, Vidal's essays, Updike's paragraphs, Mailer's polemics, Plimpton's sketches, Bellow's sermons, Didion's metaphors, Styron's sentences, Heller's one-line jokes. Not that these writers haven't succeeded in the longer forms of the history, the novel, and the tract, but they achieve their most memorable effects under the cover of brevity. Instead of staging long sieges, they conduct brilliant raids. Sometimes the raids entail a criminal arrest or an appearance on the Donahue show; sometimes, on more fanciful or clandestine occasions, a parachute and a plume of blue smoke.

HARPER'S MAGAZINE,
*May 1986*

# HUGO, *MON AMOUR*

GIVEN THE STATE of the art of prime-time television, I wouldn't be surprised if next season's hit dramatic series presented as its hero a brave and handsome suitcase. Obviously the suitcase would need to be expensive, from Vuitton, Gucci, or Mark Cross, and large enough to carry most of the toys and products synonymous with American success. Maybe it couldn't accommodate a Mercedes-Benz, but certainly it would be spacious enough for cashmere coats, silver flatware, digital stereos, Mont Blanc pens, silk scarves, top hats, delft tiles, and linzer tortes.

By casting a suitcase as the hero, the producers could do away with the increasingly tiresome and irrelevant business of portraying human character, feeling, and motive. All concerned could move directly to their passion for the objects ennobled by happy association with status and money.

The preoccupation with things is color-coordinated with the spirit of the age. The obsession shows up in the policies of the Reagan administration as well as in the photographs published by *Architectural Digest* and the short stories published by *The New Yorker*. But, as with so much else, television can come more crassly to the point.

Reduced to their properly ceremonial roles as acolytes in the sanctuaries of wealth, the supporting actors could pack and unpack the suitcase while miming appropriate responses to the merchandise. The opportunities for dramatic expression encompass the entire arc of emotion of which prime-time television is capable, and the actors could choose among an inventory of attitudes and poses:

**110**

*Wild and reckless joy*—while packing the suitcase with a dress by Halston or a suit from Dunhill.

*Elegiac melancholy*—on unpacking Grandmother's set of Lowestoft china.

*Domestic happiness*—while folding a flannel nightgown or a child's school uniform.

*Disgust*—on being obliged to touch a plastic raincoat bought at Sears.

*Lasciviousness*—while fondling satin lingerie.

*Fear*—on finding a severed head among the new shirts from Turnbull and Asser.

*Humor*—while packing feather boas and old baseball mitts to be given away as prizes at a charity auction in Palm Springs.

*Tragic sorrow*—on discovering at the bottom of the suitcase a threadbare Chanel blouse bought twenty years ago in Cap d'Antibes when the world was young.

The telling of the suitcase's many heartwarming and poignant stories undoubtedly would require the art of Aaron Spelling. Perhaps the richest and most successful impresario of prime-time comparison shopping, Mr. Spelling already has introduced his audiences to the opulence of the goods and services displayed on "Dynasty," "Fantasy Island," "Love Boat," and "Hotel."

Presumably the suitcase would have a name, and I think the name Hugo has the right sound. The name Hugo implies a reassuring degree of affluence and carries with it the faint air of passivity thought to be attractive among the children, as well as the possessions, of the rich. Nobody could mistake Hugo for a third-rate vinyl suitcase used to staying in motels on the outskirts of Mobile, Alabama. Hugo is a genuine-leather suitcase, a distinguished and self-assured suitcase accustomed to being carried through the lobbies of first-class hotels.

If Hugo could speak, he would sound a lot like Gerald Ford or

Blake Carrington. The audience instinctively would know this because Hugo resembles Gerald Ford and Blake Carrington in stature and manner. Things just sort of happen to Hugo, in the same way they just sort of happen to Gerald Ford and Blake Carrington, and Hugo responds with the same intensity of expression.

Fortunately, it isn't necessary for Hugo to speak. Hugo's silence is more eloquent than words. The mere sight of Hugo is enough to convey the state of Hugo's feeling. If Hugo is seen being reverently packed with jewels and caviar and silk, then the audience knows that all is well. Conversely, if Hugo is seen being loaded down with broken cameras and dirty sneakers (i.e., as if his condition in life were no different from that of a common shopping bag), the audience knows that Hugo is in trouble.

Spelling's scriptwriters have been assigned more preposterous tasks, and they shouldn't have much trouble devising plot lines that entangle Hugo in the romance of the world. I can imagine Hugo rescued from a sunken yacht, Hugo sold at Sotheby's, Hugo in a plane wreck, Hugo in the hands of the KGB, Hugo submitting to the indignity of a search by Turkish customs agents, Hugo abducted by fur thieves, Hugo placed with the servants' luggage during a weekend house party in East Hampton or Monte Carlo.

Nor would it be impossible to involve Hugo in the kind of transient love affairs that distract or amuse the protagonists of police and detective dramas. Like the champions of liberty who wander around Los Angeles in search of new adventure, Hugo never has time to stay. The camera could see him reclining briefly but meaningfully behind a concierge's desk with a sexy little overnight bag; in other episodes Hugo could be trapped in an elevator at the Ritz-Carlton with a sable coat, or spend the night with a matched pair of Samsonite cases in the luggage bay of a 747 en route to Japan.

The casting of a suitcase as hero offers a number of further advantages to the owners of the show. A suitcase is always a contented and thoroughly professional member of the creative team. Unlike Joan Collins, a suitcase has little use for hairdressers or chauffeured limousines. Also, it is easier to arrange personal appearances for a suitcase, not only in shopping malls and on the Carson show but also in cameo roles in Spelling's other entertainments—Hugo rowed ashore to "Fantasy Island," Hugo lost in the lobby of "Hotel," Hugo rolled up the gangplank of "Love Boat."

Were Hugo to become a star, then, at about the same time he appeared on the cover of *TV Guide*, Spelling's business people could begin to charge usurious fees to the merchants who wish Hugo to be seen carrying their products to San Francisco or Zanzibar. Let the show run for three or four years, and Hugo's endorsement might elect a president.

HARPER'S MAGAZINE,
*January 1986*

# SCULPTURE IN SNOW

O VER THE NEXT few years the press undoubtedly will come under heavy criticism, most of it arising from the romantic misconceptions of people who expect the daily papers to furnish them, at a cost of twenty-five cents or less, with wisdom, statesmanship, and truth. Against the baying of the familiar hounds—among them the corporate buyers of public opinion and politicians with no other issue at their command—I have begun to collect notes for the defense.

Relatively few people like to make the argument on behalf of the press, because the virtues of the profession consist in its raucousness, its incoherence, and its gall. Honest praise sounds so much like criticism that it offends not only the laity in search of oracles but also the clerks and scribes who construe themselves as an aristocracy of conscience.

At random intervals in the nation's history one or another of the liberal occupations attracts a claque of admirers eager for simple answers. In the 1950s it was thought that psychoanalysis could resolve the enigma of human nature; in the 1960s it was the physicists who were going to steal the fires of heaven and the lawyers who were going to reform the laws and manage the nation's foreign policy; the most recent surge of hyperbole has placed the mantle of omniscience on the profession of journalism. For the last fifteen years journalists have enjoyed a reputation for knowing how the world works. This is silly. Reporters tend to show up at the scenes of crimes and accidents, and they take an imbecile's delight in catastrophe. Few of them know enough about the subject under discussion—whether politics, music, or the structure of DNA—to render a definitive opinion about anything other than the menu at the nearest Marriott Inn. But to concede the shallowness and ignorance of the press does nothing to diminish its usefulness or importance. Even the most mean-spirited criticisms fail to answer the question as to why anybody would bother to read or write the news. Why not wait a hundred years, until the archives have been opened and the historians have had time to arrange events in an orderly and patriotic sequence?

Any plausible defense of journalism rests on a modest presumption of what it provides. As follows:

1. If the writing of history resembles architecture, journalism bears comparison to a tent show. The impresarios of the press drag into their tents whatever freaks and wonders might astonish a crowd; the next day they move their exhibit to another edition instead of to another town four miles farther west. Their subject matter is the flux of human affairs, and they achieve their most spectacular effects by reason of their artlessness and lack of sentiment.

Years ago I formed the habit of collecting newspaper items in file folders organized under such rubrics as "mullahs," "absurdity," "campaign promises," "sensational crimes," "allies," "weapons," "scientific discoveries," "the end of the world." Maybe I expected the accumulation of news to achieve critical mass, or that the particles would combine into a coherent organism. This has yet to happen, and I doubt it ever will. Journalism is the data of experience, a substance comparable to the immense population of primeval elements out of which the higher forms of thought evolve. It is the best that can be done at short notice. The antagonists of the press like to pretend that some other intellectual agency (the social sciences, say, or the White House Press Office) could perform the task as well, but this also is a delusion.

When I read through the scraps of crumbling paper in the file folders, some of them long since gone yellow in the light, I notice that it is always the seemingly inconsequential stories that retain their life. The front-page news about treaties signed and generals traveling to China has been superseded by other treaties and other journeys of state; most of the editorial opinion has been proved wrong, and the melodramatic generalization turns out to have missed the point. But the stories toward the back of the paper, about a lost child or a woman paying alimony or the New York City police catching stray madmen in nets, lose nothing with the passage of time.

The press makes sculptures in snow; its truth dwells in the concrete fact and the fleeting sound of the human voice.

2. Two years ago the publishers of Dr. Henry Kissinger's memoir, *White House Years*, publicized the book with the claim that "for eight years, the story of his life was the history of our times." This sort of inflated rhetoric has kept par value with inflation of the currency, but there remains something grotesquely comic about it. Carr Van Anda, the first great editor of *The New York Times* in the twentieth century, was once asked why he didn't decorate the paper's news accounts with the reporter's byline. *"The Times,"* said Mr. Van Anda, "is not running an employment agency for journalists."

What would he have said about the wreaths of celebrity placed on the heads of men who read news bulletins into television cameras? In the United States at this moment there are men and women whose names will live as long as the history of Western civilization—the Nobel laureates sifting the strands of genetic sequence or imagining the inner processes of the stars. Their names remain the property of only a few of their peers, and they dwindle into rushlights when compared with the radiance of Dolly Parton or John Chancellor. It is as if the audience of a Greek tragedy had confused the names of the protagonists with those of the messengers.

3. Journalists hire themselves out as journeymen, not as immortal artists. It would be fair to compare them to a troupe of medieval stonemasons traveling the circuit of unfinished cathedrals with a repertoire of conventional forms. They can carve figures of the saints fifty feet above the nave, but nobody would expect them to impart expression to the face.

Or, to take a metaphor more likely to recommend itself to the Republicans now in Washington, journalists possess the social graces of Pony Express riders—resolution, ingenuity, punctuality. They bring the news from Ghent or California, and they do their readers no favor if they try to shape it into a work of literature. Maybe this is why the books that journalists feel compelled to write, about the war in Algeria or last year's election campaign, so often read like a definitive study of a formation of clouds.

4. The critics of the press complain about its pessimism, its cynicism, its unwillingness to recommend a program of political advancement. Every now and then a reader of *Harper's Magazine* writes to say that the magazine should publish sermons. "Be more positive," says a correspondent in Oklahoma. "Imagine that you have been proclaimed king," says a correspondent in Florida, "and submit your blueprint for Utopia."

They send their requests to the wrong address. The reader in hope of inspiration can study the collected works of Saint Augustine or Bishop Paul Moore; he can listen to Billy Graham defy the foul fiend or sit in rapturous contemplation of an elm tree or a whale.

William Randolph Hearst once complained to Dorothy Parker that her stories were too sad. To this objection (not very different from the admonitions circulated by vice presidents in charge of public relations), Miss Parker replied: "Mr. Hearst, there are two billion people on the face of the earth, and the story of not one of them will have a happy ending."

If a man drinks too much and his doctor tells him that one of these days he will fall down dead in the club car on the way to Westport, is the doctor a pessimist? Is Israel a pessimistic nation because it bombs the Iraqi nuclear installation southeast of Baghdad, or is it an optimistic nation because it accepts the conditions of its existence? Is it pessimism to say that the theories of supply-side economics have little basis in fact, or that American novelists don't write very good novels?

Journalism, like history, has no therapeutic value; it is better able to diagnose than to cure, and it provides society with a primitive means of psychoanalysis that allows the patient to judge the distance between fantasy and reality.

5. Why is it that people demand a tone of optimism when discussing the large and safely abstract questions of national policy—what was thought to be the splendid little war in Vietnam, for example, or the incalculable benefit certain to derive from an economic policy that places an intolerable burden on the weak, the old, the poor, the ignorant, the young, and the sick? If somebody advised the same people about their own prospects in so blithe a tone of voice, they would think they were talking to a child or a fool.

The question is never one of optimism or pessimism. It is a question of trying to tell the truth, of the emotions required of the teller and of the emotions the attempt calls forth in the reader. If the news, no matter how bad, evokes in the reader a sense of energy and hope, then it has done as much as can be said for it. The unctuous recitation of platitudes usually achieves the opposite effect, instilling in the reader a feeling of passivity and despair.

Great power constitutes its own argument, and it never has much trouble drumming up friends, applause, sympathetic exigesis, and a band. In his commencement address at West Point last May, President Reagan was pleased to announce that the American "era of self-doubt" had come to a satisfactory end. The rest of his speech could have been accompanied by a fanfare of trumpets and drums.

But a democracy stands in need of as much self-doubt as it can muster and as many arguments as possible that run counter to the governing body of opinion. The press exerts the pressure of dissent on officials otherwise inclined to rest content with the congratulations of their retainers.

6. The media offer for sale every conceivable fact or opinion. Most of these objects possess a dubious value, but it isn't the business of the journalist to distinguish between the significant and the worthless.

During World War II British raiding units pressed far behind German lines in the North African desert in search of stray pieces of metal. The patrols collected anything that came to hand—a shell casing, a broken axle, a button torn from the uniform of a dead corporal. The objects were sent to Cairo for analysis, and by this means British intelligence guessed at the state of German industry.

So also with journalism. The data are always fugitive and insufficient. To treat even the most respectable political ideas as if they were the offspring of pure reason would be to assign them, in Lewis Namier's phrase, "a parentage about as mythological as that of Pallas Athene."

7. Without an audience, the media would cease to exist. Even if people don't read the same papers and periodicals, the media provide the connective tissue holding together the federation of contradictory interests that goes by the name of democracy. How else except through the instruments of the media could the surgeon and the labor leader, the ballerina and the stock-car driver, form even a distorted image of one another? The media present a spectacle infinitely more crowded than Balzac's *Comédie Humaine*—the rumors of war on page one, followed, in random succession, by reports of strange crimes, political intrigues, anomalous discoveries in the sciences, the hazard of new fortunes.

Just as every nation supposedly gets "the government it deserves," so also it makes of the press whatever it chooses to imagine as its self-portrait. If the covers of all the nation's magazines could be displayed in a gallery, and if the majority of the images reflected dreams of wealth or sexual delight, a wandering Arab might be forgiven for thinking that the United States had confused itself with the Moslem vision of paradise.

The newspapers yield only as much as the reader brings to his reading. If the reader doesn't also study foreign affairs, or follow the money markets, or keep up his practice of foreign languages, then what can he expect to learn from the papers?

8. The press in its multiple voices argues that the world of men and events can eventually be understood. Not yet, perhaps, not in time for tomorrow's deadline, but sooner or later, when enough people with access to better information have had an opportunity to expand the spheres of reference. This is an immensely hopeful and optimistic assumption. Defined as means rather than an end, journalism defends the future against the past.

HARPER'S MAGAZINE,
*August 1981*

# MULTIPLE CHOICE

I N OCTOBER OF 1957 the United States discovered, much to its amazement and distress, that its educational systems weren't as good as most people had been content to believe. The Soviet Union placed the first artificial satellite in space, and by so doing demonstrated to an alarmed American public that there were more things in heaven and earth than had been dreamed of by the English department at Yale. The revelation inspired an immense and optimistic assignment of funds to the cause of higher learning.

Twenty-five years have passed, and the United States once again has discovered the failure of its schools. This second revelation has a pessimistic cast, prompting the Reagan administration to dismantle the academic establishments with as much eagerness and haste as accompanied the work of construction.

For the last few months, in the midst of the demolition and the subtraction of federal money, educational authorities have been making piteous moans—about the loss of privilege, about football coaches (mere base mechanicals) being paid $150,000 a year, about the humiliations inflicted on the dignitaries who guard the temples of "the humanities," the speculative sciences, and "the liberal arts."

If the schools commanded either the electorate's confidence or its respect, I doubt whether the Administration would find it so easy to take away so much from so many. The impassive silence on the part of people without a specific interest to protect suggests that the maxim taught to young military officers—"never reinforce failure"—also has its civilian uses.

It isn't very difficult to find the reasons for the general disillusion with what passes for an American education. The students graduated from the nation's schools and universities over the last twenty years received as expensive a course of instruction as any nation has ever bestowed on a rising generation. Nothing was too good for the children of fortune. They enjoyed access to laboratories that surpassed anything known to Einstein or Planck, to libraries that couldn't have been imagined by Euripides or Voltaire, to a syllabus of academic studies as elaborate as a medieval bestiary.

Given the cost of so extravagant an undertaking, even a patient man might be goaded into asking for an account. Did the students so blessed with the implements of knowledge learn to read more intelligently than Jefferson, who had only a candle and an antique pen? Did they learn to write an expository prose that puts to shame, by reason of its clarity and force, the mere scribbling of the Federalist's Papers?

Ask those questions of a parent who paid upwards of $100,000 for the education of his children, and the poor fellow will give way to demented laughter. He counts himself fortunate if his son can write well enough to fill out an application to business school, if his daughter can do enough math to solve Rubik's cube.

If the schools and universities have failed in their task over the last two decades, it is because their employers (i.e., the society as a whole) neither wished nor expected them to succeed. What in heaven's name did the society want with people who knew how to think? The triumphant American supremacy thought it already knew all the answers, at least about important things like real estate and politics and money and weapons. People who knew how to think could only cause trouble, so why not let them play with the toys of art and literature collected in the sandbox of Western civilization?

The teaching of the liberal arts in American universities reflects the common assumption of their precious irrelevance. Instead of making the acquaintance of their own minds, the students learn to admire and applaud the exquisite greatness of the objects set before them by the curators in a museum. By presenting the realm of thought as a cabal (somewhat similar to the boardroom of the Chase Manhattan Bank), the schools encourage an attitude of passivity and apprehension.

Before it finds itself surprised by yet another revelation of its pedagogic inadequacy, the United States might try to define the purpose of an education. This should be to awaken the student to the value of his own mind, to instill in him intellectual courage.

As a first step the schools might give up the idea of "the educated citizen." To the best of my knowledge, I have never met such a person. I can conceive of a self-educating citizen, and I have had the good fortune to meet a number of people to be so described. Without exception they possess the valor of their acknowledged ignorance, conceiving of education neither as a blessed state of being (comparable to membership on the Council on Foreign Relations) nor as a commodity sold in a store but rather as a ceaseless process of learning and relearning. If in sixteen years they have spent 10,000 hours in a classroom (roughly the equivalent of thirteen months), they expect to spend another fifty years revising what they thought they had learned at school, turning what they know toward the future, not the past.

THE WASHINGTON POST,
*February 1982*

# THE SPOILS OF
# CHILDHOOD

E VERY NOW AND then the press comes across the news of abused
or neglected children, and for a period of days the editorial columns
fill with tears. The melodrama has been running its customary
course in New York this week after it was discovered that several
custodians of a day care center in the Bronx allegedly had been
molesting the children under their supervision.

The newspapers and television stations have been issuing their
usual proclamations of indignation and alarm. Also as usual, the
resident moralists choose to define the incident in the idiom of
partisan politics; they blame the Koch or the Reagan administration, complain about the lack of money in the welfare systems,
assert that Americans truly love their children and that if it were not
for the military budgets and the federal deficit, all would be well.

I wish I could still believe the official expressions of sympathy.
Given the proofs that come so easily to hand, I have begun to
suspect that American society has little liking for its children, that
more often than not children find themselves cast in the role of
expensive enemies.

If this is so, then it makes a kind of dismal sense that the United
States sustains a rate of infant mortality higher than that in sixteen
other nations, that 17 million American children live in conditions
of ignorance and squalor, that producers of Hollywood movies look
for excuses to portray children as agents of the anti-Christ.

Nor is it an accident that child care specialists receive the same wages as dog pound and parking lot attendants, or that the Los Angeles Police Department estimates that a labor force of 30,000 children, many of them under the age of five, is at work in the local sex industries. Nor is it an accident that so many studies and reports bear witness to the decay of the nation's schools, the declining standards of literacy, the rising incidents among children and adolescents of alcoholism, drug addiction, abortion, and suicide.

Why does nobody ever suggest that maybe these phenomena proceed from a common cause, that maybe they attest to the savagery of the war between the generations for the spoils of childhood?

Men and women in their forties contend with their children for domination in the kingdom of the department store and the mail order catalogue. To a throng of aging infants, the consumer society holds out the promise of eternal youth, of an enchanted mirror in which the customer can see himself reflected in the transfiguring light of immortality.

Children obviously make a shambles of this enterprise. They remind their parents of too much that is unpleasant—of death, time, and unpaid bills—and so they come to be seen as unwelcome messengers.

The precepts of child rearing undergo revision every few years because the parents have no wish to define themselves. They prefer to continue the game of let's pretend—trying on new clothes and moral attitudes, jogging away from the nanny who, like the angel of death, comes looking for them in the park. They stamp their feet and ask the question dear to the hearts of headwaiters: "If I am not immortal (which is very, very unfair), then why shouldn't I do what I please?"

Among people so reluctant to make peace with their own deaths, children come to stand as surrogates for a future often portrayed as something dark and unclean.

In a society imbued with the sense of its own helplessness and inadequacy, children offer themselves as victims over whom even the powerless hold power. The press reports only the most sensational instances of abuse and neglect, usually on the part of parents who themselves suffer the cruelties of poverty, illiteracy, and disease. But the same pathology shows up in the more affluent and supposedly enlightened neighborhoods where the children serve as objects of experiment.

If the age demands a belief in self-expression, then a generation of schoolchildren must endure the rituals of progressive education. If the theories of social equity come to weigh more heavily in the balance than the accomplishments of art or scholarship, then another generation of schoolchildren must suffer the effects of lowered standards and expectations. Whatever will make the parents feel happier with themselves, that is the price their children must pay.

The children in the Bronx pay the price of this society's rage against the future. As with the need for immense ministries of justice in societies renowned for the practice of injustice, the large number of government agencies administering love to children attests to the society's incapacity to solve the problem that so many institutions have been called on to ponder and alleviate. These political agencies define children as a social evil (comparable to pollution or crime in the subways) rather than as the embodiment of the nation's strength and only hope of rescue.

THE SUN, *Baltimore,*
*August 1984*

# THE SENIOR
# PRACTITIONER

EVER SINCE I was foolhardy enough to accept your invitation to attempt the rhetorical procedure known as a commencement address, I've been reading through the case histories of Western civilization in search of a suitably instructive text. Like most everybody else of my age and acquaintance, I tend to feel intimidated in the presence of doctors—even by doctors who have been doctors for only twenty minutes—and so I hoped to arm myself with the proofs of an unimpeachable wisdom. You can take it as a symptom of my apprehension that instead of one text I came up with three—taken from authorities as well-traveled as Rudyard Kipling, Marek Edelman, and Seneca.

In the autumn of 1908—at about the time that he was writing *Plain Tales from the Hills*—Kipling was called upon to say a few inspiring words to the medical faculty at Middlesex Hospital. I suspect that he had some presentiment of the forthcoming events on the western front because he dressed his remarks in military uniform. Being a tactful speaker, and bearing in mind the bias of his audience, he divided mankind into only two significant classes—doctors and patients. The patients he described as noncombatants relying upon the medical forces to wage the campaign against death. It was the doctor's duty, he said, to fight a long diversionary action, postponing and delaying the inevitable defeat, and—at the end, when all else failed—making sure that death claimed its victory under the rules of civilized warfare.

**126**

Mindful of the hardships synonymous with the profession of medicine—especially the belief among the noncombatants that doctors could be called upon to perform heroic feats at any hour of the day or night—Kipling observed that doctors were the only class of people in the society paid to tell the truth. The other professions—most notably the lawyers and the journalists—were paid to lie. Doctors had no choice but to look their enemy squarely in the face and call things by their right names. Sooner or later even the most artful physician had to bow to the superior technique of "the senior practitioner"—the pale and humorless figure whose judgment was final and whose presence announced the sack of the capital city.

Something of the same stoic philosophy runs through the text of a recent series of conversations with Dr. Marek Edelman—an eminent Polish cardiologist as well as a leader of the Solidarity movement and one of three or four Jews who survived the uprising in the Warsaw Ghetto in the spring of 1943. Several months prior to that uprising the Nazis conducted what they called "the liquidation" of the ghetto. Every day for forty days, between July 26 and September 6, 1942, 10,000 Jews were loaded onto trains leaving, at four o'clock in the afternoon, for the crematoria at Treblinka. The long lines of the condemned gathered in silence in the Umschlagplatz, and it was Edelman's singular and terrifying fate that as a boy of twenty he was obliged to select out of the lines the few people—one in every ten—whom it was permissible to redeem. He was employed at the time as a messenger for the authorities of the ghetto hospital to whose discretion the Nazis had given 40,000 "life-tickets"—little pieces of white scrap paper marked with a mimeographed stamp and entitling the bearer to miss the train. Thus Edelman played the part of bureaucratic angel, charged with the handing out of exemptions at the gate of the Underworld. I leave it to you to guess the weight of his anguish through a succession of forty afternoons during which he remembered that it never once rained.

After the war Edelman was one of a handful of Jews who returned to Poland. Against his will he became a doctor—a heart surgeon— and found himself again standing at the same gate, pulling people out of the same lines.

In a book of conversations that will be published this autumn, he describes his predicament as a doctor.

"God is trying to blow out the candle, and I'm quickly trying to shield the flame, taking advantage of His brief inattention. To keep the flame flickering, even if only for a little while longer than He would wish. It is important; He is not terribly just. It also can be very satisfying, because whenever something does work out, it means you have, after all, fooled Him. . . ."

Earlier in the same passage he makes a corollary point: "And when I can't accomplish anything else, there is always one thing left: to assure them the most comfortable death possible. So that they might not know, not suffer, not be afraid. So that they need not humiliate themselves."

Seneca, the Roman essayist and politician from whom I borrow my third text, wrote his letters to a Stoic in A.D. 65 for the specific purpose of teaching himself to meet his own death in a manner that he wouldn't find humiliating. He was almost an exact contemporary of Christ, born in Spain around the year one in the Christian calendar, and by the time he came to write his letters in moral philosophy, he already had survived—by reason of a prolonged exile on Corsica—the death sentences imposed upon him by Caligula (in A.D. 37) and by Claudius (in A.D. 41). Recalled to Rome on the accession of Nero, he became the young emperor's tutor and the de facto ruler of the Empire. By all accounts he was an extraordinarily gifted administrator and provided his pupil's subjects with several years of sound government. Nero as he grew older succumbed to the example of profligate and vicious companions. Seneca retired to his country estate to write the letters that expressed the sum of his thought, continually returning to the ideal of a life that doesn't cling to the toys of fortune or chance.

"To rehearse death," he says, "is to study freedom. A person who has learned how to die has unlearned how to be a slave."

Or again, "I'm making ready for the day when the tricks and disguises will be put away and I shall come to a verdict on myself, determining whether the courageous attitudes I adopt are really felt or just so many words, and whether or not the defiant challenges I've hurled at fortune have been mere pretense and pantomime."

Or again, comparing his life to some rich man's house that he has been asked to leave: "I'm in the process of being thrown out, certainly, but the manner of it is as if I were going out."

Seneca's preparations were not in vain. Nero turned increasingly cruel—first murdering his mother and his sister before commanding his tutor to commit suicide. The imperial herald found Seneca in the company of his friends, engaged in one of his habitual discourses on the consolations of philosophy. His acceptance of the news of his death is the subject of one of the most famous scenes in Roman history. Tacitus, in his *Annals*, reports that Seneca's expression didn't betray the slightest tremor or fear or sadness. He scarcely interrupted the course of his thought to ask his doctor to bring him a scalpel. After he had made incisions behind his knees, as well as in his ankles and his arms, he continued to talk as calmly as before—checking the tears of his friends, reviving their courage and inviting them to nourish their spirits by the manner of his going out.

I offer these texts as exemplary tales because if I try to imagine the balance of suffering that you will be asked to redress over the next forty-odd years, I figure that you'll need all the help you can get. As you know, most of your fellow countrymen choose to look upon death as a mistake—an accident distinctly un-American. We construe physical well-being as the highest and most perfect of earthly goods, and we spend more money on health than we spend on any other service or commodity in the inventory of human happiness—more than we spend on cosmetics, cocaine, or weapons rumored to be invincible.

For the promise of immortality—even a false promise made by an itinerant quack or an unlicensed saint—we will pay not only handsomely but also in cash. Among those of us so foolish as to imagine that we can buy protection from the human weather in the world—as if death were a crooked politician and disease an agent of Qaddafi— it has become the common practice to remand our disappointment to the law courts. The national unwillingness to call things by their right names weighs heavily on the whole of society, but on no other class in the society does the projection of the magical wish fall as vividly as it falls on doctors. The noncombatants decline to accept the limits of medicine. They expect not only perfect health but also a cure for death. Incompetent armies deify the commander, and an alarmed civilian population assigns to its protectors the powers of Zeus or Bruce Springsteen. The exaggeration greatly increases the levels of fear in the national bloodstream, and if I were to draw any moral from my three texts, I would try to shape it into a phrase about treating the metaphysical as well as the physical illness, about addressing the patient by name as well as by type.

Even during my own lifetime I've seen hospitals become alien places into which, if I had any choice in the matter, I'd rather not go. So trembling a thought never would have occurred to me when, as a boy of eleven, I used to accompany an older cousin on his Sunday morning rounds through the wards of the public hospital in San Francisco. He was in his first year of residency and not much older than yourselves. Occasionally he arranged for me to sit with the students in the surgical amphitheater, and I remember a sequence of doctors performing various operations on patients too poor to claim violations of their rights to privacy. Over a period of time I learned the rudimentary mechanics of the human anatomy, but I also learned to think of a hospital not only as a refuge but also as an arena in which doctors waged an adventurous guerrilla war against a common enemy. I don't remember any specialists. Probably I was too young to know what a specialist was. But I remember that everybody talked to everybody else—even to the patients. The walls were badly in need of paint, and nobody ever had enough of anything except courage.

I formed the same impression of a hospital in New Haven, Connecticut, where, as a freshman at Yale University in the spring of 1953, I was pronounced all but dead on arrival. Somehow I had managed to contract an especially virulent form of meningitis that attacks the blood cells and that, if left unmolested, kills the patient within forty-eight hours. The disease is easily confused with lesser degrees of illness, and so the trick is in the diagnosis. If it hadn't so happened that on that particular morning at 3 A.M. the medical student on duty at Yale Infirmary hadn't been reading about the disease, I wouldn't have lived to hear, much less deliver, any commencement speeches. I stayed in the hospital for the better part of three months, and again I found myself in the company of people whom I admired not so much for their skill—which I didn't understand well enough to judge—as for their compassion and generosity of spirit. Almost every morning before dawn one of the younger residents stopped by my room—undoubtedly in violation of the rules—to review the night's performances in the operating theater. He was an amateur musician who liked to draw analogies between the technique of the presiding surgeons and the styles of well-known composers. Although he could appreciate the romanticism of two surgeons whom he compared to Schumann and Beethoven, he preferred the classical forms of the late eighteenth century, and I remember that he once interpreted a stomach operation as a variation on a Mozart piano sonata.

If my more recent encounters with hospitals in New York can be taken as a fair measure of the prevailing conditions—and if at least some of the press accounts current in the last several years bear even a partial resemblance to the facts—it appears that a good many hospitals these days provide an ordeal by committee rather than a hope of refuge. The practice of medicine seems to have become one of the high and more inhuman technologies—a dreaded ritual that casts the patient in the role of paying victim. If this is indeed so, then I'm afraid that it is another of those ills that can be alleviated only by physicians in their capacity as sympathetic individuals. Certainly you will get no help from lawyers, nor from the institutional entities—governments, insurance companies, corporations—that make it their business to translate human truth into the fictions of property.

When I was younger I thought of the twentieth century as the miraculous end point of human history. I now think of it as a still primitive beginning. From the perspective of the thirtieth century, if mankind manages to survive for another millennium, I expect that historians will look back upon the works of our modern world as if upon sand castles built by gifted children.

Consider the changes that have taken place in my own lifetime— between the present tense and the world of 1935 in which man in his infinite ingenuity had still to invent World War II, laser light, penicillin, Treblinka, DNA, or the hydrogen bomb. Over the next fifty years the technical changes are likely to be even more dramatic, but the human dilemmas will remain much as they were in the first century A.D.—few of them obedient to the genius of the medical or weapons laboratory. Without meaning to belittle the wonders of science, I do not think they can absolve mankind of suffering, desire, madness, and death.

No matter what the season's performances in the political or cultural amphitheaters, the argument going forward in the United States is the same as it always was, in the twentieth century as in the twelfth, in China as in the Soviet Union or Imperial Rome. It is the argument between the past and the future, between the energies of the human mind and the inertia of things as they are, between the reaching of the imagination (whether expressed with a paintbrush or a scalpel) and the ancient and implacable enemies of human freedom. Invariably heavily armed, the old enemies have been called by many names—"the Inquisition," "the vested interests," "the monarchy," "the government in Moscow or Washington." No matter what their honors and titles they constitute the incumbent majority, and they depend on their traditional alliance with man's egoism and fear. The impressive weight of their authority sometimes has an intimidating effect on younger people—even if the younger people happen to be doctors—who don't yet know enough about the foolishness of the world to have confidence in the strength and possibility of their own voices. To the degree that you learn to trust in yourselves, you will find that by precisely that degree the future will seem less frightening. Think of yourselves as being embarked on your last cruise and your first voyage, in the company of all the wondering men and women who have gone before you, on behalf of a society that sorely needs your help.

*Northwestern Medical School,*
*June 1987*

# POSTMODERN

*No degree of dullness can safeguard a work against the determination of critics to find it fascinating.*

—Harold Rosenberg

T HE NEWEST OF the new plays in New York City this season abandons the foolish and antiquated device of a stage. The omission conforms to the specifications of a minimalist aesthetic that distrusts strong feeling and aspires to the satisfactions of a knowing smirk. Of what use is a stage to actors who have nothing to say? Or to an audience that expects from its playwrights more or less the same sort of comforts that it expects from its department stores?

The play that isn't a play goes by the name of *Tamara* and takes place in the Seventh Regiment Armory at Park Avenue and East Sixty-sixth Street. Judging by the solemn *explications de texte* in the cultural press, the entertainment resembles an expensive game of charades or an evening in an emotional theme park. The cast of ten inhabits an ornate set that replicates ten luxurious rooms of an Italian villa once occupied, in the 1920s, by Gabriele d'Annunzio—romantic poet, extremist politician, and merciless libertine. Sumptuously dressed in the costumes of the period, the performers wander from room to room, admiring themselves in the mirrors, teasing or berating one another with lines of oblique dialogue, chasing the images of their art deco desire through what *The New York Times* described, fondly, as an atmosphere of "good-natured decadence."

The theatergoers—necessarily limited to the happy few who can afford to pay as much as $135 for a ticket—also traipse through the villa in pursuit of whichever character excites their fancy. Upstairs

**133**

and downstairs, along the hall to the library and around the tapestry into the lady's bedchamber, the audience follows at a distance appropriate to Robin Leach or a treacherous valet. The management encourages the guests to wear evening dress and tennis shoes. Evening dress because, during the entr'acte, the audience joins the cast for a buffet supper in d'Annunzio's dining room (the champagne and the smoked salmon come with the price of admission); tennis shoes because the actors sometimes move as quickly as startled trout.

Even the most agile eavesdroppers, of course, cannot see all the scenes and hear all the gossip. Everybody must make existential choices, a task possibly meant as a commentary on Mussolini or Adorno but one that also arouses the hope of revealed orgy. D'Annunzio was known for the cruel brilliance of his sexual conquests, and at least a few members of the audience (not as high-minded as the critic from the *Times*) presumably expect to see a set of variations on a theme by Casanova.

Thus the guests who accompany d'Annunzio into the bedroom might see him attempt the seduction of Tamara de Lempicka (a Polish artist arrived to paint the poet's portrait) but fail to hear him say, in the kitchen to the maid, "Aelis, get me some zucchini." Other members of the audience might elect to follow Aldo, the fascist policeman who humiliates the ballet dancer, or Mario, the communist chauffeur, who occasionally pauses on his rounds to shout, for reasons unknown, "No one in Italia is innocent."

Billed as "The Living Movie" and playing to a full complement of guests for the better part of a year, *Tamara* quite clearly takes place within the realm of the hybrid sensibility known as the postmodern. The critics praised the salmon (served on toast points) as effusively as they praised the carpets and the enameled surfaces of the dialogue. Fortunately for the purposes of the national arts endowments, the term *postmodern* can be applied as freely as paint to any cultural surface not otherwise marked for exhibition in the Louvre or in one of Donald Trump's hotels. Within the first thirty minutes of the opening of any artist's show in SoHo it's possible to hear the term awarded to a novella, a dress design, a dance troupe, or a *sauce mousseline*. (Under the rules of postmodern criticism, one is never obliged to see the play or taste the sauce; the critic need concern himself with only a text, not an event.)

On reading the dispatches from the avant-garde frontier on Park Avenue, it occurred to me that with a little thought I probably could make use of the idea (a.k.a. "the intellectual technology") to explain, at least to myself, the season's political campaigns. Perhaps if I could interpret the candidates properly—as works of minimalist art or as figures escaped from a museum diorama or as a story by Borges—then maybe I could appreciate the humor of what seemed to me a fairly elaborate joke.

About the aesthetic of postmodernism I already knew the rudimentary principles of collage and sardonic juxtaposition, and I could recognize the sensibility not only in commercials for Bud Light but also in phenomena as obscure as a tabloid newspaper headline (APE'S HEAD AFFIXED TO MAN'S BODY—DOCTORS OUTRAGED). I had read a sufficient number of stories on loan from the Iowa Writers' Workshop and seen enough of George Lucas's movies and Philip Johnson's architecture to know that I was presented not so much with a formal style as with a mannerist temperament that delighted in puns and allusions. Lucas derived *Star Wars* from World War II movies about the carrier war in the Pacific; Johnson decorated his buildings with illustrations from a freshman course in the history of art, and the apprentice novelists compiled notes on their reading of literary anthologies.

For years I had listened to people announce their boredom with the propositions of Freud, Eliot, Picasso, Joyce, Stravinsky, Marx, Keynes, and the Bauhaus. Their complaint was partly a revolt against authority and partly a confession of defeat. Surely, they said, there must be something else, some easier, happier sensibility that we can take to Acapulco for a weekend or to Paris for a writers' conference. We are tired, they said, of being poor and atonal; alienation is no longer fun and new; we know we should make our own portrait of reality, but who will give us a grant, and with what sort of fabric does one decorate a room in archetypal myth?

At a loss for answers to any of these questions, the postmoderns promoted the acts of criticism to the rank of high art. Henceforth it would be the critic who would play the part of Prometheus, the critic who would decide who was who and what was what, the critic who would assign every image to its correct category, choosing among the available artifacts—tones, photographs, colors, reprints, ornaments, domes, vaults, etc.—and combining them, in the manner of Hermann Hesse's Magister Ludi, into significant glyphs and ideograms. The triumph of the critical method they defined by their playfulness, their eclecticism, their belief in the supremacy of metaphor, and the refinement of their sense of irony. Irony served them both as a weapon and a refuge. If anybody questioned their motives, or, God forbid, classified them as fools, they could smile knowingly and point out, with an air of professional condescension, that they were only kidding. Nothing was serious because everything was a remake of something else.

The postmodernist authors with whom I was familiar took pride in their ability to make subtle distinctions between shades of emotion and bolts of feeling. Instead of stories they wrote meditations and commentaries, obscure parodies and fantasies so privately held as to resemble a game of hide-and-seek or a stock participation arranged by Crédit Suisse. What their characters didn't say was as important as what they did say.

Precisely the same attitudes and techniques inform the work of deconstructionist literary critics, advertising copywriters, and producers of television news. Any text can be superimposed on any other text, and it is the man with the moviola machine who changes words into things and cuts the images into the strips of preferred reality.

President Reagan proved the postmodernist thesis of the presidency as "the living movie." For eight years he read scripts, smiled or frowned on cue, rummaged through American history as if it were a theatrical trunk from which he could borrow an attitude, a hat, or a quotation out of context. Sustained by a faculty of self-interested critics, his administration existed in the realm of pure idea. Even so, he retained trace elements of an unmediated personality, and sometimes it was possible to distinguish between the man and the actor.

But in the summer and autumn of 1988 the presidential candidates passed through the alembics of postmodern journalism and were transformed into texts. Appearing as the products of critical analysis and presented as montages made for television, Messrs. Bush, Dukakis, Bentsen, and Quayle spoke the minimalist language of the photo opportunity and the thirty-second sound bite.

Just as *Tamara* suggests the probable future of the American theater, the 1988 campaign suggests the future of American politics. The impresarios of the New York stage know how to provide resplendent costume and imaginative set decoration, but scarcely a word of credible dialogue and seldom a character that can be mistaken for anything other than a symbol mounted on a stick. In the national political theater the campaign managers staged their equally brilliant effects against the backdrops of Iowa cornfields and Pennsylvania steel furnaces. As props they employed not only flags and tanks and balloons but also astronauts, Garrison Keillor, convicted felons, and Cher. Mounted on the scaffolding of the public opinion polls, the candidates presented themselves as symbols for all seasons.

During the second debate between Vice President Bush and Governor Dukakis the presiding journalists pitched their questions at an angle of portentous inanity fully comparable to the line, "Aelis, get me some zucchini." They asked Dukakis why he wasn't a more likable guy and how he would feel if his wife were to be raped and murdered by a madman. They invited Bush to contemplate the sadness of his own funeral cortege and to examine his conscience through the magnifying glass of his dead father's imaginary scorn. The contempt implicit in the questions demonstrated the presumption that the candidates had ceased to exist in any context other than the ones the critics chose to invent. The debates had become a miniseries, the campaign a lesson in deconstruction, the candidates the stuff of docudrama.

Before long I expect to see variations of *Tamara* produced not only in New York but also in Washington—astonishing sets constructed in vacant lots, warehouses, empty office buildings, and bankrupt condominiums. The miniature theme parks could appeal to every conceivable taste for phantasmagoria—Imperial Rome, Havana in the 1930s, Hampton Court during the reign of a good-naturedly decadent Henry VIII. If, after the election, anything goes seriously wrong with the economy, I can even imagine productions arranged across Park Avenue from the Seventh Regiment Armory in the duplex apartments belonging to ruined investment bankers.

Driven mad by his losses in Mexican junk bonds, the banker wanders through rooms crowded with expensive merchandise and scenes of unspeakable depravity. Prominent real estate speculators scream into telephones. Women faint and Japanese businessmen laugh. Richard Nixon appears, mysteriously, dressed in fascist uniform and carrying a riding crop. Every now and then he shouts, at nobody in particular, "In California, everybody is innocent."

HARPER'S MAGAZINE,
*December 1988*

PART **II**

# POLITICS & ECONOMICS

# POLITICAL DISCOURSE

I T IS THE height of the summer political season, and for the past
several weeks the newspaper columnists have been making their
customary moan about the torpor of the electorate. Not even William
F. Buckley, Jr., professes to understand fully the public indifference
to the presidential campaign. Here it is the beginning of a new
decade, the United States seized by ravaging inflation and beset by
rumors of war, and yet the surveys of popular opinion report wide-
spread antipathy toward the candidates, the "issues," the fate of
Western civilization, and anything else that gives off the stench of
politics. The campaign has been playing in the media theaters for
the better part of two years (complete with hundreds of millions of
words of program notes), but the audience appears to have gone
elsewhere. Mr. Buckley and his fellow seers sift the weekly polls
and ask one another momentous questions: What has become of the
Republic? What is the matter with those people out there on the
other side of the television news? Why do they fill out their question-
naires with adjectives implying scorn and disgust?

Columnists get paid to provide momentous answers to their own
questions, and they like to attribute what they call "the malaise of
the American people" to the conduct of politicians. They compare a
candidate's early statements on energy or defense policy with the
legislation subsequently amended by Congress or by a level of
applause; if the distance between the word and the deed seems to
the columnist too great, well then, obviously the candidate failed to

**141**

perform the acts of government. This explanation enjoys an enthusiastic following among the mandarins of the press and universities; aside from being sentimental and wrong, it insults the intelligence of a citizenry already afflicted with an imaginary malaise.

I sometimes think that only editorial writers employed by *The New York Times* dare to pretend to believe a politician's campaign promises. The ordinary voter would no more expect a politician to make good on his promises than he would expect to find true love and happiness on a three-day Caribbean cruise. Beyond the lawns of the bureaucracies I have yet to meet anybody who did not instinctively know that a politician makes a profession of compromising his principles and betraying last week's constituencies. That is his métier, and he deserves to be admired for the complacence with which he revises his opinions and the agility with which he bends his knee to the prevailing truth. In 1860 Abraham Lincoln received the Republican nomination on the clear understanding that he would do nothing to emancipate the slaves; Woodrow Wilson campaigned in 1916 on the slogan "He kept us out of war"; in 1932 Franklin D. Roosevelt promised to balance the budget. Once elected to office, a president has no choice but to drift with the tide of events. He finds himself constantly taken by surprise, ceaselessly forced back from his commitments, obliged to learn the names of molecules and terrorist organizations that he didn't know existed. Usually he is the last man in the room to discover the emergence of a national issue, and by the time he musters the appropriate committees and proclamations, the issue has changed into something else.

The voters recognize and accept the watery character of politics. They do so not because they are cynical (as the professors and columnists would have it) but because their own experience instructs them in the corruptibility of their fellow men. Who except Mr. Joseph Kraft has not encountered the despotisms of everyday life? Who except Governor Reagan's foreign policy advisers has not been subjected to the tyranny of an assistant vice president, the cowardice of a network executive, the ambition of a shop steward?

Any platform that any candidate may construct the voters know to be a house of straw. What they look for in political discourse is not a program of specific action but a tone of voice. They listen for a definition of liberty, for an awareness of the ambiguity implicit in the weight of things, for a rhetoric that conveys some sense of their own fleeting and precarious existences. Unlike the custodians of the political mysteries, the voters know how much they don't know. No matter how imposingly wrought the facade of permanence, the earth shifts and slides beneath their feet. One year the newspapers tell them they have the Russians for friends and the Chinese for enemies; a year later the Chinese become friends and the Russians turn out to be enemies. Somebody builds a factory and thinks he has done a fine thing for his town; a year later he hears himself reviled for having poisoned a river. Somebody else sets out with the noblest of intentions to work for racial equality; after having pursued the twists of logic into the maze of affirmative action, he finds himself arguing on behalf of racial privilege. Who could have imagined, even ten years ago, that a decision to winterize one's house would be a matter of foreign policy? Nothing remains as it was, and the voters know that their lives tremble in the balance of decisions taken by people whom they have never seen and whose names they don't know how to pronounce. Knowing themselves to be transients in a world of ceaseless change, the voters also know that no politician can resolve their doubts or put to rest their entirely reasonable fears. If a politician spoke to them as if they were consenting adults, maybe he could relieve them of at least a little of their anxiety. Maybe the voters would listen to a politician who told them what things cost, who said, with Bismarck, that nations are made with iron and blood, not with street fairs and parliamentary resolutions. Or maybe they would pay attention to a politician who said, as did Lincoln eighteen months after the Emancipation Proclamation, "I claim not to have controlled events, but confess plainly that events have controlled me."

But it is precisely this human voice that never interrupts the broadcast of the presidential campaign. It is their speech that renders politicians implausible, not their actions. The candidates address the voters in a language of street cries and press clippings. They become characters in the soap opera of the television news, their slogans and phrases worn so smooth by repeated use that they resemble ancient coins to which nobody can assign either a value or a city of origin. Instead of using words that awaken in people a sense of the unfamiliarity of what they thought was familiar (this being the prerequisite to discovery and to the hope of human possibility), the candidates use words as if they were spells and palliatives, seeking to lull the children to sleep, assuring them that the world's arrangements are fixed and certain.

If politicians speak a ceremonial language, maybe this is because their offices have become increasingly ceremonial. What, after all, can a politician actually do? President Carter and Governor Reagan might receive the fealty of the nominating conventions (in the midst of balloons, klieg lights, and loud applause), but they preside over political mechanisms that function at an ever-increasing distance from the act of governing. The Democratic and Republican parties have dissolved into so many conflicting factions that they no longer can be said to work as organized systems. If I think of what it means to comprehend the contradictions of government (even to read through the tax laws, the federal budget, the thousands of pages of congressional testimony), then I don't wonder that politicians try to compress the complexities of government into poetic phrase and gesture. So few citizens can devote the time necessary to the study of even a fragment of the political process, and the politicians despair of having to respond coherently, often within a matter of hours, to the eruption of Mount St. Helens as well as to the shooting of Vernon Jordan, the OPEC oil price, the unemployment rate, and a riot in Miami. Under the circumstances, it is not surprising that the candidates appear to be actors in a Kabuki theater. Even when safely elected to office, they continue their endless campaign. The political season never stops, and politics never goes away.

If only the candidates could emerge from behind the screens of metaphor, maybe they could engage the voters in a dialogue of ends and means; maybe they could talk about inflation as a vested interest and foreign policy as an art of war. Maybe they could say, with Machiavelli, that it is better to be feared than loved, more prudent to be cruel than compassionate.

The light-mindedness of their talk prevents them from saying that the United States stands as a force in the world not because of its collection of weapons but because it embodies an idea of liberty struggling to free itself from the overhanging debt of the past, from the encumbering and familiar lies (frequently defined as "vital issues" or "the national interest"), from the fathers who say, in effect, we all would have been so much better off if you (i.e., the voter) hadn't been so inconsiderate as to have been born.

This struggle goes on every day, and most people, most of the time, find excuses for letting it pass by. They neglect to make the distinction between the kind of fighting that civilizes the earth and the kind of fighting that reduces it to barbarism. A politician who would earn the ear of the public would need to describe this struggle in a way that draws the analogies between the lives of individuals and the histories of nations. He could say that barbarism shows itself in many forms—in the heroin traffic between Iran and Los Angeles as well as in the interest rates charged by the Chase Manhattan Bank. The hope of liberty demands a ceaseless struggle against the tendency to confuse freedom with a license to exploit, against the temptation to define self-destruction as self-fulfillment and the willingness to think that getting one's way is synonymous with inner peace. The candidate might also say to people that maybe they're not supposed to let themselves die so easily, that nobody suffers the pain of birth or the anguish of loving a child in order for presidents to make wars, for governments to feed on the substance of their people, for insurance companies to cheat the young and rob the old. So eloquent a man might also say that the toxins in the Love Canal correspond to the drug of pornography, that energy can be measured both in terms of kilowatts and misdirected rage.

If he cannot offer the voters reassurance, the candidate at least can address them as adults who know their own minds and can come to their own conclusions. The circumstances of the modern world call into doubt the maxims that large numbers of people had thought to be immutable, and so a politician who would speak to them convincingly would do well to remember that the world is larger than the architect's models made by his speechwriters.

HARPER'S MAGAZINE,
*August 1980*

# REAGAN'S
# ACADEMY AWARD

O N THE SATURDAY evening after the presidential election I was driving across New York's Triborough Bridge when I noticed, between the bridge and Yankee Stadium, a neon sign flashing the message GOOD LUCK REAGAN. The words alternated with readings of the time and temperature (5:23 P.M., 47° Fahrenheit), and they appeared at the base of a billboard raised up on the rubble of the East Harlem slum. Not knowing who owned the billboard, or who had thought it worthwhile to buy space on Mr. Reagan's behalf, I couldn't decide whether the intention was sentimental or sardonic. Depending on the inflection of the voice, I could hear the words pronounced either as a pious wish or a cynical farewell.

The ambiguity of the greeting corresponded to the irony implicit in the view to the west. From a height or a distance New York always seems a beautiful and resplendent city, and on this particular evening it was made lovelier by grace of a northwest wind that had blown away the usual burden of smoke. The dark wall of buildings glittered with light, and the sky was the color of roses. So magnificent was the effect that it might have been thought unpatriotic to observe that, in the streets below the neon sign, the going price for burning an empty tenement stood at $100 ($400 if people happened to live in the place) and that nine-year-old boys could earn $3,000 a day selling heroin to their peers.

**146**

For four days the newspapers had been describing the magnitude of Mr. Reagan's victory as if it were an event comparable in historical importance to the Norman Conquest of Britain. American opinion supposedly had shifted heavily to the right, bringing to an end something called "the era of liberalism" and bestowing upon Mr. Reagan a mandate to take down the stage scenery backing the romance of social justice. The city's most eminent journalists had retired into confused abstraction, shuffling through their notes and polls in search of an explanation for a result that none of them had foreseen. In the literary salons it was being said that the Visigoths had sacked the Senate, that the warmongering professors who ordinarily confined their adventurism to the pages of *Commentary* would soon be working out the logistics for a siege of Moscow, that the multinational corporations had hired a mouthpiece eloquent in his defense of greed, and that the evangelical rabble from the Middle West was already dragging its tents and Bibles into Washington.

Few elections offer a text so easily explicated. Mr. Reagan's "landslide" (the third such marvel in the last five elections) rested as much on paradox and contradiction as it did on the spending of Republican money for television commercials. As follows:

THE AMBIGUOUS GOOD NEWS

Mr. Reagan presented himself as the candidate bringing hope, faith, freedom, and prosperity to an electorate sorely in need of good news. As opposed to President Jimmy Carter, who spoke so mournfully about the passing of the American dream, Mr. Reagan held out the promise of a bright future. Maybe it was a fatuous promise and an illusory future, but at least Mr. Reagan gave people an excuse to believe that the next ten years might be better than the last ten years. This is probably as much of a future, or as much of a campaign platform, as any politician can be expected to provide. Certainly Mr. Reagan didn't articulate a coherent system of social or economic thought. Nor did he attempt anything so foolish as a political agenda. He made do with slogans and amiable improvisations, the charm of his persona embodied in the sweetness of his actor's voice, calmly reassuring his audience that once again all would be well, that nobody would be trampled to death in the escape from the burning theater.

The Democratic party had nothing to say about even a spurious future. Mr. Carter spoke of perils beyond measure, of poisoned seas and dwindling stores of money and light, of blacks and Jews tearing at each other in second-class restaurants, of Russians armed with invincible weapons. He cast his politics as a medical report instead of a lullaby, and the voters turned away from him as if from the specter of death.

But so also did the voters turn away from everything else that conspired against their intimations of immortality. By getting rid of Jimmy Carter they hoped to get rid of all the other ills afflicting the nation. When questioned as to their reasons for voting for Mr. Reagan, a majority of the respondents mentioned something they were against—inflation, unemployment, David Rockefeller, the Russians, taxes, abortion, real estate prices, the poor quality of hotel service, the taste of frozen orange juice.

When taken together with the 80 million eligible voters who didn't bother to go to the polls, Mr. Reagan's majority might be said to embody a mandate of rage, disappointment, impotence, resentment, and disgust—all of it directed not only against the hapless Mr. Carter but also against the very idea of politics.

If the more cheerful augurs could read in the entrails of the election a renewed faith in the prospects of American democracy, their more skeptical colleagues could as easily read the same signs as the harbingers of anarchy. A political system decays when large numbers of reasonable and high-minded people come to the conclusion that politics is beneath them, that the familiar political speech no longer answers to the complexities of the age, and that only demagogues of the worst sort would prostitute themselves to the lust for simplification. Democratic government succeeds not because majorities win elections but because minorities submit to being governed by the results. Last November the statistical majority neither won nor consented to lose; in the name of conscience it reserved the right to disobey.

CHRISTIAN VALUES

All the authorities agreed that Mr. Reagan derived much of his support from the evangelical congregations, among them Christian Voice and Moral Majority, Inc., which were determined to reawaken the Christian faith among a populace gone sick with atheistic humanism. This interpretation offers the irony of Mr. Reagan, the candidate of marriage and the family, entering the White House as the first President of the United States ever to have been divorced. One of his sons, a ballet dancer, lives in a state of sin with a young woman in New York's Greenwich Village. Given the suspicions aroused in the Christian mind by both the ballet and the artistic quarters of society, how is it possible that nobody thought to mention the subject in all those churches in which Mr. Reagan was welcomed with a grateful murmuring of amens?

Nor did anybody seem troubled by the prospect of so many Republican oligarchs buying membership in paradise as if it were a country club only slightly less restrictive in its admissions policy than Bel Air or Palm Beach. If the revival-meeting Christians take the Bible as seriously as their sermons imply, I assume that as a remedy for the feeling of envy they have frequent recourse to the nostrum about it being easier for a camel to pass through the eye of a needle than for a rich man to enter the Kingdom of Heaven. But Mr. Reagan, himself a man rich in the patronage of Mammon, stands at the head of a political party devoted to the amassing of wealth on a scale that would have embarrassed Pharaoh. The candidate referred to this acquisitiveness as "Americanism" (a good thing), as distinct from "materialism" (a bad and probably Japanese thing).

It is a credit to Mr. Reagan's grasp of American politics that he resolved the theatrical dilemma by recognizing the inseparable union of church and state. Ordinarily this is an insight vouchsafed only to an incumbent president. When Jimmy Carter campaigned for office in 1976, he promised to rid Washington of the pharisees who defiled the temples of government with their lies and wars. Once invested with the robes of office, Mr. Carter discovered what his predecessors had always known—that the crimes of government were mere illusions and that the power of the presidency was sufficiently miraculous to make the crooked straight and the rough places plain.

Addressing a congregation of the Reverend Jerry Falwell's Moral Majority, Inc., in Lynchburg, Virginia, a few weeks before the election, Mr. Reagan made a more elaborate statement of the same truth. He began by talking about the Supreme Court decision that had restrained the authorities from reciting morning prayers in the public schools. If God had not been expelled from the classroom, Mr. Reagan said, the United States would be a lot better off. He didn't explain the reason for God's expulsion, but he was quite sure that the disciplinary action hadn't been God's fault. God had not been caught stealing football helmets or selling cocaine on the playground. He had not been trapped in the act of bribery by an FBI agent posing as an Arab, nor had He been arrested, like Congressman Robert Bauman (R-MD), for making sexual advances toward a sixteen-year-old boy. No, God had behaved in an exemplary manner throughout His long attendance in American schools, and so His dismissal was obviously the result of some chicanery, probably (although Mr. Reagan didn't say so) the work of communists.

If God wasn't at His desk, then conceivably He might be a truant, wandering along a railroad track or hanging out with a crowd of delinquents in a massage parlor. But this wasn't like God. He had always been an orderly and upright youth, good at His lessons and dutiful in His service to the prejudices of the community in which He happened to find Himself, and so maybe He had become a politician.

Governor Reagan didn't pursue this line of speculation, but he gave his audience in Lynchburg reason to hope that something of the sort may have occurred when he said, "The halls of government are well nigh as sacred as the churches, temples, and synagogues of our religions."

If God has taken up residence in the halls of government, then the confusions of the last few years can be quite easily explained. God had been testing the faith of the people and weighing the coin of their belief on the scale of His opinion poll. When confronted with

Richard Nixon's iniquity, or the Christmas bombing of Vietnam, the weak and the faint of heart made lamentations in the newspapers and corrupted themselves with the luxury of doubt. But these were people of little faith, deceived by the ways in which God moved so mysteriously through the halls of government. They noticed that a host of minor politicians routinely plundered the public treasury, but they failed to understand that the politicians did this in order to prove that the riches of this earth are as nothing when compared to the rewards of heaven.

THE UNNECESSARY UTOPIA

The Democrats win elections when enough people think that the government can build Utopia in the temporal wilderness. The Republicans win elections when Utopia doesn't appear on the ballot. If the Kingdom of Heaven already stands revealed in Grosse Pointe or Palm Beach, then what is the point of going to the trouble of constructing a paltry substitute for the poor? The corollary fantasy holds that if everybody looks out for his own interest the common interest will take care of itself. Republican economists describe this process as the working of Adam Smith's invisible hand, which, like the household staff in "Upstairs, Downstairs," finds itself more generously rewarded in private service.

The most intricate of the ironies implicit in the November election thus has to do with the value placed on words. Probably what defeated Mr. Carter and elected Mr. Reagan was the obsolescence of the liberal Democratic notion that the United States could govern the world with adjectives, that for military victory and economic supremacy it could substitute the rhetoric of sublime moralism. The notion has been current for thirty years, as characteristic of leftist intellectuals walled up in the universities as of the media operatives at large in the realms of policy. To the extent that enough people thought the wealth of the United States infinite, it was possible to design schemes for redistributing that wealth on the premise that the government could impose an infinite succession of taxes. The dominant opinion held that the United States could have it both ways—guns and butter, peace and war, profit and well-being, wealth and nobleness of soul, art and fame. Under this system of childlike belief, law became an applied science and politics a department of engineering.

Unfortunately, like so many of the journalists who backed his campaign for the presidency in 1976, Mr. Carter believed in the rule of words. He had little appreciation of the sources of power different from his own, and he relied, together with the rest of the Democratic establishment, on parables and exhortations.

Although Mr. Reagan apparently also believes that the United States can have it both ways, he undoubtedly recognizes the existence of powers other than those available to the paid entertainment. Mr. Reagan is an accommodating man who has made it his lifelong habit to defer to his social and financial superiors. As an actor he makes use of words, but they do not bind him to a mythology, and he doesn't think of them as magical incantations. He reads a script, not a manifesto or a sermon. When, on the night of the election, his victory had become plain to him, he gave what amounted to an Academy Award speech on the stage of the Century Plaza Hotel in Los Angeles, accepting an Oscar for best performance by a supporting actor with the appropriate show of gratitude for the director, the grips, the costar, and all the other wonderful people who had made possible the most "humbling moment in my life."

Given Mr. Reagan's ingratiating manner, his actor's lack of interest in the meaning of words instills a sense of confidence rather than alarm. The same thing cannot be said of the political cadres employed by the fanatical right wing of the Republican party to vilify those liberal senators (Messrs. Bayh, McGovern, Culver, and Church) whom they nominated as enemies of the state. By reducing words to objects, the Christian propagandists transformed language into stone, thereby forming an ecumenical union with those totalitarian states against which they hurled the clichés of freedom.

THE NEW BEGINNING

Although I doubt that the country has become more conservative than it was two weeks or twenty years before the election, I think it probable that people wish to feel more conservative. They talk about restoring old values and old houses in the same way they talk about Mr. Reagan's economic and foreign policy. If in the 1970s it was thought fashionable to indulge an expensive habit for cocaine or divorce, in the 1980s it will probably be thought fashionable to stay married and drink gin.

During the last two decades of the twentieth century the scientific revolution that has been gaining momentum for eighty years promises to accelerate the rate of change at computer speeds. At the dawn of a new era, the United States chooses to elect a president illiterate in the sciences, a man born in 1911 (six years before the birth of John F. Kennedy), whose ideas about international affairs correspond to those of Teddy Roosevelt. In the ecological, as well as the economic and political, sciences, the lines of recent discovery point toward the existence of an interdependent world that has become, for all practical purposes, one nation. But Mr. Reagan still mumbles the threats of an antique nationalism as quaint and appealing as the Fourth of July cannonade in colonial Williamsburg.

Among Mr. Reagan's fervent admirers the wish to believe in the simplicity of the lost frontier overrides the contradictions implicit in his rhetoric. And so, for the time being at least, it doesn't matter that Mr. Reagan champions "the right to life" while promising to give full employment to those arms manufacturers who used to be called, in a simpler age, "the merchants of death"; it doesn't matter that for all of Mr. Reagan's talk about "free enterprise," the corporations that he would rescue from the toils of government regulation depend for much of their profit on government subsidy. Mr. Reagan offers to substitute happy problems for sad problems; and perhaps the most instructive of all the ironies attendant upon his election was suggested by something that Nancy Reagan said to a reporter from *The* [London] *Observer* during the last week of the campaign.

"Ronald," she said, "really hates to have conflict around him. He doesn't want to have to get on the plane having to hold his stomach."

Neither do the children in East Harlem like to have to hold their stomachs, though more from hunger than from the pangs of anxiety. Mr. Reagan will need all the luck he can get, which only a churl would begrudge either him or the rest of us, but the idea of democracy rests on incessant conflict (between old and young, rich and poor, capital and labor, city and country, yours and mine), and if Mr. Reagan doesn't have the stomach for it, then all the gold in Fort Knox and all the missiles in all the silos in Kansas won't put Humpty Dumpty together again.

HARPER'S MAGAZINE,
*January 1981*

# ESKIMO ECONOMICS

To HEAR THE media explain it, the country has become conservative. For the last two or three years the guardians of the American conscience have been worrying about the numbers of people espousing conservative economic theory and conservative religion. By now the nation supposedly swarms with conservatives of various descriptions—new, old, armed, evangelical—all of them organizing themselves around the virtues believed to be allied with the family, the pulpit, and the flag.

Perhaps this is so, but I wish I knew what most people mean by the word *conservative*. I can appreciate the secondary connotations of the word (as a synonym for disillusioned or as a euphemism for the prejudice against change), but its political meaning remains unclear, and the tracts published by the American Enterprise Institute only make it more elusive. More often than not the word seems to represent a set of passions rather than a system of ideas. People who declare themselves conservative frequently behave as if they were radicals, and when they attempt to align their doctrine with their self-interest or their emotion (usually rage), the conversation deteriorates into babble not unlike the speaking in tongues.

The discrepancy between what people say and do arises from the American talent for reducing political argument to religious dispute. The discussion usually takes place in the realm of absolutes, with as little reference as possible to the experience of any of the participants. People who advance the principles of liberalism presumably conceive of individual liberty as the highest possible good,

**155**

and yet, when given the chance to cast their principles in a political form, they invariably assign dictatorial powers to the state.

Self-professed conservatives say that they wish to protect the value of established well-being and tradition, but then, almost in the same breath, they go on to say that they also wish to conserve the spirit of free enterprise and the individualistic nature of a society that allows every man the opportunity to improve and transform himself. The two sentiments stand implacably opposed to each other. By encouraging individual initiative and ambition, the conservative allies himself with the compounds most corrosive to any established order.

Most businessmen have a romantic image of themselves as protectors of the status quo, and very few of them understand that the capitalist spirit is a revolutionary one. On the terrace of a country club they talk complacently about the marketing of a new concept or a new technology, little dreaming that the innovation might develop in ways they cannot foresee and that they might as easily have brought forth a goliath that will reduce them to penury. In 1939 the owners of *The Saturday Evening Post* had a chance to buy CBS. They listened with polite condescension to the explanation of the possibilities implicit in television, but they were in the communications business, and they didn't know why somebody would want to bother them with toys.

Except for the pessimism implicit in the enterprise, what is conservative about the reckless piling up of a nuclear arsenal already numbering as many as 10,000 warheads? If it requires only two hundred of these missiles to poison the earth, why is it conservative to go on producing them in profligate abundance? The more warheads in the international inventory, the more likely the chance of war; the more extensive the development of such weapons, the more likely that the continuing research will make them available (at bargain prices) to Muammar el-Qaddafi and Pol Pot.

The more dynamic the society and the more rapidly things change, the more difficult it becomes to reward the traditional forms of sacrifice. What does the conservative wish to conserve, and for whom? It runs against the grain of American conservatism to insist on the preservation of landed estates or social rank, and so even the most timid conservative hears himself arguing (against his own acquisitive instincts and over the passionate objections of his wife) in favor of a capitalism that Joseph Schumpeter once described as the process of "creative annihilation."

The paradox sometimes confuses even the most learned and doctrinaire conservatives. Only last week the question came up at a seminar in which a number of prominent apologists for the neoconservative persuasion (historians as well as Republican Cabinet ministers in exile) had gathered to complain about the acids of modernism. Everybody had a great deal to say about the gangsterism in the gold and commodity markets and about the way in which the carnivorous Washington bureaucracy gorged itself on the flesh of the taxpayer. The formal proceedings came to an end in a familiar chorus of recrimination, and the participants adjourned to a handsome library in which the books had been furnished at federal expense.

To one of the most eminent scholars present, a man in a three-piece suit accustomed to advising the presidents of corporations, I remarked on a stock offering that I had seen earlier the same day. The prospectus advertised stock at $4 a share in a company licensed to provide public hospitals with a cure for heart disease. The promoter wasn't very specific about how this was to be done, but it had something to do with a machine and a course of medicine. The scheme had been backed by several well-known heart specialists, and even if the program didn't make good on its promises, which it probably wouldn't, at least it would make the suckers feel better. For providing the machine and a course of treatment, the new company would divide all fees with the hospitals. Because the money would be paid under arrangement with Medicaid or Medicare, the government would pay the cost of the fraud. The promoter figured that within a year the price of the stock would rise to $100 a share.

I mentioned the proposition to my neoconservative friend as an example of the kind of thing that he so often and so loudly condemned, and I thought he might be able to make use of it in a speech to a group of concerned citizens. Instead of indignation, my friend asked for the name of the promoter. He advised me to buy as much of the stock as I could get hold of. When I pointed out that the investment was hardly a conservative one, he said that in these debased times (brought about, of course, by Democrats and the well-known "failure of nerve"), a man had no choice but to become a speculator. If he was to protect his wife and children, then he must needs take advantage of any opening vouchsafed to him by Providence.

"Satan is in the marketplace," he said, "and we must learn to play by Satan's rules." He went on to explain that once the economic system had been restored to its proper balance and perfection, he would gladly put his money in a savings account and avoid the company of swindlers.

In ordinary usage the word *conservative* implies an association with the ideas of thrift, industry, prudence, moderation, and restraint. All admirable qualities, and all of them of doubtful value in the current speculative chaos of the political, intellectual, and financial markets. The forces at work in American society over the last twenty years tend to make a mockery of the conservative virtues. The society applauds passion and immediacy, and it is in almost nobody's interest to save money or to work toward an achievement that cannot be explained between commercials on the Johnny Carson show.

If inflation consumes the value of money at the rate of 15 percent a year, a man must double his income in every fourth year in order to retain the wealth he possessed in the first year. Under such circumstances, who but a noble fool would invest in savings accounts or government bonds? If the habits of thrift threaten a man with bankruptcy, how can he transmit even a remnant of his estate to his children (or to himself ten years hence) unless he borrows heavily and hopes for a continuing destruction of the currency? Who, then, is more conservative—the man who speculates or the man who saves?

Despite the earnest alarms to the contrary, the country as a whole appears to have decided the question in favor of speculation. The national investment in the most common forms of gambling (casinos, lotteries, numbers, racetracks, etc.) now amounts to $150 billion a year, and the once industrious middle class trades feverishly in real estate, gold, stamps, furniture, paintings, and whatever else offers at least a temporary refuge against the storm of inflation. The nation's farmers, once said to embody the stalwart agrarian virtues, play the futures markets in wheat and corn.

It is probably fair to say that most people, most of the time and in most aspects of their lives, behave in a conservative manner. Nobody likes to change his habits of thought, and it usually takes a generation for people to modify their definitions of art and morality. When they say that they wish to conserve things as they are, they usually mean that they wish to conserve things as they seem.

Given the instinctive conservatism of human nature, most people become exceedingly nervous when forced to accept the gambler's risk. They suspect (correctly) that they might be pursuing a policy bound to destroy their own wealth, and their apprehension makes them easy marks for the professionals.

During this year's presidential campaign all the candidates presented themselves as conservative, in the sense that they stood willing to forgo (and would ask the country to forgo) an immediate or expedient result for the sake of a result projected forward in time across a horizon of years and decades. On this premise they rested their claim to "statesmanship," and they appended to their certificates of leadership their visions of the future and their lists of the sacrifices necessary to restore the nation's productivity as well as its moral and military supremacy.

But the candidates had to conduct their campaigns on television, which is a medium that dissolves all reference to time past and time future in the acid of the immediate present. Either the politician tells the audience what it wants to hear or he loses his ratings in the next day's polls. The candidates thus could do nothing else except speculate in the market of opinions, changing their positions on the issues in order to accommodate the specifications of the moment, selling or bidding up the price of an idea in response to the demand of the crowd.

The conservative ethos presumes an attitude of moderation and magnanimity (i.e., a willingness to restrain one's primitive appetites in the interest of civilization), but what corporation can afford to conduct its affairs on so admirable a premise? The value assigned to the quarterly statements of profit and loss obliges the corporation to measure its success on time horizons as ephemeral as those of the publishing or dress business. The shareholders expect a steadily rising value (reflected both in the dividend and the price of the stock), and so the corporations must maximize their profits from day to day and week to week. Which among them can afford to curb its greed?

Similarly, within the hierarchy of the corporation, the individuals who would further their own ambitions learn to depreciate the values of patience and loyalty. They maximize their salaries and their benefits by shifting their allegiance every two or three years, trading their services to the next employer in the manner of mercenary captains or actors playing short-term engagements.

To the extent that the forces operative in the American markets have transformed a generation of would-be conservatives into a band of predators, the economic system of the United States has come to resemble the economic system of the primitive Eskimo. On the evidence of a thousand years of careful observation (surely testimony to a conservative habit of mind) the Eskimo have learned to save nothing. If an Eskimo hunter discovers twenty-seven caribou wandering across the tundra, he kills the entire herd. His colleagues follow the same practice with regard to seals, polar bears, and whales, always on the assumption that they might never see so many animals again.

Never having had occasion to understand the principle of cultivation, the Eskimo have acquired an attitude toward consumption that bears comparison to that of the federal government. The government's taxing policies apparently follow from the assumption that never again will it find so many taxpayers foolish enough to assess their incomes honestly.

The Eskimo kept themselves in economic balance by observing the ruthless budget procedures imposed by nature. Their old people were set adrift in canoes, their deformed or surplus children left to die in the snow. The hypocrisies of American politics forbid so straightforward a statement of economic policy, but the state accomplishes the same purpose by pensioning off its older citizens on fixed incomes and by spending no more than a pittance on the health and education of its children.

The Eskimo at least had the sense to realize that their society was a profligate one and that without the means or the incentive to create new wealth they had no choice but to feed for as long as possible on the bodies of found whales. It is a tribute to the economist's art that in the United States the same policies appear in the newspaper under the name *conservative*.

HARPER'S MAGAZINE,
*December 1980*

# THE COMPLEAT
# AMERICAN

I N HIS PERFORMANCE of the presidency, Ronald Reagan plays the leading role as a series of impressions of American minor heroes. The reading of the part lends itself to Mr. Reagan's genius as a supporting actor as well as to the skittishness of an audience that has trouble following a complex narrative or subtle dialogue. Mr. Reagan offers a complete repertoire of sketches, which, when taken together, exemplify the sum of the American ideal. If some of his characters seem in conflict with others, or if they succeed one another as quickly as the scene changes in a vaudeville revue, that is the nature of a genre that exploits the American talent for paradox and the one-line joke. The more obvious routines can be described as follows:

*The Rolling Stone*

F. Scott Fitzgerald once observed that American lives have no second acts. Perhaps the gentleman had lived too long in Hollywood. American lives generally consist of nothing but second acts. It is the first and third acts that few people know how to stage or write.

What other nation in the history of the world can boast the

**162**

testimony of so many converts? The theme of metamorphosis recurs throughout the whole text of American history and biography. Men start out in one place and end up in another, never quite knowing how they got there, perpetually expecting the unexpected.

The figure of the enthusiast who has just discovered jogging or a new way to fix tofu can be said to stand or, more accurately, to tremble on the threshold of conversion, as the representative American. The citizenry reveres movement for its own sake, as if in the mere act of going from one place to another a man might stumble across the ineffable. In the nineteenth century Americans placed such a high value on speed that hundreds of them died in railroad accidents and steamboat explosions. The loss of acceleration filled the passengers with uneasiness (somebody else might be getting there first), and they would urge the captain or the engineer to force his engines beyond the limits of the boilermaker's art.

Corporate vice presidents change their affiliation and place of residence almost as often as army officers or Mexican field hands. The practice of serial monogamy, brought to the dimension of a light industry in Mr. Reagan's adopted state of California, sustains the illusion of romance through the disappointments of middle age.

Like his ancestors before him, Mr. Reagan preserved his options, moving west or east, left or right, as the season or opportunity beckoned. An actor and a liberal Democrat at the age of forty-three, Mr. Reagan had not yet begun the study of politics. Twenty-seven years later he had become president of the United States, a conservative . . . Republican, and an enthusiastic convert to an economic theory as fantastic in its design as the aerodynamics of a UFO.

Mr. Reagan's predecessor in the White House was a willing but not quite so adept student of the quick change. Mr. Carter made his entrance on the political stage in Georgia as a self-proclaimed realist, a once-upon-a-time naval officer who let it be known that he wouldn't mind taking fortified positions against Russians, black people, New York intellectuals, and miscellaneous agents of the devil. By the time he became president his militancy had softened into the posture of a moralist who preached the blessings of human brotherhood to the South Africans and discounted the specter of international communism as a paranoid delusion. Before he left office he had moved stage right once again, delivering his exit lines against the tanks in Afghanistan and the treachery of Moslem holy men.

The impulse toward transformation corresponds to the frontier strategy of real estate speculation, a strategy summarized in the advice "settle and sell." Before the roof had been put on the church it was time to move farther west. The contemporary markets in political and cultural theory operate on the same principle. Mr. Irving Kristol, the dean of academic capitalism, once prided himself on the purity of his faith in Trotsky. Several of Robert Kennedy's lieutenants in the war against crime consoled themselves for the loss of that war by serving as attorneys for the mob. Charles Colson, who offered to run over his grandmother if the action would serve the interests of the state, now travels with Billy Graham's television troupe, preaching the virtues of Christian conscience to grandmothers threatened with the loss of their pensions. Jerry Rubin has given up street revolution for the more profitable anarchy of the stock market, and Eldridge Cleaver, who had spoken for the Black Panthers, went on to speak for God through Word, Inc., and the Eldridge Cleaver Crusade.

*The Booster*

The romance of the intrepid American individual as a solitary figure bearing west into Utah appears to have been an invention of the literary East. The country was settled by people moving in groups, by transient communities mounted on wagons and making up their laws and customs as they passed, arguing violently, through the forest. Such people chose for their captain a man who could organize and persuade, who knew how to get folks doing things together from their own volition and interest, who could rekindle their guttering enthusiasm with descriptions of an imaginary Eden lying in wait just over the next line of hills. Of this paradise the captain was as ignorant as anybody else in camp, and so he had to have the confidence man's gift for improvisation. The westering caravans had little use for leaders in the European sense of the term, men distinguished by a unique ability for bravery, learning, eloquence, or greatness of soul. The development of extraordinary capacities assumed the scaffolding of authority and class distinctions that Americans had left behind in the wreck of the Old World. People learned to travel light, and the chroniclers in the western deserts constantly reported great numbers of dead horses and abandoned wagons on the trail. What was wanted was a salesman and a booster, a good fellow on the order of George F. Babbitt or Ronald Reagan, somebody with shallow roots who could attach himself to whatever enterprise promised the hope of profit.

In a nation of strangers it was necessary to insist on a severe degree of conformity. Without the implacable enforcement of what de Tocqueville called "the tyranny of the majority," the crowd might break up into its component languages, nationalities, professions, and sects. Because the American association was voluntary, because people had come because they wanted to come, because those present literally had brought the country into being, they had no choice but to accept the dictum, abridged, in the idiom of bumper stickers, to the phrase "Love it or leave it."

James Q. Wilson, the eminent student of American government and politics, once remarked that he had spent much of his life confined within three authoritarian institutions—the Catholic Church when he was a child, the United States Navy when he was a young man, Harvard University as a tenured professor. As a totalitarian system demanding conformity of thought, the greatest of these, he said, was Harvard.

The desire to be and to act like everybody else shows up in the American passion for borrowed identities, for joining clubs and wearing clothes stamped with safe labels, for not daring to risk an opinion at odds with those of the presiding majority. The suspicion of a man acting alone or thinking for himself remains deeply rooted in the American character. Mr. Reagan recites his golden commonplaces in the full knowledge that success comes most readily to the individual who merges his own interest with the interest of the town, the project, or the team.

*The Cockeyed Optimist*

The doctrine of the second chance and the new beginning carries with it the good news that the battle is never lost. On the wagons moving west into Oklahoma in the 1890s, the tattered signs read, "In God we trusted, in Kansas we busted. Now let her rip for the Cherokee Strip." Americans hold that talent and grit overcome all obstacles, and if a man can put together a future out of whatever lumber he finds lying around on the bank of the Pecos River, nothing is impossible. The foolish optimism implicit in this attitude is as characteristic of Mr. Reagan as it is of the improving spirit of reform.

The attitude has its obvious strengths. People who believe that nothing is impossible sometimes succeed in accomplishing the impossible. Mr. Reagan struck precisely the right note in early September when, having called together his economic advisers to demand further reductions in the federal budget, he said that he knew he asked a difficult and unpleasant thing, but, "If not us, who? If not now, when?"

The weakness of the approach lies in its use of the past as an armory of comforting fables rather than as a reminder of the vastness and strangeness of the world. The national theology grants the primacy of hope over experience. The conviction that the world can be made new as of noon tomorrow accounts for the naïveté, not to mention the crackpot smiling, of the recent convert to a newly minted theory.

Mr. Reagan apparently never lost faith in the promises of glory. His father was a failure, his childhood by all accounts a model of small-town cruelty and unhappiness, and yet, in defiance of Freud and Skinnerian schools of human behavior, the circumstances seem to have left Mr. Reagan unharmed. He went west, rose in the world, cut his opinions to fit the cloth of the new country, fixed his eye on the main chance, dyed his hair, and offended nobody. He passes grinning through the labyrinths of government and the terror of assassins, makes friendly jokes as he cancels the federal subsidies of widows and orphans, exhorts Congress, with modest self-effacement, to arm the less stable nations of the earth with weapons more barbarous than all the hordes of Genghis Khan, listens with serene contentment to the quack geopolitics of General Alexander Haig, bestowing on the nation unsound public finance as if it were a school prize. Mr. Reagan announces the glad tidings of what F. Scott Fitzgerald described, in a somewhat different context, as "the orgiastic future," a future in which all wrongs would be righted, all differences resolved (presumably by a committee of foundation officials), and where everything would be synonymous with everything else. In such a dream of heaven the present exists solely as a point of departure, a depot linking the nonexistent future with a nonexistent past.

HARPER'S MAGAZINE,
*November 1981*

# ECONOMETRICS

I N A POPULAR journal the other day, I noticed a statistic, cited with the obligatory alarm by a professor of economics, to the effect that only 68 percent of the nation's industrial capacity is still in use. The lost 32 percent, measured in rusting assembly lines and empty factories, apparently has fallen into ruins as melancholy as those of ancient Rome. The professor cast the familiar prophecy about the dying of the American light.

Variations on this mournful text appear in so many articles and news broadcasts that I wonder why nobody ever makes the same sort of estimates about the nation's moral and intellectual capacities. Admittedly, the statistics would be hard to come by and difficult to arrange in the ritual form of a data base. How is it possible to measure the emptiness of a human mind? Most people recognize the phenomenon when they see it; they also know when they are looking into the faces of weakness and greed. But how is it possible to translate these certainties into numbers acceptable to the stock market, the econometric models, and the Defense Department?

Judging by what I can see in New York, not only in the faces of the resident oligarchs but also in the pages of both the tabloid and literary press, I think it is probably fair to guess that the nation has remaindered about 50 percent of its capacity for thought and moral effort. The booming of the market in cocaine testifies to the urgency of the retreat from reason, and the political nostrums so far promulgated by the Democratic candidates seeking the presidency in 1984 bear out the suspicion that their speechwriters still hold fast to the belief that nothing much has changed in the world since the election of 1964.

Lacking specific recommendations, the candidates join the professors in the crying of doom, which, as has been explained to me by Georgie Garbisch, a reader in Maryland, allows them to avoid the even more dismal prospect of having to think. She went on to make the further observation that as Americans, "We do not ask nearly enough of ourselves—not of parents, not of children, not of women, not of men, not of our institutions, not of our talents, not of our national or our personal character, not of our Constitution's promise, which we betray." In that one sentence, she says most of what needs to be said about the emptiness of the nation's factories and the hollowness of the nation's politics.

George Orwell once observed that almost everything that goes by the name of pleasure represents a more or less successful attempt to destroy consciousness. The United States now spends upwards of $350 billion a year for liquor, tobacco, pornography, and drugs. The Cold War against the American intellect thus constitutes a more profitable business than the traffic in nuclear weapons.

Subsidized by the state and supported (sometimes with the First Amendment) by the peep show operators of the mass media, the continual state of siege works against man's hope of freedom. The sadomasochistic entertainments hold the mind in chains. Tethered to the posts of sexual fantasy, intimidated by the confusions of lust, murder, and fear, the imagination cannot escape the bureaucrats and the soothsayers.

The pox of the national debt reflects the inability of a democracy to make choices. Like the deficit, now running to approximately $200 billion a year, the debt stands as bleak testimony to the fraudulence of the nation's politics. Few politicians have the courage to refuse payment of the ransoms demanded by the interests that maintain them in office. None of them can distinguish between luxury and necessity—for the good and American reason that one man's luxury (the tobacco subsidy, say, or the interior electronic decoration of a Trident submarine) is another man's necessity, and who but a despised elitist can choose between them?

If the present dilemma were to be resolved in a peaceful or benign manner, it would be necessary not only to distinguish between luxury and necessity but also to keep in mind the distinctions (suggested in 1927 by Ezra Pound) between transient, durable, and permanent goods. Transient goods include fresh vegetables, F-16s, rock concerts, legal fees, tennis lessons, pornography, and MX missiles. Durable goods include well-constructed buildings and roads, decent education, intelligent farming, and afforestation. Permanent goods include scientific discoveries and works of art.

Having assigned the rest of the world the task of providing durable and permanent goods, the American economy derives its wealth from the sale of perishable commodities (wheat, television images, ammunition) and the manufacture of transient luxury. American mothers who nurture dreams of avarice on behalf of their sons no longer tell exemplary tales of industrialists, surgeons, merchants, and ship captains. They speak instead of actors, ballplayers, dress designers, maîtres d'hôtel.

Few people bother to define real capital as the capacity to do real work, or real credit as the reserve of energy and industriousness available to the mind of the nation.

The idea of freedom stands in as much need of revision as the geography of the supposedly lost frontier. Within the circles of advanced opinion, it is taken for granted that high tech will save us all, that man has vanquished Nature, that his machines have made nonsense of the seasons and subjugated the tribes of Paleolithic instinct. The illuminati who make these confident announcements then proceed to talk in a lighter and more conversational tone of voice about the corporate cul de sac in which they find themselves penned like so many sheep, about the faithlessness of their husbands, the forgery of their tax returns, the silence of their children.

They neglect to associate the violence of Nature with man's inability to know, much less to conquer, himself. Most people have the same hopes and aspirations—work in which they can find meaning and a way in which they can express their capacity to love. And yet, in this most advanced of nations and most enlightened of times, how few people manage to achieve those deceptively modest ends.

The rescue from insolvency and sloth also presupposes the asking of further questions about the function of government, the purposes of taxation, and the uses of money. By what right does the state borrow instead of lend? In whose interest does the government manipulate the value of the currency? How does it come to pass that among all of mankind's wonderful inventions (art, science, law, religion, family, and medicine), men reserve to money the supreme privilege and the highest place? In the American scheme of things, why is the usurer (i.e., the financial magnates on the covers of *Business Week*) thought to possess the rank of a duke and the loveliness of a child?

If we could stop thinking of ourselves as omnipotent, perhaps we could relocate the frontier to that point in time where men can sense, but cannot quite see, the looming shape of the future. Suppose, for instance, that the frontier could be understood as being always and everywhere present—as near at hand as the wish to murder, cheat, steal, lie, and generally conduct ourselves in a manner unbecoming in an ape.

Suppose that we could learn to recognize it in the death of a child in the next street, in any afternoon's proceeding in any criminal court, in the faces of people stupefied by anxiety. Think how many of its large and various capacities the United States could put to use if only it knew why it was doing so.

THE WASHINGTON POST,
*March 1983*

# MR. WORTHINGTON
# GOES TO WASHINGTON

**B**EFORE BECOMING A political theorist, A. Lawrence Worthington served as an adviser to families rich enough to worry about the deportment of the heirs. He successfully defended so many fortunes (against the stupidity of banks, the swindling lies of stock market touts and the impertinence of the Internal Revenue Service) that, over the years, he came to be known as the Great Conservator.

In the fullness of time, Mr. Worthington's name was brought to the attention of the Reagan administration and, when the estimates of the federal deficit passed $150 billion, he was invited to Washington to perform a miracle. It was thought that if he could protect the assets of a sugar-refining family certifiably insane, surely he could do something on behalf of the U.S. Treasury Department.

Among all the flaws of character that could be displayed by the heirs to important fortunes, what Mr. Worthington had learned to fear most was the tendency toward idealism. The trait could become especially destructive if it was joined with an energetic and activist temperament. No matter what their motives (to redeem themselves in the eyes of their father, to inject an element of compassion into the manufacture of Kleenex, to rescue the nation from illiteracy or racial hatred), the heirs who sought to manage the family business inevitably reduced it to penury.

"They mean well, of course," Mr. Worthington said, "but they haven't got the knack for the game; they were brought up too soft, and their instincts are all wrong."

Having seen the damage done by good intentions, Mr. Worthington insisted that the heirs under his supervision be placed on a strict regimen of self-indulgent behavior and superfluous spending. If his charges were young gentlemen, he encouraged their interest in racehorses, shark fishing, Scandinavian women, fast cars, gambling, and cocaine; when young ladies were assigned to his care, he tutored them in the same subjects but also provided supplemental courses on jewelry, designer clothes, Impressionist paintings, and New York divorce lawyers.

The benefits of a misspent youth he had reduced to four principles of sound finance:

1. No matter how profligate an individual's taste for luxury or perversion, the expense never exceeds the cost of large-scale social engineering.

2. The impulsive redistribution of wealth rewards the deserving members of the middle class who operate hotels, supply champagne, fix broken tennis rackets, and compose sonatas for violin and automobile horn.

3. Displays of extravagance reassure the populace by confirming their faith in capitalism and giving to money the luminousness of something new.

4. The regular outbreak of scandal provides the relatives with a steady source of gossip. They would rather talk about Amanda's current love affair than listen to an explanation, complete with charts and quotations, of the transformation of the company and the uplifting of the common man.

"I'm sure you can see," Mr. Worthington said, "all that needs to be done is to transfer these principles from the private to the public sector."

Although he hadn't been long in Washington, he was heartened by what he had seen. Certainly President Ronald Reagan and the

Pentagon purchasing agents had an aptitude for the insouciance that Mr. Worthington hoped to establish as a model of political conduct. He thought it promising that the Air Force already knew how to spend $7,622 for a coffee-maker, and he approved of Mr. Reagan's dozing inattentiveness. He was glad to see that so many officials in the Administration already had smeared themselves with some kind of bad news.

"All good signs, but still not enough," Mr. Worthington said. "The proper attitude must be implanted in the Congress. It is the idealists in Congress, especially the ones still in their youth, who cause the trouble."

He had been introduced to a few people on Capitol Hill and had been appalled to discover so many dreamers in their midst.

"You can't imagine the folly that some of those people have in mind," he said. "Why, only yesterday, I met a man who wanted to fill the sky with metal. Last Monday I spoke to a man who wanted to teach every child in America to read. I've met senators who want to turn black people into white people, who think they can provide medical insurance that buys immortality."

What needed to be changed, Mr. Worthington said, was a habit of mind. If the Congress could learn to squander the money on itself, then all would be well. The spending could be easily seen and therefore easily understood. The newspapers would have more parties to photograph, and at least once a week the headline writers would count on discovering a very important person in a smoke-filled room or a public fountain.

Politics could play as it was meant to play (i.e., as entertainment and as inspiration to thieves), and the serious money in the bulk of the federal Treasury could accrue interest at a serene and dignified rate.

THE GLOBE AND MAIL, *Toronto*,
*September 1984*

# THE LOVE SONG OF
# JAMES EARL CARTER

**D**URING HIS FOUR years in the White House Jimmy Carter kept a faithful diary. An eager and voluminous diary. A lover's diary 5,000 pages long and bound in eighteen precious volumes. He made so many notes that it is a wonder he had time to do anything else. Apparently, he was forever writing in a corner, jotting down his thoughts and observations, preserving his impressions of historic moments. An idealist or a Republican might say that this was not a proper occupation for the President of the United States, but so stern a judgment would fail to make sympathetic allowance for the Wagnerian magnificence of Mr. Carter's passion. He was writing about himself, and the subject so captivated him, so consumed him with the fires of love, that he abandoned himself to it in the way that lesser men abandon themselves to their enthusiasms for stamps or butterflies or Civil War cannon.

Now that Mr. Carter has made a book of his diary, an adoring memoir entitled *Keeping Faith*, the notes read like a collection of letters sent from scout camp. Arranged in chronological sequence, they tell the story of a boy and his mirror. The young and upright Jimmy Carter goes north to Washington, and there, among the cruise missiles and the cherry blossoms, he has a wonderful time. He meets wonderful and important people; he thinks wonderful thoughts (some of them statesmanlike, others merely warm and human); he travels to romantic, far-off lands; he lives in an old and

**175**

famous house; sometimes he is sad, but most of the time he is happy and brave. Once or twice he saves Western civilization.

The book continues in this voice for 596 pages, and except for Jimmy Carter's mother I don't know who could bear to read the whole of the correspondence. Presumably it is his mother that Mr. Carter has in mind as his perfect reader, and I'm sure that she also enjoyed looking at the candid snapshots (Jimmy in the Oval Office, Jimmy at Camp David, Jimmy among dignitaries, etc.) stuffed into the pages like blurred photographs of the camp baseball and swimming teams. For the purposes of a review, it is enough to read the first sixty-two pages (all of them introductory and advertised under the heading, "A Graduate Course in America"), and then to look at random through the rest of the collection. The tone never varies, nor does the scout's unfailing ability to achieve a subtlety of perspective comparable to that seen on a postcard of the Lincoln Memorial.

The scout concedes in his preface that he has no wish to write "a history of my administration." Not only would this be too difficult and boring a task, but, even worse, it might interrupt the diarist's elegiac contemplation of himself. Instead of a history he writes what he calls "a highly personal report of my own experiences" because he wants to share (certainly with his mother and maybe with a few other ladies in Plains, Georgia, who wonder how he's doing up there in Washington) the "feelings of gratitude and pleasure" that he has gathered as keepsakes during his visit to the nation's capital.

The opening chapter is meant to be a dramatic account of Mr. Carter's last few hours in office. It is the morning on which his agents arrange to transfer almost $8 billion through the Bank of England in return for the release of the American hostages in Teheran. Given the events in question, another writer might have endowed the scene with liveliness and force. Mr. Carter reduces it to dullness by the simple expedient of staging the action in the theater of his emotions. What is important is the play of the scout's feelings, not what is happening in Algeria, England, Germany, or Iran. Nobody else in the room attains the status of reality, and before he has gotten to page 8, Mr. Carter has reverted to extensive quotation from his beloved diary. At 1:50 a.m. he begins "jotting down some rough notes." The presidential stenography continues unabated for four pages until 10:45 a.m., when, "from Rosalynn: 'Jimmy, the Reagans will be here in fifteen minutes. You will have to put on your morning clothes and greet them.' "

During the intervening eight hours and fifty-five minutes Mr. Carter has jotted down twenty-five dutiful notes, and the reader is left to ask who, if Mr. Carter was serving as recording angel, was acting the part of President? The notes reveal the temper of the scout's mind. As for example:

> 7:55 a.m. . . . I am personally receiving reports on radio traffic halfway around the world—between the Teheran airport control tower and three planes poised at the end of a runway. The airport is on the outskirts of the capital city of Iran, and only a few months ago it was one of the busiest in the world.

I would like to think that Mr. Carter revised this entry when getting it ready for the printer, augmenting the excitement of "I am personally receiving reports" with the geopolitical dimension provided in the phrase, "The airport is on the outskirts of the capital city of Iran," but I'm afraid that the notation appears as Mr. Carter wrote it that morning in the White House, holding the telephone in one hand and scribbling notes with the other in order that his mother should be apprised of momentous events until the very end, until finally Rosalynn had to come and tell him that scout camp is over and that it is time to go home.

I quote the passage at length because it offers a fair example of Mr. Carter's method as well as the sound of his complacence. Whenever possible, he mistakes the novelties of technology for the substance of diplomacy; because he can listen to an air traffic controller "halfway around the world," he thinks he has become fully informed across the entire spectrum of Islamic affairs.

On page 19 the scout establishes the major key of pious self-approbation in which he composes the rest of his ballad to the lost loveliness of the Carter administration. He is describing his wonderful, wonderful inauguration day, and as he and his wife "approached our new home," he remembers the following colloquy:

I told Rosalynn with a smile that it was a nice-looking place. She said, "I believe we're going to be happy in the White House." We were silent for a moment, and then I replied, "I just hope that we never disappoint the people who made it possible for us to live here." Rosalynn's prediction proved to be correct, and I did my utmost for four solid years to make my own hope come true.

On page 23 he completes the sentiment:

As we walked through the living quarters on my first day as President, we were properly awestruck—but comfortable, and at home.

Within the span of the next thirty-nine pages the scout effectively destroys his credibility as a witness to anything other than his own innocence. He compares himself, flatteringly, to President Wilson, and then, a few pages later, he expands the comparison to embrace Presidents Jefferson, Madison, and Jackson. He confides to his diary the thrilling experience of seeing his first movie in the White House; he admires his humility as exemplified in his wanting a policy of "no Ruffles and Flourishes or honors being paid to me"; feeling slightly sheepish, he confesses to the pleasure in hearing the military bands play "Hail to the Chief." The technological luxuries available to the President move him to little cries of wonder and delight. He is as pleased with "the quality of the notes" (i.e., the memoranda prepared by the household clerks) as he is with "the procedures for responding to nuclear attack." The same Christmas shopper's mentality animates his discussion of the men whom he chooses to serve on his staff and in his Cabinet. Into none of their characters does he evince the least glimmering of an insight. Ham and Jody and Charlie and Bert, of course, he knows from the old days in Georgia; these wonderful fellows professed their belief in Jimmy Carter before he was elected President, and so obviously there can be no question about their worth and talent. His Cabinet officials he looks upon as items of elite merchandise. He chooses them because of their titles and credentials, because he has seen them advertised in the pages of *The New York Times* and the catalogues published by the Trilateral Commission, the Aspen Institute, and the Council on Foreign Relations. The scout collects the ornaments of the policy-making establishments in the way that twelve-year-old boys collect the portraits of baseball heroes found in packages of bubble gum. He thinks of them as giants, as leaders, as Very Important People who have been to NATO and the Bohemian Grove. It never occurs to him that he is dealing, almost without exception, with the personifications of the same toadying mediocrity that distinguished the administrations of Presidents Nixon and Ford. Impressed by the merit badges sewn on the sleeves of the older scouts, the diarist marvels at their sophisticated banter with the camp counselors. He conceives of Zbigniew Brzezinski as "a first-rate thinker" and a master of expository prose. Mr. Brzezinski undoubtedly possesses many talents, but thinking and writing, at least in English, are not among them. To the scout this is unimportant. He believes what he reads on the labels, and it is enough that Brzezinski can find the Russian Army on a map.

By the time he comes to page 54 the scout has persuaded himself that he knows most of what needs to be known about "history, politics, international events, and foreign policy." He tells his diary that he likes nothing better than to sit around with "Ham and Jody and Zbig," talking wonderfully important talk about the fate of mankind. He's been at camp for little more than a month, hardly time enough to unpack his catcher's mitt, but already he can "disagree strongly and fundamentally" on questions of state; already he has become the peer of Kissinger and Castlereagh, and guess what, Mama, these Very Important People, these veteran scouts who can read a menu in French, they nod and smile and listen to what he has to say. All of it is pretty big-time stuff, Mama, for a boy who, before coming north, thought that history was for girls.

"Next to members of my family," he explains in one of his letters home, "Zbig would be my favorite seatmate on a long-distance trip; we might argue, but I would never be bored."

And then, of course, there were Fritz and Cy—the most expensive objects displayed in the catalogues. Wonderful, wonderful Fritz Mondale, who was a man of such stature, and Cy, good old decorous Cy. About Cy, the scout can't say enough.

Among all the members of my official Cabinet, Cy Vance and his wife, Gay, became the closest personal friends to Rosalynn and me. He and I were to spend many good times together—talking, fishing, skiing, playing tennis—as well as less enjoyable hours negotiating a Middle East settlement and working and praying for the hostages.

Later in the camp term the scout humiliates Cy in a particularly nasty and mean-spirited way, but this is Cy's fault, and by that time the scout has taken to referring to him simply as Vance.

On page 39 the scout briefly addresses the dilemma of nuclear war and responds with his customary self-satisfaction:

I wanted to understand our defense organization . . . and my myriad special responsibilities in the control and potential use of atomic weapons. This is a sobering duty of the chief executive of our country, and every serious candidate for this office must decide whether he is capable of using or willing to use nuclear weapons if it should become necessary in order to defend our country. Under those circumstances, I was ready to perform this duty.

That's about as far as the scout gets with the question, which, fortunately for all concerned, doesn't exceed the moral capacities required of a first-year camper. Nor does the scout have much trouble making decisions. On page 57 he explains that once he had found his way to the lake and athletic fields, he felt pretty confident with the camp routine.

. . . I realized that my ability to govern well would depend upon my mastery of the extremely important issues I faced. I wanted to learn as much as possible and devoted full time to it, just as I had done as a young submarine officer, a businessman, a governor, and a political candidate running against enormous odds to be elected President.

Because he "devoted full time to it," the scout assumes that he has reached complete understanding. How could it be otherwise? The scout believes that his time is not like other men's time, that he has been blessed with omniscience and grace. He also enjoys a close and long-standing acquaintance with God, to whom he "prayed a lot—more than ever before in my life." The alliance between his own sublime competence and God's political tips removed from his mind "any possibility of timidity or despair." Thus he could make quick work of the business of state ("option papers describing the choices I had to make rarely stayed on my desk overnight") and get back to the more urgent and poetic task of writing bulletins to his diary.

It isn't that Mr. Carter perjures himself in the first sixty-two pages of his memoirs but rather that he shows himself so incapable of self-knowledge that his words lose all hope of relation to the events he chooses to describe. Except as the odd expression of mind afflicted with terminal narcissism, how is it possible to accept the testimony of a man who believes that the White House is a fun and comfortable place, that Zbigniew Brzezinski is a first-rate thinker, that the arts of government devolve automatically, with the desk and the telephone system, on the occupant of the Oval Office?

If any doubts remain as to Mr. Carter's delusions of moral grandeur, he puts them to rest with the repeated references to himself as "a populist," that is, a humble man of the people, winning the prize of the presidency against the all but insuperable obstacles raised against him by the northern and eastern establishments. This is so ludicrous a misstatement of the facts that it changes the venue of Mr. Carter's self-serving fictions from the arena of political chicanery to the amphitheater of clinical pathology. As a populist Mr. Carter was a fraud. In the campaigns of 1976 he enjoyed the full faith and backing not only of the northern media but also of the eastern financial interests. He was the candidate boomed by *The New York Times,* by *Time* magazine, by David Rockefeller's Trilateral Commission, by the entire apparatus of eager Democratic office seekers who hoped for nothing better than a chance, after eight years of eating nuts and berries in the Republican wilderness, to return to the picnic tables of federal patronage. The Democrats that year lacked the moral and intellectual energy to go to the trouble of staging even the pretense of debate. What difference did it make? What was there to say except that it would be nice to be back in

Georgetown? Against Gerald Ford, the heir presumptive to Richard Nixon's disgrace, the Democrats figured they could win with any candidate willing to spend the required period of time in Holiday Inns. Carter would do as well as anyone else, largely because the media had become enchanted by a fairy tale of their own invention in which Jimmy Carter appeared as the avatar of the old-fashioned rural virtues believed (at least among city folks) to reside in small towns. It was the bicentennial year, and the media were in a mood to listen to homespun sermons and country guitars. To the editors of *Newsweek*, Jimmy Carter looked like the political analogue of the Beverly Hillbillies and the Nashville Sound. The scout passed his preliminary examinations with people like Cyrus Vance and Douglas Dillon and Paul Austin, persuading those fine gentlemen on the admissions committee that he possessed the traditional Southern qualities that William Faulkner attributed to the Snopes family— small-minded and mean, only too eager to do what he was told in order to protect the Yankee investment in the cotton fields. Two years later, after it became painfully obvious that the scout also believed his Sunday school nonsense, the media turned away from him in scorn and disgust. By the autumn of 1979 Mr. Carter had become so peripheral a figure in American politics that he had to push his way into the locker room at the end of a World Series game in order to attract the notice of the television cameras. In November of that year he was rescued from oblivion by the divine intercession of Allah.

The chapter headings of *Keeping Faith* indicate that beyond page 62 the scout discusses China and Bert Lance and human rights and the energy crisis and the Panama Canal and Camp David and God knows how many other topics of pressing concern. I couldn't force myself to read the text. Neither would I willingly listen to a narrative of the Wilderness Campaign told to me by some poor soul imagining himself to be Ulysses S. Grant.

Glancing at the diarist's notes that continue throughout the book, I see that the scout persists with his relentless discovery of the obvious. Sometimes he marks the spot with an exclamation point. He learns that the press is irresponsible, that the Congress puts its private interests ahead of the public interest, that the Arabs and the Jews don't like each other, that the Russians have a lot of guns.

Whenever something goes wrong, it is invariably somebody else's fault. Senator Edward Kennedy prevents him from giving the country a wonderful, wonderful health-care program; Walter Sullivan, the American Ambassador in Teheran, causes him to suffer the agony of the hostage crisis; the Ayatollah deprives him of re-election in 1980; the American people fail him throughout his Administration because they concentrate too much on their own selfish interests and refuse to understand that he had come among them as their savior and redeemer.

All in all, despite the world's ingratitude, the scout still manages to have a wonderful time. Toward the end it gets a little hard to find enough people who properly appreciate the gift of his person. During his last week in the White House he presides at a banquet for the happy few who remain loyal to his vision of a world that might have been. The evening is a wonderful, wonderful success. After dinner the guests go into the ballroom to listen to John Raitt sing hit songs from *Carousel* and *Oklahoma!*; several of the guests come forward to whisper compliments into the scout's eager ear. Of these flatteries "the most memorable of all" is presented by Mstislav Rostropovich, the cellist recently arrived in the United States as an exile from the Soviet Union. The scout thinks the phrasing especially fine because Rostropovich is "a courageous man . . . and special friend of ours" who has suffered the cruelties of a police state and therefore knows what life is all about. The praise of Rostropovich is worth ten thousand times the praise of *The Washington Post*. So delighted is the scout with the music of the cellist's "heavily-accented" voice that he must have found it difficult to wait until everybody left before rushing upstairs to tell his diary the wonderful, wonderful news. The entry deserves to be quoted in its entirety:

Slava Rostropovich gave an excellent little speech at our table, pointing out that the masses of people were often wrong—that what was significant was the personal relationship that developed between leaders or performers or artists and others. He said that we had meant more than anyone in the United States to him and his family when they came here from the Soviet Union. He pointed out that the masses made a mistake on November the 4th, as they had when they rejected Beethoven's Ninth Symphony, rejected *La Traviata*, and in the first performance of *Tosca* the audience reacted against it so violently that they couldn't even raise the curtain for the third act. He said history was going to treat my administration the same way they did Verdi, Puccini, and Beethoven. It was beautiful.

Diary, January 13, 1981

This notation all but ends the scout's reverie; it appears on pages 593 and 594, in the place that a musical composition would reserve to the coda. Nothing more needs to be said about the deranged melody that Mr. Carter plays on his two-string banjo. I'm told that the book was accorded respectful reviews in *The New York Times*, *The New York Review of Books*, and a number of other journals supposedly interested in the direction of American politics. If this is true and not merely a vicious rumor put about by right-wing extremists, then the nation probably can look forward within the next few years to the election of a President capable of composing even crazier music for drums, cymbals, and atomic bomb.

THE AMERICAN SPECTATOR,
*March 1983*

# BAND MUSIC

*It is a great art to know how to sell wind.*

—Baltasar Gracián

ABOUT A MONTH before the staging of the Fourth of July pageant in New York harbor, the television networks fell to quarreling about the division of the jingo's spoils. ABC had purchased exclusive rights to most of the attractions—among them, President Reagan's awarding of the Medals of Liberty and Chief Justice Warren Burger's administering of the oath of allegiance to three hundred petitioners for citizenship—and the other networks complained about unfair restraint of the image trade. Executives at CBS and NBC dressed up their self-interest in the patriotic costumes of the First Amendment. Somebody said something about the Fourth of July "belonging to the American people"; somebody else said something equally idiotic about how it was getting hard to tell the difference between a politician and a circus performer.

That particular distinction was lost a long time ago, but it's conceivable that CBS and NBC might have been worried about losing access to the President and the Chief Justice for even as long as twenty minutes. What if one of Colonel Qaddafi's assassins managed to set off an explosion that wasn't part of the fireworks display? For the price of a special entertainment, ABC would have bought an option on a historical miniseries.

David Wolper, the Hollywood promoter who assembled the four-day spectacle and sold it to ABC for $10 million, didn't bother to invoke the sanctity of "the people's right to know." Most of the events taking place on Liberty Weekend, he said, belonged to him. He had hired most of the musicians and had had at least something

**185**

to say about the placing of the aircraft carriers. He had taken the trouble to engage President Reagan and Chief Justice Burger as props for two of his occasions, and he didn't see why he should lend his props to anybody else's puppet theater.

"I'm paying for the Medal of Liberty," he said. "I created it."

His point was unassailable. Out of the clay of a press agent's dream he had forged the coin of publicity, and he deserves the compliment of grateful imitation. Let other networks follow his example and acquire the rights to any holidays that haven't yet been sold to the Japanese. I can imagine NBC presenting a national strike on Labor Day, complete with well-choreographed riots in nine major markets during which National Guard units fire on angry mobs. The network, of course, would own all subsidiary rights—interviews with the wounded, books, movies, T-shirts, paperback reprints, audio cassettes, the bottling of the widows' tears, etc.; the network's ad salesmen wouldn't have much trouble selling the commercial spots to pharmaceutical and insurance companies as well as to the Business RoundTable and the teamsters' union.

If CBS obtained the rights to Christmas, it presumably could claim ownership of the entire national collection of toys, lights, tinsel strings, wreaths, and performances of Handel's *Messiah*. In the same way that David Wolper agreed to lend some of his Fourth of July footage to the other networks for their evening news broadcasts, I'm sure that the executives at CBS would make an equally gracious gesture on Christmas Eve. They might allow a few representative orphans to appear on a rival network to open a few representative presents. They might even permit limited use of their videotape of President Reagan dressed as Santa Claus.

For having found yet another way to make something out of nothing, Wolper probably should receive one of his own Medals of Liberty. But I wonder if he, or anyone else, has yet considered the promotional opportunities recently made available in the United States Congress. Now that television cameras have been admitted into the Senate as well as the House of Representatives, the politicians in both amphitheaters must take a little more thought about their manner of dress. Obviously they cannot continue to wear the drab and miscellaneous suits in which they're accustomed to making a bankrupt shambles of the national enterprise. Nor can they be trusted to wear uniforms of a vaguely military air. Each of the states, and possibly some of the larger congressional districts, almost certainly would insist on designing uniforms to fit the specifications of regional pride, and I can all too easily imagine a garish profusion of gold braid worked into the figures of symbolic birds, vegetables, mottoes, animals, and trees. Although Thomas "Tip" O'Neill might look convincing in epaulets and a feathered helmet, the sight of Senator Alphonse D'Amato under a comparable weight of ornament might expose the gentleman to the danger of ridicule.

No, I'm afraid what's needed is something a good deal more straightforward and all-American, and I think the members of Congress would be well advised to wear jumpsuits of the type worn by drivers in the Indianapolis 500. The costume has the advantage of an egalitarian uniformity distinguished only by the sportsman's gradual accumulation of worth and merit. Every congressman would begin with the same bolt of empty canvas, but as he became more practiced in the art of raffling off fractions of the public interest, his jumpsuit would bloom with the endorsements of his grateful patrons and owners. Within a month of his arrival, or as soon as he can cast his first patriotic vote for a weapons appropriation, the apprentice maker of laws might be seen wearing the letterhead of the Lockheed Corporation or the trademark of Pepsi-Cola. Before the end of his first year he might add patches awarded by General Dynamics, Mobil Oil, and the Association of American Dairy Farmers. Over a period of time the truly accomplished members of Congress would acquire the dignity of totem poles. I imagine majestic figures dense with emblems, decals, and monograms, almost magical beings embossed with all the sacred names in the iconography of American enterprise.

During roll-call votes each congressman would be expected to wear a baseball cap bearing the insignia of the principal lobby or special interest that he stood ready to defend against the ingratitude of the poor. Any congressman worth his weight in campaign contributions would own an impressive collection of caps, but his choice of a particular cap on a particular occasion would alert the newsmen dozing in the broadcast booth to the issues at stake in the afternoon's play.

It's a pity that the jumpsuits couldn't have been made ready in time for the Fourth of July. Wolper might have rented a few senators as parachutists dropping onto the deck of an aircraft carrier just as a Marine band (wearing the patches of ABC Sports) concluded its rendition (available for $14.95 on disc or cassette) of "The Star Spangled Banner."

HARPER'S MAGAZINE,
*August 1986*

# POTOMAC FEVER

*What grimaces, what capers, leaps and chuckles prime
ministers, presidents and kings must indulge in, in the
privacy of their bedrooms, so as to avenge their systems
on the daylong strain imposed on them!*

—Valéry, *Tel Quel*

WITH THE ONSET of the presidential campaigning season,
Nicolson falls victim to one of the common delusions of his trade.
On most days of most seasons Nicolson goes dutifully about the task
of writing newspaper editorials meant to keep the country safe from
communists and fleas. But in the autumn of every fourth year, when
the weather turns cold and the public opinion polls move their rigs
north into New Hampshire, Nicolson imagines that he was born to
be a statesman instead of a journalist.

Most journalists worthy of their rank suffer low-grade and chronic
symptoms of the same pathology, but in Nicolson the affliction takes
a peculiarly virulent form. During the worst of his seizures he
believes he would enjoy being President of the United States. His
hands sweat and he thinks he hears the cheering of crowds. He
broods about the ingratitude of a society that places so much of its
trust and so many of its helicopters at the disposal of dolts. His
humor turns choleric and he wonders why nobody asks him to make
commencement speeches.

Fortunately for his wife and children (who otherwise might be
condemned to a sequence of forced marches through the nation's
shopping malls), Nicolson has the wit to know that unless he takes
severe measures he would end like one of those garrulous derelicts
sometimes seen explaining their geopolitical theories to ash cans in

**189**

the park. Several years ago Nicolson devised a list of questions intended to restore his sense of democratic proportion. He presents the list to obliging friends with the instruction that they conduct the interrogation in a matter-of-fact voice appropriate to the reading of a catechism or police report.

When Nicolson showed up in the office the other day it was obvious that he had not been having an easy autumn. A tall and stoop-shouldered man, who once walked from Panama to Mexico City, he seemed drawn and pale, his eyes clouded by a distant stare. He pushed the familiar typescript across the desk and then, without saying a word, settled himself uncomfortably in a chair. After taking a few moments to light his cigarette, he indicated with a laconic nodding of his head that he was ready to answer questions. I began, as always, at the top of page one.

*What is it that presidents do?*

They keep up appearances and wear the iron masks of power. They tell the necessary lies with which other, more high-minded men would rather not incriminate themselves.

*What is the condition of a president's existence?*

Fragmented and incoherent. Somebody is always tugging at his sleeve, trying his patience, and nibbling at his time. He's lucky if he can remember his name, much less the capital of France.

*With whom do presidents consort?*

Mostly with the kind of people that decent citizens choose to avoid—with flatterers, office seekers, crooked lawyers, assassins, touts, arms merchants.

*Do presidents understand the workings of modern science?*

No.

*Of weapons and languages?*

No.

*Of art or culture?*

No.

*Do presidents possess extraordinary gifts of wisdom or perception?*

On the contrary, their ignorance is their strength. If they knew what they were doing they would find it impossible to act.

*How would you describe a presidential election?*

An ordeal by klieg light.

*How does the electorate reach its judgment?*

On the basis of the single slogan or facial expression that the audience can be counted upon to remember for more than fifteen minutes, because of the color of the candidate's tie or the nervousness of his hands.

*Name the attributes of a winning candidate.*

Stamina, courage, energy, and a strong stomach. The candidate must travel thousands of miles, bear the insults of ill-informed experts, eat the food in Holiday Inns, submit to the charade of a debate, answer (in twenty words or less) questions that cannot be answered in 100,000 words, display under all circumstances and any weather not the least sign of fear or disgust.

*What is the cost of a president's ambition?*

Ruinous and of two kinds. First, the cost to the nation. Presidents must be seen doing great deeds, and these inevitably require huge sums of money. The waste is as colossal as the president's appetite for praise.

Second, the heavy tax on the lives of the people in the President's immediate vicinity. The governor of even a small New England state marks the passage of his career with an emotional desolation as bleak as the wreckage behind the caravans of Genghis Khan. Look into the face of a candidate's wife, and you look into an abyss.

*List the attributes of a successful president.*

Selfishness and a cold egoism. A willingness to sacrifice other people's interests to one's own. Also a talent for dissimulation, a capacity to endure boredom and to turn one's back on the unlucky or unsuccessful. Better the man who can order the incineration of cities with a cozy smile than the man who worries about the death of whales.

*What is the president's reward for these crimes against conscience and humanity?*

Applause, the servility of all those who approach him, a lot of space in the papers, and a lot of time on television. Also the comfort implicit in a surrounding din of gossip, sirens, cheering, and noise.

*What does a president hope to achieve? Toward what vision of the future does he push his way through the crowd?*

He doesn't know. He moves instinctively deeper into the labyrinth of his megalomania, snuffling toward the scent of something more—more weapons, more friends, more secrets, more lies, more power.

*Why should we feel grateful for the services of men blessed with such a monstrous appetite and rare pathology?*

What other kind of men could bear the weight of our expectation?

At this point Nicolson's eyes had begun to clear. His expression seemed less furtive, his voice more confident and kind. There were a few additional questions on his list, but Nicolson indicated that the delusion had passed; for the time being, at least, he could follow the political news without feelings of envy or resentment. Happy to be relieved of his burden, he picked up his text and went off to write what he referred to as "a pawky, God-fearing, patriotic sort of piece" for the Sunday edition.

THE WASHINGTON POST,
*October 1984*

# BOILING THE WHALE

*Money is a kind of poetry.*

—Wallace Stevens

SOONER OR LATER it undoubtedly will occur to somebody in the Reagan Administration to put the federal government up for sale in a series of leveraged buyouts. Given the Administration's childlike faith in capitalist mechanics, as well as the budget director's unhappiness with the idiot economics of the nation's schools, farms, and military establishment, I'm surprised that the First Boston Corporation hasn't already been hired to plot the courses of destruction.

Within a week of the first sale, the deficit and the national debt would vanish as if in a magician's smoke. The Dow Jones industrial average would gain 4,000 points in a matter of days, and everybody lucky enough to command the necessary lines of credit and political patronage would make a truly American killing.

The financial play makes sense once government is defined as a "smokestack industry." Government so defined meets all the specifications of a dying enterprise—heavy debt, inflated wages and pensions, incompetent management, noncompetitive prices, dwindling markets for its product. Relatively few people still take the trouble to vote, and the population under the age of twenty-five has learned to think of Washington as a stage set for a Sunday morning television show in which six journalists talk to one another in a language almost as weird as Latin.

Government's decline into senescence has been apparent for a generation. It is the reason Ronald Reagan has been twice elected President, why the public schools resemble vacant lots, why Bernhard Goetz was not indicted for the attempted murder of four black

**193**

adolescents on a New York subway train. Private companies now operate prisons as well as aircraft control towers and fire departments. In their effort to teach the help to read and write, American corporations spend as much on education every year ($60 billion) as all the public and private universities in the country. Last year the nation paid $21.7 billion for the varieties of private police protection, as opposed to $13.8 billion for public law enforcement.

The Administration's current budget proposals lack the courage of both its greed and its convictions. It isn't enough merely to sell Amtrak, eliminate the Job Corps, dismantle the Small Business Administration, curtail payments for student loans. Although admirable as symbolic gestures, none of these subtractions supplies the virtue of additional revenue. Nor do the President's investment counselors show a proper respect for the entrepreneurial spirit to which the President's speech-writers pay the homage once owed to Caesar and the king of England.

For several years now the speculators on Wall Street have been giving regularly scheduled lessons in the arts of pillage and extortion. Hardly a day passes but that some undervalued oil or communications company doesn't fall prey to Ivan Boesky, T. Boone Pickens, or the Bass brothers.

The simplicity of the leveraged buyout complies with the norms of low cunning that appear to be habitual among the gentlemen so comfortably seated in the boardrooms of the Reagan Administration. When correctly managed, the transaction redistributes the wealth to the already rich, which, as every college sophomore knows, is the great and guiding purpose of the American dream.

The acquisitors begin by identifying a company that holds assets worth a good deal more than its purchase price. They then borrow the money to buy the property, but instead of trying to preserve it they reduce its various productive organs to the liquid forms of cash and tax manipulation. The process is not dissimilar to flensing, boiling, and trying out the carcass of a sperm whale.

The acquisitors repay their loans with the money distilled from the liquidation of the assets; they also pay off the company executives who expedited the sale, ushering them safely to the door with goodbye presents often worth $10 million or $20 million. After subtracting these tax-deductible opportunity costs, the acquisitors divide the remainder of the spoils and issue a press release about the great blessing they have conferred upon the stockholders and the American future. In New York they sometimes pose for photographs with Mayor Ed Koch.

The federal government clearly is an undervalued asset. The budget director, David Stockman, recently described it, with an accountant's air of faint distaste, as a "blooming, buzzing mass of programs, projects, commitments and purposes." Testifying before Congress about the arithmetic of the deficit, he seemed to blame the government for chronic disorderliness. Certainly he thought of government as a nuisance; conceivably he hoped that somebody, perhaps the Koreans, would win it in a raffle.

Among its various possessions, the government owns one third of the nation's landmass as well as 2.6 billion square feet of office space (equivalent to all the office space in the country's ten largest cities, multiplied by 4; the government is also the world's largest hospital system operator, shipowner, and insurer. Measured by anybody's appetite the federal body politic offers a feast for 1,000 crows.

Before dismembering the corpse it first would be necessary to incorporate the entity in Delaware and to assign it both a trading symbol (USA) and an opening stock price. Some of the subsequent deals would be easier than others.

The real estate, especially the California, Florida, and Long Island beaches, presumably would attract syndicates organized by the Administration's friends—by Frank Sinatra, Betsy Bloomingdale, the Bechtel Corporation, Jerry Zipkin, Johnny Carson, and the Heritage Foundation. A few Third World states (those that minded their ideological manners) could be given an interest in the agricultural properties, which would improve their trade balances as well as reduce their debts to the New York banks.

The sophisticated deals might require a little more thought, but I can imagine at least a few of the prospective buyers and possible lines of commercial reasoning.

MT. RUSHMORE—The Chrysler and Trump organizations almost certainly could be inveigled into a competitive auction. The chief executive officer might wish to carve his own image into the face of the cliff.

THE INTERNAL REVENUE SERVICE—Merrill Lynch and American Express presumably would wish to extend the range of their financial conveniences. All debits and credits would appear on a single monthly statement, and customers could return to the happy condition of children living on an allowance.

THE NUCLEAR ARSENAL—The Soviet Union would make a generous tender offer, probably through a Swiss intermediary, but some of the more provincial members of Congress undoubtedly would object for reasons of fear or conscience. This might require selling the inventory, in odd lots and at less attractive prices, to the Germans, the Japanese, or a consortium of South American colonels.

THE STATE DEPARTMENT—Harvard University could receive it on terms offering extremely favorable tax advantages. The university could approach the alumni with yet another unprecedented appeal for funds. McGeorge Bundy and John Kenneth Galbraith could explain why the State Department would serve as an important research facility for the John F. Kennedy School of Government.

THE CAPITOL AND THE WHITE HOUSE—*The Washington Post* or Walt Disney Company might buy one or both buildings as a corporate headquarters.

THE MILITARY SERVICES—These could be offered to the larger corporations, both domestic and foreign. Because most wars come about as a result of economic quarrels, the multinational corporations, like city-states of the Italian Renaissance, should have the decency to pay their own troops. The soldiery could be fitted out in splendid uniforms bearing the insignia of Sony, CBS, Volvo, IBM, and British Airways. Some of the smaller formations (the Marine Corps, say, or the Coast Guard) conceivably could be sold to wealthy individuals, to big-city governments, or to Arab princes.

THE CIA—Perceived as an archive of scripts, the agency ought to attract excited bidding from HBO, Simon & Schuster, Tri-Star, and Warner Communications.

HARPER'S MAGAZINE,
*April 1985*

# POLYGRAPHS

T HE UNLIKELY PASSION for truth telling appears to have become obsessive in the whispering galleries of the federal government. Before too long I expect an especially zealous functionary to recommend lie-detector tests for every American man, woman, and child. Secretary of State George Shultz presumably had something of the same worry in mind when he threatened to resign if anybody asked him to take so foolish an examination.

Shultz knows a bad idea when he sees one. He also knows bureaucrats. Allow them to pursue their fantastic notions of a safe and orderly world, and with a little luck they can wreck almost anything.

Suppose the polygraph machines actually worked, and that they could catch the duplicitous citizenry in its daily and necessary lies. Within a week the economy would fail; at the end of the month the Russians would be in Washington.

Consider first the damage done to the nation's domestic life. Imagine wives obliged to give straight answers to their husbands, or husbands forced to admit the truth to their wives. How many marriages could bear the weight of so much earnest confession? Anybody who survived the initial breaking of furniture would be on the phone to his or her lawyer, but the lawyers, of course, would be out of business.

The professional code of legal ethics—affirmed by acclamation at the last two annual meetings of the American Bar Association—

requires lawyers to tell as many lies as might be convenient to the purposes of their clients. To whom would they speak, in voices choking on the bones of truth, and what judge could listen to their pleadings?

I don't know about other jurisdictions, but in New York the judges would have been obliged to place one another under indictment. Most of the police force would be in jail.

Certainly the stock market couldn't function. Deprive a broker of his right to circulate rumors or insist that corporate vice presidents refrain from inside trading, and the market would empty of both buyers and sellers.

If forced to make honest bids, the nation's weapons contractors couldn't afford to employ enough people to manufacture ammunition for antique hunting rifles. The construction trades would depart into bankruptcy, and so would the businesses dependent upon the vanity of the public. What hairdresser would survive an afternoon's appointments? What tailor could sell another suit?

Nor would the media continue to exist. Who could write an advertisement for an automobile or a foreign policy? Who could falsify a filmed image of New York Governor Mario Cuomo or a cheeseburger? The few journalists still at large would be reduced to making lists of yesterday's football scores and temperature readings. Nobody could write a commencement address, bestow a Pulitzer Prize, or make a speech accepting an Academy Award.

Think what would become of Congress, or the conduct of the nation's diplomacy. The politicians would sit for hours with electrodes strapped to their forearms, reciting the long and dingy tales of votes sold and favors granted. White House spokesmen presumably would stand in front of unescorted microphones making guileless confessions about the movements of the nation's submarines.

The question remains as to who would examine the evidence. Who could pass the tests of virtue?

The operatives at the CIA undoubtedly possess the necessary firmness of mind, and so presumably do the Reverend Jerry Falwell's congregations within the Moral Majority. But they would need help, not to mention a great deal of technical support.

The government undoubtedly could recruit volunteers among the young Republican clubs at the nation's better universities, but these enthusiasts might tend toward harsh and callow judgments. Unless properly watched—by teams of backup examiners—they might make the mistake of arresting their own financial advisers and confiscating their own trust funds.

The experience could transform them into liberal Democrats, and, as Shultz well knows, that result could be hazardous to the nation's health.

Clearly, the trend toward truth telling must be stopped as soon and as emphatically as possible. By refusing to sit for his portrait before a polygraph machine, Shultz sets a staunch and patriotic example.

Ever since men first learned to speak and write, they have had good reasons to be careful about telling the truth. The truth nearly always makes trouble for oneself, if not for somebody else, and most people know that happiness consists in being well and artfully deceived. If they didn't know this, Ronald Reagan wouldn't be President, and the country would be broke.

THE SUN, *Baltimore,*
*January 1986*

# UPTOWN

*In politics nothing is contemptible.*

—Benjamin Disraeli

F ROM WHAT I can see and hear of the nation's Democratic politicians this autumn, it seems that most of them would rather be Republicans. Somewhat belatedly they have discovered what the voters learned as long ago as 1968—namely, that the Democratic party can too easily be confused with a crippled beggar or a vacant lot.

In March of 1985 a number of anxious politicians organized the Democratic Leadership Council as an antidote to the Democratic National Committee. The committee tended to associate itself with the grievances of minorities and the old-line liberal rhetoric that had done so much damage to the party in the presidential elections of 1972, 1980, and 1984. Obviously it had lost touch with the plutocratic spirit of the times, and the trendier Democrats wanted an ideological wardrobe signifying their arrival in a more exclusive neighborhood.

The council recruited a hundred and forty Democratic officeholders (among them Senators Gore, Nunn, Biden, and Chiles, as well as Representatives Wright and Gephardt) and asked itself why the party lacked a coherent theory of what it wants and believes. All agreed that they had to shift their doctrine several compass points to the right, but it wasn't immediately clear how this was to be accomplished. What candidates should the party endorse? What villains could it denounce? What issues should it submit to the decision of the opinion polls? Was it still correct to ask Sidney Poitier to dinner or cast a vote against the bomb? Was it safe to drive a BMW and read *The New Republic*? In the dingier quarters of Pittsburgh, could bartenders be relied upon to pour a decent glass of white wine?

Such terrible questions always have disturbed the comfort of the *nouveaux riches*, and I'm sure the council's deliberations caused some of the members to think seriously about changing their tailors. In August the council released a preliminary sketch of its revised image, but on reading the newspaper dispatches from Washington it occurred to me that the new line of intellectual dry goods, although certainly admirable in its intention, still lacked the proper Republican style. The effect was somehow too gaudy and too new, as if the opinions had been too recently acquired from the haberdashers at Brookings or the Aspen Institute.

As was to be expected, the council embraced, as eagerly and straightforwardly as the Reagan Administration had done, the feet of Mammon. The members professed themselves bored by the squeakings of conscience and shocked by the threadbare idealism that the Democratic party has been wearing ever since the days of the New Deal. They supported government deregulation, favored restraints on foreign trade and the easing of the antitrust laws, blamed the country's misfortunes not only on the capitalists in Wall Street but also on the greed and sloth of the labor unions, recanted the romantic and mischievous nonsense about taking from the rich to give to the poor, ignored the farmers, and allied themselves with the entrepreneurial realpolitik said to be in vogue among the country's wealthier real estate operators. A few of the more excitable members offered the reckless suggestion that salaries somehow be connected to competence; other members, even more radical, went so far as to say that retired corporate executives should forfeit their pensions if, after their departure and because of their failure to provide for everlasting prosperity, their companies fell upon hard times. Were either of those two rules to be applied to Democratic officeholders, of course, all of the council members would be obliged to seek job retraining (possibly as short-order cooks), but the newspapers thoughtfully omitted any disrespectful remarks on the point.

Alas, it's no easy trick to move to the right of Pat Robertson or the Heritage Foundation. To announce one's intention to take military reprisals against any weak or impoverished nation that stands in the way of the American light is good, rousing jingoism (reminiscent of Teddy Roosevelt's discovery of Cuba as "a good, safe menace"), but the sentiment isn't new enough to impress the media. Nor is it sufficient to promise the dismantling of the few social programs that survived the Reagan Administration's *auto-da-fé*. Already accustomed to the ruin of widows and orphans, the electorate yearns for measures considerably more dramatic.

I'm afraid that the Democratic party hasn't come quite far enough along its pilgrim's road to moral reawakening. Over the course of the next year I'm sure that wiser and better paid consultants will come up with grander designs, but for the moment I can think of at least three gestures likely to assure a still suspicious public that the party—at long last and after much travail—has moved into the better part of town.


1. Nominate Richard Nixon as the Democratic candidate in the 1988 presidential election. Clearly the man is capable of miraculous transformations, and for the right price I expect he would consider presenting himself in the costume of yet another "new Nixon." He commands the respect of most of the world's dictators and enjoys a high degree of name recognition among voters over the age of forty-five. Last spring in San Francisco he received a standing ovation from the American Newspaper Publishers Association, a sign as certain as a voice from heaven that his politics remain perfectly tuned to the wisdom of the age. Best of all, the man could win.

2. Recognize the Soviet Union as the nation's newest friend and truest ally. Just as the Republicans have long understood that the best foreign policy follows the lines of commercial interest and racial suspicion, so the Democrats can announce that sooner or later it will come down to a matter of the Occident against the Orient. If Japanese money and technology arrange a joint venture with the Chinese market, Western civilization can look forward to a century of bankruptcy, humiliation, and defeat. Both the Russians and the Americans profess a materialist faith in progress and grant the

supremacy of bureaucratic procedure to the unstable lurchings of the unaffiliated human imagination. Any savings of money brought about by the reduced manufacture of weapons can be distributed as gifts to American citizens earning over $100,000 a year.

3. Define the poor as works of art. Nobody ever knows what to do with the poor. For years the Democrats squandered enormous sums on the dream of social justice. The Republicans haven't done much better. They have tried to render the poor invisible by ignoring their presence and closing down their access to education and medical care, but the poor have neglected to vanish. They still can be seen through the windows of limousines, cluttering the sidewalks and taking up too much space in the parks.

The Democratic Leadership Council might profit by the example of the artist Christo. Christo wraps large objects in cloth or plastic, thus imparting to otherwise ordinary things the value of transient masterpieces. He wrapped a bridge in Paris and a promontory in Australia, and for all I know he has wrapped bears and deserts and islands in the Caribbean.

Why not wrap the poor? Bundle them up in denominations of 500 or 1,000 and sell them to wealthy collectors looking for a reason to set a trend. If not enough collectors can be found, the bundled poor could be donated to museums and classified as tax deductions. Instead of subtracting from the sum of the society's wealth, the poor could be counted as additions to the gross national product. Safely and attractively wrapped, they might serve as ornaments in the nation's office plazas and hotel lobbies.

I know that none of these suggestions can be accepted within a matter of weeks or months. At first they might seem too visionary, a little difficult to explain to the contributors of campaign funds. I don't think I'd like to be the Democratic politician sent to introduce the theory of Richard Nixon's candidacy to the ACLU or David Letterman. But the suggestions at least should prompt the party's speechwriters to bolder metaphors. Maybe if the Democratic Leadership Council hired Michael Deaver as its lobbyist in Texas or

California, or if it could devise a way in which the hunting of illegal aliens could become a professional sport (available on prime-time television), the newly revived Democratic party might find its way to the higher ground of a modern and victorious politics.

HARPER'S MAGAZINE,
*October 1986*

# BEWARE THE
# DEADLY ENDIVE

*A joke is an epitaph on an emotion.*
—Friedrich Nietzsche

THE REAGAN ADMINISTRATION always has had a talent for staging masques and *tableaux vivants*, and from the beginning of its run in Washington it has more often resembled a theatrical company than a government. The performance opened with an inauguration conceived along the lines of an Academy Awards ceremony; it ends by transforming the geopolitical doctrines of the last forty years into postmodernist farce. Few governments in recent memory could have accomplished so stunning a *coup de théâtre*, but then few governments in recent memory have possessed the requisite degree of economic illiteracy or so sure an instinct for burlesque.

The joke, as well as the appreciation of its point, turns on the juxtaposition of the two principal stories that have been playing on the front pages of the news since last Christmas. The first story is the one about the near anarchy in the international currency markets and the imbalances in the scale of the world's trade. The other story is the one about the Iranian arms deal and the delusions of Napoleonic grandeur drifting through the asylum of the National Security Council. Understood as parallel subplots in the same comedy, the two stories wonderfully explicate the folly of the Cold War. They suggest that geoeconomics has replaced geopolitics as the preliminary study of Armageddon, and they argue that, as indices of strategic power, the rates of bank interest and the throw-weights of foreign debt bear more directly and more ominously on

**206**

the status quo than the velocities of cruise missiles or the number of aircraft carriers in the eastern Mediterranean.

Anybody doubting the change of venue has only to consider the contrast between the gaudy summit conference staged last October in Iceland by President Reagan and Soviet Premier Mikhail Gorbachev and the January meeting in Washington at which the American and Japanese finance ministers discussed, very quietly, the strained diplomatic relations between the dollar and the yen. After talks described as cordial, James A. Baker, the American secretary of the Treasury, and Kiichi Miyazawa, his Japanese peer, approved a joint communiqué so artfully contrived that it managed to say precisely nothing about their respective currencies and mutual suspicions. They smiled into the few cameras present and agreed that "developments in exchange markets warrant monitoring." The gentlemen clearly meant no harm, but within an hour of their bland announcement the dollar lost another fraction of its worth against both the yen and German deutsche mark.

The finance ministers spoke as enigmatically as oracles because everybody knew they were talking about the very real possibility of the very real devastation of very real targets. President Reagan and Premier Gorbachev struck histrionic poses because everybody knew they were speaking the language of military romance. Not that their weapons and their armies don't retain considerable symbolic value, but I doubt that many people in Moscow or Washington intend them for actual use. They're far too precious, too obviously meant as ornamental pieces in what has become an expensive but fanciful game of capture the flag. In both the United States and the Soviet Union, of course, the arms trades continue to support the political and economic pretensions of the state. The weapons sustain the imagery of power, and the military employers provide make-work for large numbers of people who otherwise might be obliged to paint post office murals or play the zither.

The primacy of economic over military ways and means long ago became apparent to the proverbial man in the street. An opinion poll conducted last year among Americans unaffiliated with the State or Defense Department showed that the respondents thought they had more to fear from a credit card than they did from nuclear energy. Interpreting the statistics to fit the bias of my own argument, I like to think that most people understand, quite properly, that the burdens of debt (their own and the federal government's) constitute a graver danger to their health, safety, and welfare than any or all of the Soviet armored divisions posted on the plains of northern Europe.

Throughout the winter and early spring reports from Brussels, New York, Washington, and Geneva confirmed a similar ordering of the hierarchy of the public alarm. The dollar fluctuated like a cork on the current of rumors about imminent meetings of the Group of Five, and the hectic speculation in the New York stock markets brought to mind the feverish ravings of somebody about to die of a tropical disease. The sight of once prominent investment bankers being summarily arrested on charges of criminal fraud contributed to the feeling that something had gone pretty seriously wrong with the dreams of avarice.

During a round of trade negotiations in the last week of January the American envoys in Brussels threatened to impose punitive tariffs in the amount of $400 million on the import of French cheese, British gin, and Belgian endive unless Spain and Portugal agreed to buy 2.8 million tons of American feed grains. The meeting convened on a Monday; by Tuesday the economic ministers were talking about an Atlantic trade war, and by Wednesday it was clear that the NATO alliance had less reason to fear the Russian army than to beware the deadly endive.

On February 2, in Washington, Paul Volcker, the chairman of the Federal Reserve Board, informed a congressional committee that any further decline in the value of the dollar might entail "high costs and risks." Mentioning the prospect of both an inflation and a recession, he pointed out that if the dollar falls too far, the suppliers of foreign loans might take their money elsewhere, and so wreck the Potemkin village of this country's borrowed prosperity. At the close of his remarks the prices of Treasury notes and bonds fell by as much as three-eighths of a point.

Volcker's testimony contradicted the statements of Secretary Baker, who, speaking out of another side of the government's mouth, has been saying for the last eighteen months that the devaluation of the dollar is a godsend for American business. Alarmed by the grotesque size of the nation's trade imbalance, which amounted to $170 billion in 1986, Baker has held to the belief that as the dollar becomes cheaper so also will Americans find it easier to sell their products abroad. As yet the promised miracle has failed to take place, and the available evidence suggests that it isn't likely to take place.

By Valentine's Day the International Trade Commission had agreed to consider placing restrictive tariffs on foreign flowers (particularly Colombian carnations), and the bookstores were touting as the season's most perceptive economic analysis a work of fiction entitled *The Ropespinner Conspiracy*, in which the author blames the greed in Wall Street on two communist agents who infiltrate the Racquet Club and seek to put an end to capitalism through the sale of junk bonds.

Newspaper columnists of all political castes and persuasions were remarking on the broad decline in the American standard of living, which, when plotted on a graph, compared unfavorably with the equivalent measurements in such supposedly bankrupt countries as Britain and Italy. More often than not, the observations were accompanied by the familiar series of unhappy questions that fall into the rhythms of liturgical chant. Why has the nation's productivity declined? Why is the debt so heavy ($2 trillion and rising) and still so many people out of work? How does it come to pass that the American steel industry has lost $7 billion since 1982? How is it possible that the United States has been reduced to offering as its principal exports the bulk cargoes of scrap iron and wastepaper? Who made off with the spirit of American enterprise?

None of the questions invite practical, or even plausible, answers, which perhaps explains their function as ritual. Every few days President Reagan issues another fatuous proclamation in favor of "American competitiveness," and the more excitable members of Congress demand to know why nobody can devise the economic analogue of a raid on Libya. Their rhetorical initiatives lose most of their meaning and much of their force when subjected to a competition with the facts.

The truth of the matter is that the United States cannot compete in a free market because it has been accustomed for so many years to trading in the rigged markets provided by its own government and its larger corporations. Established on the premise of permanent war, the American economy renders roughly one third of all its goods and services to a federal bureaucracy that seldom thinks to ask what anything costs. Just as the television networks enjoy the privileges of monopoly, so do the automobile companies, the banks, and any corporate entity rich enough to set prices and manage the demand for its merchandise.

Nor can the Congress take much comfort in the hope of protective tariffs. Too many votes already have been sold to foreign owners. Within the last decade foreign companies have invested roughly $1 trillion in the United States—$250 billion in assembly and manufacture, $200 billion in Treasury bills, $450 billion in bank assets, and $100 billion in land and real estate. The majestic stillness of that kind of money tends to muffle the objections of democratic conscience.

Without asking too much of the analogy, I think it's probably fair to say that under the nostalgic and reactionary tutelage of the Reagan administration the United States in 1987 has managed to achieve the economic condition of the antebellum South. In the years just prior to the Civil War the Southern gentry also believed that they had all the time in the world and that they were favored by fortune. Not caring to dishonor themselves with the indignity of commerce, content to buy their luxuries and manufactured goods from Europe and the mercantile North (i.e., from the Taiwan of the day) and to leave the management of their affairs to their agents in the seaport towns (i.e., to men not dissimilar from those now being arrested in Wall Street), the Southern cavaliers retired to their plantations to read the romances of Sir Walter Scott and think that a war wasn't much different than a duel.

President Reagan's friends presumably read the novels of Ian Fleming and the biographies of Teddy Roosevelt. Otherwise they might as well be mounted on cavalry horses under the magnolia trees.

Within the larger and demonic context of a global economy quite clearly beyond the comprehension, much less the control, of its innumerable sorcerer's apprentices, the old geopolitical adventures begin to look like nostalgic pageants paraded across the battlefield at Gettysburg. They constitute a kind of wishful thinking, expressive of the desire to restore the world to the simplicity of a child's game of toy soldiers. Whether it's the American counterrevolutionaries in Nicaragua or the Russian troops in Afghanistan, the military objective is the same—the defeat of the future and the defense of the past.

HARPER'S MAGAZINE,
*April 1987*

# THE SAGE OF
# SADDLE RIVER

*Life is a glorious cycle of song*
*A medley of extemporania*
*And love is a thing that can never go wrong*
*And I am Marie of Rumania.*

—Dorothy Parker

IN AUGUST OF 1974, fourteen years ago this month, President Richard M. Nixon quit the White House in disgrace, generally perceived by the national media as a crooked politician so thoroughly paranoid and corrupt that anything he said could be construed as a lie. This summer he appears before the American public in the role of elder statesman and sage, generally perceived—by the same national media—as a wise diplomatist remarkable for his telling of geopolitical truths. Thus the thief becomes the oracle, and the hanged man changes into the king of wands. The metamorphosis is wonderful to behold, but without meaning to slight Nixon's attainments as an actor (especially his gift for the pious gesture and the unctuous phrase), I suspect that his rescue from oblivion can be largely attributed to the media's delight in fairy tales.

Certainly it was a task accomplished against difficult odds. Even in the best of times, Nixon's performances in the national political theater tend to totter precariously toward the comic and grotesque. Look at him askew or in an odd light, and it is frighteningly easy to mistake him for an old vaudevillian pretending to play King Lear, an inspired clown traipsing around the stage declaiming stately gibberish. Very little evidence in the record of his presidency supports the pretension to statesmanship. A close reading of the small print suggests that he could be relied upon to break any promise, deny any conviction, betray any ally or nominal friend for the sake of a selfish advantage. Nor was he thought to be particularly intelligent. The commentaries that he scrawled on state papers, late at night and in an unsteady hand, tended to lack subtlety—"The man is a goddamn fool" or, more emphatic, "Bomb them." Henry Kissinger used to make fun of Nixon's insufferable egotism and "meatball mind." To his more sardonic confederates Kissinger liked to read aloud from the President's memorandums, laughing at the pomposity of the language in which Nixon dressed up the banality of his thought.

It's true that as President, Nixon pursued the opening to China, which, given the circumstances, was a feat of diplomacy comparable to conceding the existence of the Pacific Ocean. It's also true that most of the time he knew whose telephones to tap. But on the larger questions of character and history, Nixon was almost always wrong. He believed, devoutly, in the chimera of the "domino theory," and he thought the United States could win the Vietnam War if only it dropped another twelve tons of explosives on another four peasants. He was wrong about the effects of the bombing and invasion of Cambodia—the North Vietnamese "sanctuaries" that he meant to destroy didn't exist—and he didn't understand the economic consequences likely to follow the separation of the American dollar from the gold standard. Consistently ignoring intelligence reports that didn't confirm his own theories and suspicions, he was wrong about Allende and the Shah of Iran, wrong about the Russians and the trustworthiness of Kissinger (a first-rate charlatan but a third-rate strategist, as treacherous as Nixon himself), wrong about the Arabian oil cartel and the nature of the communist conspiracy. Most of his attempts at realpolitik ended in failure, and at the end he was even wrong about the character of the American people, misjudging their response to his complicity in the Watergate burglaries.

But in the enchanted never-never land of the big-time media, the historical memory counts for as little as last year's debutante. The makers of the presiding myths shape their images in the evangelical present in which the crippled boy wins the lottery, the chorus girl studies ancient Greek, and the lessons of experience never contradict the miracle of paradise regained. The United States grants the favors of the second, third, and fifty-seventh chance, and its citizens remain free to invent for themselves whatever character draws a crowd or pays the rent. Convicted drug salesmen do their time in jail and two years later, having met God in Cell Block E, join the editorial board of *National Review.* Ambitious young women who begin by selling their smiles on the street end as society hostesses frowning about the state of the country's morals. A bankrupt passes through Chapter 11, and on his way out of the courthouse finds himself accosted by a banker eager to set him up with a new loan and another American Express card.

Self-important as well as credulous, the more prominent figures in the national media never tire of admiring their own significance, and if Nixon learned one new trick during the years of his exile it was the one about paying court to the ladies and gentlemen of the fourth estate. He learned the trick from Kissinger, and when he shifted his theater of operations from San Clemente to Saddle River, New Jersey, he began giving small dinners for those few journalists (the happy, precious few) to whom he would say that only they—alone among all the world's editors and columnists—understood the true meaning of the twentieth century. The journalists, of course, accepted the praise from Caesar with the dignity befitting their rank and station. All too easily I can imagine the appalling solemnity of the conversation, and after dinner I'm afraid that somebody was sent to fetch the maps.

The hymn of adulation began rising in the media in late 1986 (respectful interviews in *Time,* the excited announcement in *Newsweek* that "He's Back!") and reached a crescendo in the spring of this year with the publication of Nixon's latest memoir, *1999: Victory Without War.* The leading newspapers welcomed the book with flattering reviews ("dramatic . . . timely," *New York Times*; "Nixon, He's Still the One," *Washington Post*; etc.); *Life* magazine published passages from the text, and the author graciously consented to appear on both the "Today" show and "Meet the Press" (for the first time in twenty years) for an exchange of views at the highest levels of imperial cliché. During the month of April, Nixon delivered speeches (all variants on chapters in his book) to hushed audiences crowded into ballrooms in Dallas, Chicago, Orange County, and Detroit. The critic for the *Chicago Tribune* praised him for his "kingly world view"; in other towns, reporters were astonished by his "resolute cadence" and amazed that he could speak for an hour without looking at his notes. In Washington the eight hundred editors assembled at a convention of their own kind awarded him a standing ovation. By the beginning of May the book had arrived on the best-seller lists, and the nation's syndicated columnists ("supremely realistic," Jeane Kirkpatrick; "powerful . . . illuminating," Brian Crozier; etc., etc.) were glad to report that Nixon had returned from the years of his penance as a statesman blessed with the stature of Churchill or de Gaulle.

The encomiums struck me as so preposterous that I thought it only fair to read the book. It was conceivable—not likely, but conceivable—that Nixon had put aside the practice of calculated lying that had informed all his utterance for fifty years, that yes, Virginia, there was a Santa Claus, that the chorus girl really did read Greek, and that Nixon had written an honest book. The hope of a miracle expired on page 4. Having tried three times to read the book all the way to the end (by no means an easy thing to do), I cannot understand how anybody could describe it as anything other than sanctimonious drivel. The writing is poor, the arguments specious or trite, the author's voice as sententious as that of a latter-day Polonius.

A single paragraph on page 27 serves to illustrate both the tone and method of the prose. At line 20 Nixon says, "But perfect peace—a world without conflict—is an illusion. It has never existed and will never exist." At line 22 he slightly varies the sentiment—"Real peace is not an end to conflict but a means to living with conflict"—and then, at line 35, he joins both commonplaces in a harmony worthy of Andrew Lloyd Webber, "Perfect peace assumes the end of conflict. Real peace is a means of living with unending conflict."

The repetitions continue throughout the book's 321 pages, and so does the belaboring of the obvious. All eight-year-old girls, of course, know that "perfect peace is an illusion"; so do most eight-year-old boys and a fair percentage of the world's better-informed dogs. But to Nixon, very pleased with himself in his wizard's hat, the discovery is big news. He goes on to tell his readers that the Russians cannot be trusted, that a surprising number of people exist in a state of poverty, and that war isn't a game of Parcheesi.

The argument of the book can be reduced to a few standard notions about the primacy of the American national security state and the holy crusade of the Cold War. Nixon welcomes the "titanic struggle" between the U.S. and the USSR—good for developing youthful character, good for military spending, good for business—and he is very, very distressed by what he calls the new "isolationist strain" in the American character. Neo-isolationists he defines as people who don't want to "step up" to the country's "global responsibilities," who don't think that it is America's business, now and forever, to play "a central international role" and lead the world to freedom and not-so-perfect peace. After about thirty pages of this sort of rhetoric, it becomes clear that what he means by the new "isolationist strain" is the impulse toward good sense and common decency. Nixon is keen to preserve the game of nations, in which people like himself get to dress up in delusions of grandeur, and he expects the American people to pay for his amusement with their taxes and the blood of their children. Any American who doesn't want to play the grand game is either a traitor or a deluded fool.

Throughout the book Nixon interrupts his explanation of current events to offer uplifting remarks about the American ideal of liberty and the spirit of hope that informs the American purpose. Against these virtues he opposes the Soviet vices of tyranny and fear. Such piety is especially repulsive in the mouth of a man who, during his entire term of office, showed nothing but contempt for the American republic and every principle for which it stands. His first act on becoming President was to set up the National Security Council with de facto and de jure authority for the making of foreign policy, preferably in secret and without reference to either the Congress or the Constitution. Whenever possible he substituted palace intrigues for open and honest debate. He used the CIA to subvert foreign politicians and taught the Air Force to falsify the records of the secret bombing of Cambodia. His hatred of free speech was apparent in his every gesture and expression, and I suspect that he felt truly at ease only when he found himself in the company of his own toadying courtiers or in the presence of military despots like Marcos and the Shah of Iran. Confronted with an obstacle to his will, he invariably exhibited the autocrat's instinct to coerce, break in, lie, and suppress. I think it probable that he envied the Soviets their freedom of totalitarian maneuver, and I'm fairly sure that his obsession with the evil of the Soviet empire follows from his recognition, in men such as Gromyko and Brezhnev, of portraits of himself.

Possibly because I happened to be reading Nixon's book in conjunction with the news dispatches about President Reagan's journey to Moscow, I was struck by how little Nixon seems to have learned since he was a young congressman in the 1950s snuffling out proofs of communist conspiracy for the House Un-American Activities Committee. Clearly the world has changed a good deal in the last forty years, but in Nixon's mind, it is still 1948. He doesn't seem to have noticed that the familiar nineteenth-century illusion of grandly conceived wars and alliances has become irrelevant to a world in which no nation can guarantee the stability of its currency or defend its borders against the drug trade and acid rain. Apparently Nixon hasn't concerned himself with the revolutions in the technologies and the sciences. Nor does he wish to consider the possibility that the Cold War might be over and that the questions raised in the Soviet press, about Lenin as well as Stalin, might have been asked in good faith. Like tolerance and compassion, good faith is a neo-isolationist trait that deserves to be placed under surveillance and possibly charged with crimes against the national security state.

Because Nixon insists that all the old myths remain comfortably intact, his book confirms the media's childlike belief in the world outside of time. In the enchanted garden of a never-ending talk show, Nixon sits across a table from an ancient Soviet general with whom he has been exchanging documents for forty years. Only by constantly threatening one another with nuclear destruction (and thereby, not incidentally, all the other inhabitants of the globe) can they maintain the facade of their omnipotence. It is a facade that the attending journalists have come to think is real, and if a stagehand took away the set, they wouldn't know where to look or what to say.

HARPER'S MAGAZINE,
*August 1988*

# A DWARF FOR
# ALL SEASONS

> *Man an' boy I've seen th' Dimmycratic party hangin' to*
> *th' ropes a score iv times. I've seen it dead an' burrid an'*
> *th' Raypublicans kindly buildin' a monymint f'r it an'*
> *preparin' to spind their declinin' days in th' custom*
> *house. I've gone to sleep nights wonderin' where I'd throw*
> *away me vote afther this an' whin I woke up there was*
> *that crazy-headed ol' loon iv a party with its hair*
> *sthreamin' in its eyes, an' an axe in its hand, chasin'*
> *Raypublicans into th' tall grass. 'Tis niver so good as*
> *whin 'tis broke, whin rayspictable people speak iv it in*
> *whispers . . .*
>
> —Mr. Dooley

> *There is a demand today for men who can make wrong*
> *appear right.*
>
> —Terence

**D**URING THE WHOLE of the year prior to this season's primary
elections, the troupe of presidential candidates received such unan-
imously bad press notices that it's fair to ask what the critics thought
they had reason to expect. Against what standard of performance
was the company of wandering mimes being measured? What ideal
figure of the perfect politician did everybody have in mind?

Certainly the critics didn't feel hesitant about giving voice to their
sarcasm and contempt. For twelve months the editorial pages of the
nation's better newspapers offered condescending remarks about
"the seven dwarfs" and "the car pool" on the Democratic side of the

field and found among the Republicans either wimps or lunatics. The high-minded columnists complained about the candidates' lack of substance, charm, sense, force, wit, and stature.

Reduced to its fundamental harmonic structure, the criticism that filled the pages of *The New York Times*, *The Washington Post*, and *The Wall Street Journal* could be stated as follows: "Who dares present us with loutish amateurs? What pigsty of a republic has the effrontery to send us so tawdry a band of would-be kings? Look at them in their identical blue suits and cheap red ties—aping the manners of their betters, mouthing inane promises, reciting lists of dreary statistics, boring us with their interminable debates, grinning their foolish, provincial grins. How can we take them seriously—we who have said good evening to Ted Koppel and discussed the weather with Donald Trump?"

When Gary Hart had the gall to return from oblivion, the tone of fluttering indignation ascended to the pitch of a falsetto whine. What was merely bad taste had become deliberate insult. The columnists clucked their tongues like dowager aunts reminding their nieces and nephews about the rules of sexual protocol and saying that the solemn ritual of a presidential campaign must not be turned into trivial burlesque. A. M. Rosenthal in *The New York Times* and Gail Sheehy on public television suggested that Hart might do well to consult a psychiatrist. *The New Republic* found Hart utterly devoid of *gravitas*, a sideshow freak who belonged not in the stately rooms of first-class celebrity but in the circus tent of the *National Enquirer* along with Elvis and Liz and Joan and the two-headed baby born in an alien galaxy.

The complaints betray a dismal ignorance of American history and a profound fear of the democratic idea. None of the latter-day critics apparently knows, or cares to remember, that most American presidents have proved themselves as resolutely second-rate as Benjamin Harrison, James Buchanan, Rutherford B. Hayes, Grover Cleveland, and Millard Fillmore.

During the middle passages of the nineteenth century the politician stumping through the American forest in search of a vote was already an object of ridicule. The Whig diarist George Templeton Strong noted as long ago as 1856 that the stump speech depended for its claptrap effect on "pathos and bathos delightful to see." Most stump speeches, he said, made him "sick and sore with laughter."

Then as now, elections had less to do with questions of grave consequence than with mummery and graft. William Henry Harrison carried the election of 1840 on the catchy but meaningless tune of a phrase, "Tippecanoe and Tyler Too," and in 1884 James G. Blaine, an eminent and self-satisfied Republican, lost the election because a preacher in his employ made the mistake of referring to the Democrats as the party of "rum, romanism and rebellion."

Nor, apparently, do the latter-day critics know, or wish to know, that in the arena of our national politics, mediocrity is the norm, not the exception. An American politician belongs, by right of birth, in the sawdust of the *National Enquirer*, to the ringmasters and gossip-mongers who delight in Princess Di and write headlines that say SOVIETS FIND LOST CITY ON MARS or ANGRY WIFE PUTS PIRANHA FISH IN HUBBY'S BATHTUB or SUNBATHER BURSTS INTO FLAMES; ALL WE'VE GOT IS A SCORCHED BLANKET, BAFFLED POLICE SAY.

How could it be otherwise? Mediocrity is the common clay of the human condition. As in politics, so also in medicine, finance, and literature. Most people (i.e., the presiding majority) do not possess exceptional talents—not for making money, not for governing, not for writing sonnets or hitting baseballs. A state governed according to the whim of genius (i.e., by the exceptional minority) would descend within a matter of weeks into anarchy.

The democratic principle holds that the business of the state can be conducted by ordinary men, subject to the ordinary failures of character as well as to the moments of ordinary courage and intelligence. The lack of divine intervention in the affairs of men is what Lincoln meant by a government "of the people, by the people and for the people." It is what Mark Hanna meant when he compared President William McKinley to a tin railroad shed and what Joseph Alsop meant when he praised Richard Nixon as a "workable plumbing fixture."

Under this republican definition of government, this season's primary candidates meet the historical standard of blind presumption. Governors Dukakis and Babbitt could stand in the shoes of Presidents Garfield and Harding; so could Representative Gep-

hardt, Vice President Bush, and General Haig. Each of the gentlemen also could do creditable duty as the president of Citibank, the
editor of *Newsweek,* or the president of Yale University.

If their language is dull and their images too earnest, at least they
make an attempt at substantive discussion and the teaching of
impromptu civics lessons. Ten years ago the newspaper moralists
complained about the superficiality of television advertising that
summed up the nation's dream of heaven in thirty seconds of commercial agitprop. Now that the candidates endure the penance of
debates, the critics find them as boring as the testimony in front of a
school board or a tax commission—in sum, as tedious as any other
honest labor of representative government.

Why, then, the mincing smirks among the political gentry in New
York and Washington? Why do the elder statesmen of the Democratic party (people like Cyrus Vance and Robert Strauss and Walter
Mondale) whisper to the media their disappointment in "the dwarfs"
and "the car pool"? Why do the media devote so much of their
limited span of attention to the two candidates—Jesse Jackson and
Gary Hart—who stand not the slightest chance of winning next
November's election? Why do they persist in imagining that Governor Mario Cuomo and Senator Bill Bradley—absent candidates as
thoroughly mediocre as the ones already present—might somehow
improve the presidential campaign with the facade of dignity?

The answer has to do with both the social and the financial
motives of what has become a privileged class. During the years of
the American supremacy (roughly 1945 until the present), the
country's leading plutocrats adopted the attitudes they thought con-
sonant with their newly arrived importance as proconsuls of a newly
arrived empire. Arrivistes of all denominations (whether merchants
or literary intellectuals) never have much sense of humor, especially
with regard to themselves, and it wasn't long before everybody who
was anybody (in Washington as well as at CBS) forgot what could be
reasonably expected of politics. They had learned to ride in limousines and comb their hair for the television cameras, and they
didn't want to be reminded of two-headed babies or dancing bears.

Prior to the advent of Henry Luce's "American Century," the
country's writers didn't feel obliged to confuse politicians with the

equestrian statues in a public park. To his journal in 1853, Thoreau remarked: "The oldest, wisest politician grows not more human so, but is merely a gray wharf rat at last."

Mark Twain, Ambrose Bierce, and Mr. Dooley weren't much more sanguine, and Henry Adams, an appalled guest in Teddy Roosevelt's White House, while writing a letter to a friend in 1902, observed: "What makes a long residence in Washington so bad for one's temper is the horrible display of vanity, especially among the men. If ever, once, in all those forty years that I have known statesmen, I had met one solitary individual who thought, even at intervals, of anyone or anything but himself, I would forgive him as a sad example of human eccentricity, and say no word against him."

Nearer to our own time, Richard Reeves, a political columnist known for his occasional lapses into plain statement, said: "Politicians are different from you and me. The business of reaching for power does something to a man—it closes him off from other men until, day by day, he reaches the point where he instinctively calculates each new situation and each other man with the simplest question: What can this do for me?"

So unflattering an assay of a politician doesn't conform to the inflated expectations of the age. The current generation of patrons feels it deserves a political figure more in keeping with the splendor of its department stores—somebody suitable for framing in the pages of *Architectural Digest*, a statesman as grand as the Pan Am building and as wise as Alvin Toffler. The condescending tone of voice expresses the disgust of a nouveau riche plutocracy for what it perceives to be the vulgarity of the common man as well as the rich man's deep-seated fear of popular—a.k.a. "democratic"— government. The happy few yearn for the proverbial man on horseback, the glittering Caesar who will astonish them with his resemblance to John Wayne and relieve them of their boredom.

The ceaseless belittling of the primary campaigns also expresses the wish to take the presidential nomination back into the back room. Back where it safely and properly belongs—among the people who, by virtue of subscribing to *Newsweek* and knowing the difference between clams *oreganato* and Julian Schnabel, congratulate themselves on the refinement of their taste in politicians. If no candidate comes to the convention with enough votes to ensure his nomination, then the dealers in influence can divide the spoils without having to bargain with the agents of an illiterate mob.

Once the candidate has been anointed, of course, the laughter stops. Candidates can be seen as clowns in primary campaigns, but not in general elections. What was a domestic comedy becomes, overnight, a solemn romance.

Prior to his appointment as Richard Nixon's successor in the summer of 1974, Vice President Gerald Ford had been perceived as an amiable but stupid congressman as likely to fall off a dais as to walk into a glass door. Once arrived in office, Ford was assigned—together with the Marine guard, the nuclear codes, and the Great Seal of the United States—a reputation for sagacity. Nobody went quite so far as to describe him as a philosopher-king, but the Washington press corps immediately recognized in him the lineaments of the homely wisdom traditionally ascribed to rural folk and the singers of country songs.

The media perform the ritual of purification, changing the worm into a butterfly and telling their patrons that a giant has been born. Let a single name emerge from the confusion in Iowa and New Hampshire, and within a matter of hours the hagiographers at *Time* magazine will begin to write the autumn fairy tale—the free world trembling in the balance, questions of grave significance caught in the telecommunications nets, the marsh lights of power glimmering in the Washington mist. The man who can make wrong appear right must first be dressed up in the veils of innocence.

HARPER'S MAGAZINE,
*March 1988*

# AFTER 1984

*Practical men, who believe themselves to be quite exempt
from any intellectual influences, are usually the slaves of
some defunct economist. Madmen in authority, who hear
voices in the air, are distilling their frenzy from some
academic scribbler of a few years back.*
—John Maynard Keynes

DURING THE SUMMER of a presidential campaign the national
media abandon themselves to their passion—always present but not
always so rapturously expressed—for the American national security state. In story after story and newscast after newscast, as
incessantly as the cicadas singing in the acacia trees, the media
murmur their anthem of praise to the great and inexpressible power
likely to shift, like the golden serpent in Apollo's golden cave, on
the morning of November 8.

The intensity of the current belief in the power of the sovereign
state would have surprised even so practiced a skeptic as George
Orwell. Never mind that the belief bears little or no resemblance to
the facts, or that the witnesses to the revelation might as well be
testifying to their faith in the wizardry of elves. Never mind that the
genius of twentieth-century technology has rendered the pretensions to nineteenth-century empire as defunct as General George
Custer. The authors of the country's news wish to believe in the
existence of a state sufficiently omnipotent to see the world as a
reflection of itself and to change the singing of insects into a stately
music for stringed instruments and drums.

Ever since World War II it has been customary to believe that the
world is held in thrall by Leviathan. Grotesque bureaucracies in six

**225**

or seven cities presumably make all the decisions of consequence. The poor, helpless sap of an individual doesn't stand a chance against the omnipotence and implacable inhumanity of the modern state. Orwell had said so, and so had Kafka; eight American presidents believed them, and so did three generations of English professors.

As the reader no doubt will remember from English 104, Orwell's satirical novel *1984* presupposed a world divided among three totalitarian states, each of them imposing on its subject population the conditions normal to a penal colony. The food was bad; so were the water and the conversation. Nobody was permitted to think, make love, or take notes.

So omnipotent had these states become, so efficient and surehanded in the techniques of oppression, that no mere individual would dare to commit an act of the imagination. The reigning despots presided over bureaucracies so perfect that they could make both time and the world stand still.

For some years now this literary revelation has failed to correspond to the text of events. Although the news apparently hasn't been widely circulated among the American political cadres, it isn't as if anybody has been trying to withhold classified information. Within the last generation, the Chinese have endured at least two revolutions, the Soviets have been put to considerable trouble and expense to preserve the semblance of empire, and the Americans have failed to impose their theory of democracy on a single one of the Central American states.

Even within the precincts of Washington, the federal government has trouble enforcing the disciplines of the national security state. On Capitol Hill a House subcommittee last year held hearings at which two prominent American corporations (General Motors and General Electric) sought permission to negotiate their own treaties with the Soviet Union. Both companies manufacture communications satellites, but the United States at present cannot provide them with a means of lifting the satellites into space. The Soviet Union, however, offers launchings on seven different types of rockets at prices as reasonable as $30 million, and the American companies wished to sign contracts and entrust their satellites to the engineers at Tyuratam in Soviet Kazakhstan.

American law forbids the hiring of Soviet space vehicles, on the grounds that the practice might compromise the nation's security. Both GM and GE dismissed the objection as jingoistic nonsense and asked that the State Department rescind the law. Their executives argued, in effect, that the American government obstructs the free expression of free enterprise. Besides, they said, if they postpone deployment of commercial satellites, they will lose the business to the Japanese or the French.

Their testimony suggested that the United States now stands in the same relation to its larger corporations as the United Nations stands in relation to the United States—that is, that the smaller and more coherent power (IBM say, or Mobil) consents to the fictional dominion of the nominally larger but more diffuse power (the United States) in return for the right to do as it damn well pleases.

By sapping the authority of the centralized state, the new technologies have shifted the locus of decisive action to the more modest concentrations of intellect and will. These smaller organisms can be defined as the transnational corporation, as the merchant city-state (Singapore, Taiwan, Hong Kong), as militant causes (the PLO or the IRA), even as individuals as intransigent as Manuel Noriega or Muammar Qaddafi. Israeli tank commanders, Colombian drug dealers, African despots, Turkish assassins, and Lebanese terrorists—all these unlicensed individuals blithely carry on their wars and coups d'état without receiving so much as a written excuse from the faculty deans in Washington, Beijing, or Moscow. As yet, nobody has drawn a map that reflects the new order, but if somebody were to do so, I suspect that it would look more like medieval France than nineteenth-century Europe.

Despite the systems of modern communications (or perhaps because of them), the hierarchies of international capitalism resemble the feudal arrangements under which an Italian noble might swear fealty to a German prince, or a Norman duke declare himself the vassal of an English king. The lords and barons of the transnational corporation become lieges of the larger fiefs and holding companies, owing their allegiance less to a government (any government) than to Sony or McDonnell Douglas or Citicorp. It is the company that pays their pensions, insures their lives, bestows on them their titles and badges of identity.

The frontiers run between markets and spheres of commercial interest, not along the boundaries of sovereign states. If a company is large enough and rich enough (commanding assets worth several billion dollars and employing more people than lived in fourteenth-century Venice), the company, of necessity, conducts its own foreign policy. In part, this is because the nation-state can make good on so few of its promises.

What nation can defend its borders against disease, ballistic missiles, the drug trade, or the transmission of subversive images? What nation can hold harmless its air or its water against the acid rain drifting east across Canada or the radioactive cloud blowing west from Chernobyl? What nation can protect its currency against predatory speculations on the world's money markets?

Central bankers returning from abroad wish they could find even a scrap of evidence for Orwell's theoretical stasis. They talk instead about the chaotic entangling of the international lines of trade and credit, about the aboriginal bankrupts of the Third World holding the civilized banks hostage like so many missionaries sitting in cannibal pots. In the sciences, the news is the same. The correspondents on the frontiers—of physics, of biology, of astronomy, of genetics—speak of violent revolution, of fundamental changes following so fast, one upon the other, that nobody can conceive of a reality so tidy as Orwell's totalitarian housing development.

Even within the arena of American politics, where the sorrowing professors find all too many proofs of the Orwellian truths, the levers of power fall into the hands of men from nowhere, who, like Presidents Carter and Reagan, mount their campaigns on little more than ideological enthusiasm, the sweetness of a voice, or the earnestness of a smile. In this year's Democratic primaries Michael Dukakis represented a constituency not much larger than his own ambition, and Jesse Jackson cast himself as the leader of a Third World nation that happens to be located within the boundaries of the continental United States. He appears before the faithful as an American

Nkrumah or Tshombe, a charismatic figure in a safari suit embracing Yasir or Fidel, making overtures to Syria and the Sandinistas, not on behalf of the United States but on behalf of the imaginary state of *l'Amérique Noire*.

Why, then, against the evidence available on any city street, do the intellectual classes insist on the dark and terrible beauty of Orwell's iconography? Partly, I suspect, it is because *1984* is one of the few books that the schools forced on two generations of recruits to the banners of the Cold War. It is also likely that the Orwellian state represents, although unfortunately in a malign form, a view of the world so satisfying to the literary and political mind, in which words take precedence over things.

HARPER'S MAGAZINE,
*September 1988*

# NOUNS AND
# PRONOUNS

*State business is a cruel trade; good-nature is a*
*bungler in it.*

—Marquis of Halifax

O F ALL THE lies that President-elect George Bush so obediently told during the autumn election campaign, none was more preposterous than the one about how he wished to change America into "a kinder and gentler nation." I can understand why a politician would tell the customary lies about clean water, lower taxes, and the flag; but what would prompt him to think that a nation—especially a nation remarkable for its military prowess and its frenzied devotion to money—can acquire the virtues properly associated only with individuals? An abstract noun neither smiles nor sings nor tells bedtime stories. The promise of human feeling on the part of any institution—whether a bank or an infantry regiment—debases the language and props up the effigy to whom George Orwell gave the name "Big Brother." When governments claim the rights of individuals (just as when individuals claim the prerogatives of government), it usually means that the rule of law has been supplanted by the rule of men.

The question remains as to what it was that Bush—or, more likely, his speechwriters—had in mind. Were they being cynical or elegiac? Had they become so contemptuous of native opinion as to think that by saying so they could change cruise missiles into birthday balloons? Or, having become frightened by what they had seen of the moral squalor of the Reagan Administration, were they promoting a happy return to Christianity and the third grade?

**230**

Given the barbarous lessons of the twentieth century, I don't know how anybody can still pretend that any nation-state—whether American, Soviet, or Chinese—can afford the luxuries of mercy or compassion. Cruel by nature and dishonorable by definition, the state recognizes no law other than its own need. Were the state to be cast in an animal form it would be seen as a hideous and mutant thing—reptilian, stupid, rapacious, and half-blind.

Surely even Bush must know by now that the state doesn't play by the same rules as those in effect at Andover or a Connecticut country club. As director of the Central Intelligence Agency he presumably had occasion to reflect on the ways in which the United States was obliged to sacrifice human life and happiness (in Cambodia, say, or Iran) on the altar of its perceived interests. During the eight years of his service in President Reagan's household guard, Bush undoubtedly had further occasion to notice that the United States sometimes found it expedient to abandon its allies (among them Ferdinand Marcos and Manuel Noriega), debase its currency, default on its debts, repudiate its treaties, cheat its own citizens (of medical care, a school lunch, and a decent education), betray the principles of its Constitution (for reasons of state, in Nicaragua and Iran), forward the shipment of cocaine to Shreveport and points north, and lie—repeatedly and complacently—about the environmental catastrophe leaking out of the government's nuclear weapons factories in Ohio, Colorado, and South Carolina.

If this were not instruction enough, Bush certainly had occasion to study the mechanics of political chicanery during the course of his presidential campaign. He proved to be a diligent apprentice.

Prior to the Republican convention in New Orleans last summer, it was thought that Bush didn't have much talent as a demagogue. Everybody knew that he would do and say what he was told to do and say, but could he convince the television cameras?

The nominating conventions bear comparison to the medieval practice of readying a knight for battle. Just as the knight's squires raised him onto his horse and forced over his head the iron mask of power, so also the candidate's political valets dress him in the glittering plates of armed cliché. For the Republicans in New Orleans, the mounting of Vice President George Bush presented the awful possibility of clownish parody. The plumed helmet was too big for the candidate's head, and his grooms knew that he was likely to slide off the other side of the horse. Never was there a novice captain so unsuited to the illusion of command.

By all accounts a once decent man—attentive to his family and friends, as well intentioned as the first day of school—Bush unfortunately possessed none of the attributes expected of an equestrian statue in a public park. His manner was that of the eager and perennial sophomore, and his voice, which was thin, carried the overtone of upper-class privilege in tennis clothes. Despite his considerable experience in government service, Bush conveyed the impression of boyish fecklessness undisturbed by the labor of thought.

Well aware of their candidate's weaknesses, Bush's attendants in New Orleans relied on the arts of advertising. If they couldn't turn him into bronze or stone, they could transform him into a salable product, which, in a commercial society, is the next best thing to immortality. The problem was so well understood by the political cadres in New York and Washington that they spoke of Bush (as they also spoke of Dukakis) as if he were a soft drink, a spray cologne, or a Japanese car.

The marketing plan devised in New Orleans made use of the two principal strategies known to the sellers of what Madison Avenue calls "message icons": "comparative advertising" (slurs directed at the competing product) and "brand-imaging" (lies about the wonders of one's own product). In the service of the former strategy the Republicans broadcast a series of television commercials depicting Governor Dukakis as a dreaming liberal sympathetic to rapists and as a dangerous fool who didn't know the difference between a Russian and a Smurf. The latter strategy entailed tying Bush to the saddle of his horse, padding his helmet with enough Styrofoam to hold it in place (at least until November), and dressing him up in the costumes of the common man. Bush dutifully denied any connection to his point of social origin or to the monied interests that paid for the fabrication of his image, and for three months, following the script, he presented himself as a regular, straight-shooting kind of guy who "cries easily" at sentimental movies, admires Loretta Lynn and the Oak Ridge Boys, pitches horseshoes, cares a lot for "mainstream values," subscribes to *Bassmaster* magazine, delights in his motorboat, and never misses "Monday Night Football."

Never once during the campaign did Bush say or do anything that suggested gentleness or kindness. When he wasn't fatuous, he was dishonest. He slandered his opponent, mocked the generously idealistic tradition in American politics (a.k.a. the "L word"), and wondered why women who received abortions weren't being sent to prison. As often as possible he appeared before small-town rallies in the company of Hollywood strongmen, among them Arnold Schwarzenegger (a.k.a. "Conan the Barbarian"), who assured a crowd in Hackensack, New Jersey, that Bush was "no wimp." The endorsement implied that Bush could be relied upon to maim or kill anybody that his country ordered him to maim or kill.

Even so, despite the thousands of flags and the incessant spectacle of Bush waving a brave hello to the nation's bright and invincible future, I never could dispel the feeling that his smile was fraudulent and that Bush was frightened both by his political associates and his horse. Behind the visor of his plumed helmet, which looked to be made of tin instead of iron, I could too easily imagine him being afraid of what else he would be asked to do. How many other lies would he be forced to tell? Of the little that was left to him of his conscience, how much more would he be required to place in escrow?

In the same acceptance speech in which he promised to make America "a kinder and gentler nation," Bush also said, speaking of the American people as a whole, that "we must be good to one another." The phrase had a plaintive sound, as if Bush were speaking about himself and hoping that the American people would be good not to one another but to him. It is, I suspect, a forlorn hope.

Too many people have learned too well the brutish lessons of the twentieth century, and they have taken as their beau ideal not the strength of character once admired in a virtuous individual but the technological perfections of a nation-state. Encouraged by the squalid example of the Reagan Administration, the captains of finance most closely identified with the spirit of the age aspire to the moral vacuum of the rigged stock deal and the slick ad campaign.

A few days before Bush's election I was introduced to a representative member of the species—a young and callow investment manager, adept in the maneuvers of the leveraged buyout, the merger, the takeover, and the corporate raid. Having raised $100 million for a university library and research laboratory, he had summoned a delegation of alumni to show them drawings of the buildings that he had endowed with the ornament of his name. The view looking west was of the Hudson River, and after the stewards had served the coffee and passed around the Cuban cigars, the host explained the advantages of setting oneself up as a government. Having adopted a program of deficit spending, and being comfortably burdened with a portfolio of heavy bank loans that he had no intention of paying off, he compared our federal fiscal policy with his dealings with restaurants and department stores. Because he had run up his debts to genuinely alarming levels, he had achieved, at least among the cognoscenti at Citibank and Le Cirque, a status comparable to that of Brazil.

What was especially fine about constituting oneself as a government, he said, was the way in which it relieved a fellow of a sense of guilt. He submitted the rapacity of his appetite (for power, for goods, for services) as proof of his magnanimity. It was expected of nation-states, he said, that they should live beyond their means, that they should be spendthrifts as well as liars and cheats. The dean of the university had provided him with a reading list, and he had collected an anthology of quotations from diplomatists as mordant as Francis Bacon and Georges Clemenceau.

"A state neither loves nor hates," he said. "It pursues its interests. You would be surprised how simple this makes the negotiations with women and children."

He was a man much pleased with himself, and at the time I remember being reminded of Donald Trump. In retrospect I'm reminded of Vice President-elect Dan Quayle. It is to people such as these that Bush can expect to make his little speeches about "a kinder and gentler nation." No wonder he seems a trifle anxious when he frets about the state of the nation's imaginary soul. I think it probable that he cannot distinguish his enemies from his friends. He was elected as a constitutional deity—a wax figure made for television, meant to be briefly worshiped, and then, like the annual kings of the ancient corn harvest, sacrificed to the expedience of the moment and the changing of the political seasons.

HARPER'S MAGAZINE,
*January 1989*

# PAPER MOONS

*Many a man would rather you heard his story than
granted his request.*

—Lord Chesterfield

**A**T THE ST. REGIS HOTEL in New York last October I had
occasion to attend another of those mournful conferences about the
ruinous imbalance of the nation's trade. The debit at the time
amounted to $152 billion, and the gentlemen on the dais were
talking about protective tariffs and the good old-fashioned wages
still being paid in the sweatshops of Singapore. During a brief
recess in the proceedings I ran across four consultants comparing
prophecies in the bar. Among them I recognized Townsend, an
intellectual mercenary with whom I'd become acquainted on his
previous campaigns as a hired voice in the employ of the Strategic
Defense Initiative and supply-side economics. Townsend is a large
and shambling man, nearly always dressed in a rumpled suit but
blessed with an evangelist's talent for sincerity and a sophist's gift of
phrase. He greeted me with boisterous laughter, and then, noisily
moving glasses around the table, invited me to join the company for
a drink and an exchange of rumors.

"A wonderful gig," he said, speaking of his new commission.
"Expenses and $500 a day for complicated explanations of the
obvious. My God, it's better than the energy crisis."

The other consultants, younger and more earnest, smiled nervously at Townsend's little joke. They hadn't marched to the music
of as many different drums in the ideological wars. The woman had
only recently received her doctorate from Harvard, and the two men,
both wearing bow ties and suspenders, were drinking tea.

The one with the thin and expensive briefcase said, "Say what

**236**

you like, Townsend, but the country's in trouble. Pretty damn serious trouble, if you ask me."

Townsend patted him reassuringly on the arm.

"Of course the country's in trouble, Murray; the country's always in trouble. If it wasn't in trouble, we'd all be eating fried rice and teaching freshman math in Oklahoma."

In answer to my question about the occasion for the conference, he explained that it was being sponsored by several alarmed and public-spirited corporations in need of a public-spirited reason to fire, collectively, 50,000 workers. A public relations firm had rounded up the usual crowd of reliable authorities—economists, government bureaucrats, doom-ridden journalists. Townsend was delighted with their expressions of professional despair.

"They've noticed that the country has lost most of its heavy industry," he said. "Everybody's got a set of statistics and a sad story to tell. You know the sort of thing—companies going bankrupt, cheap foreign labor, the price of the dollar, the enormity of the debt . . ."

"All true," I said.

"Of course, all true," Townsend said, "but not important. The Americans never were much good at making things."

The woman looked startled, and the academic gentlemen frowned. The smaller of the two (the one who wasn't Murray) mumbled something about dangerous communist nonsense, but Townsend held up both hands in a gesture of appeasement.

"Nothing unpatriotic intended," he said. "But what is it the Americans really know how to make and sell? Not cars. Our cars are junk. Not rockets. Our rockets blow up. Not steel, or textiles, or furniture, or electronics. We can't afford to pay the help."

The woman from Harvard looked at her notes and said, "What about services?"

Townsend smiled his oracular smile.

"Yes, good, but what kind of services?"

"Fast-food restaurants," Murray said.

Townsend, still smiling, shook his head.

"Fashion?" said Murray's colleague. "Videotapes? Ammunition?"

Townsend kept smiling and shaking his head until the lesser consultants subsided into respectful silence. Murray was kind enough to ask the straight man's question.

"Okay," he said, "what is it that the Americans know how to make and sell better than anybody else in the world?"

Townsend drank deeply from his still tax-deductible drink, and then, after a majestic pause, he said: "Metaphors, my dear Murray. Metaphors and images and expectations."

For the next twenty minutes he expounded his theory of economic salvation, and although I can't remember all of it, I remember wondering whether Townsend had ever considered opening a storefront church.

If given a choice in the matter, he said, Americans prefer something that isn't there. They're in love with the idea of a thing, not the thing itself. Of those who buy jogging shoes, 70 percent don't jog. The menu in most American restaurants is more interesting than the food. A television commercial is an artifact far more subtly made than the product it advertises. Apartments on Fifth Avenue sell for $4 million not because the buyers want a place to live but because they seek a state of grace. The diamond in the Tiffany box is infinitely more precious than the same diamond bought on West Forty-seventh Street. Entire vocabularies of unintelligible jargon—literary as well as military and academic—describe kingdoms of nonexistent thought. Political promises belong to the realm of surrealist fiction. Like the government in Washington, the economy floats on the market in abstraction—on the credulity of people willing to pay, and pay handsomely, for a domino theory, a stock market tip, or any other paper moon with which to furnish the empty rooms of their desire.

"Consider," Townsend said, "the American genius for making money, which is the talent for making something out of nothing. What is money? A piece of worthless paper. A number seen fleetingly on a screen. An act of faith."

Before the other consultants could muster a coherent response, Townsend glanced at his watch and said that he had to get back to the conference room for the evening presentation. He signed the check with a princely flourish, and then, laughing his large and jovial laugh, he said, "My God, what do you think they're paying me for? Expenses and $500 a day for what? For a puff of wind."

He stood up from the table and started for the door, but the young woman newly arrived from Harvard wasn't at all happy with the way the conversation was being left. It was obvious that she thought Townsend insane. If he wasn't insane, then clearly she was in the wrong profession.

"Wait," she said. "You're forgetting the weapons budget, $300 million a day for armaments. Missiles, tanks, submarines—solid objects."

Townsend bestowed upon her the most beatific of his Buddha's smiles.

"More jogging shoes," he said. "Heavier than adjectives, or even balanced phrases, but still metaphors. Metaphors of power."

HARPER'S MAGAZINE,
*December 1986*

# OLD GLORY

*War is the health of the state.*

—Randolph Bourne

**E**VER SINCE THE Soviet Union announced its intention to withdraw from the Cold War, the American government has been hard-pressed to discover or invent a substitute for the lost crusade. It isn't only a question of money, although the money is by no means paltry—$300 billion per annum watering the desert of the American economy; nor is it merely a matter of reaffirming the doctrine of American virtue expounded in the universities and the news media. Largely and most importantly, it is a question of the government's need for a patriotic folktale. Under what flags and banners can the government arm itself with the powers to which it has become accustomed during forty years of continual crises? What raison d'etat can provide so useful a compendium of slogans, half truths, self-justifications, excuses, and moral purposes?

The Cold War supplied both the economic and iconographic staples of American politics, and the belief in the Soviet Union as the Land of Mordor furnished the cover story for official sleights of hand that otherwise might have been seen as dishonest, stingy, or murderous. If somebody was rude enough to ask why the government set up surveillance of its own citizens, or why the state collected so much data pertaining to an individual's behavior, or why so many Americans had to go hungry, invariably the answer turned on the nostrum: "Yes, but think how much worse things would be in Russia."

Take down the Wagnerian stage set of the Evil Empire and it's conceivable that the American people, free of the melodramatic distraction and no longer listening to the music of doom, might

**240**

remember their right to self-government. They might find other uses for their political energy and imagination. What, then, becomes of the permanent American government that so complacently relied on the guarantee of permanent war?

Together with its dependents, subcontractors, apologists, and friends, the permanent American government now consists of several hundreds of thousands of people searching anxiously for a cause around which they can rally their mutual self-interest. Absent the Russians, who or what can be assigned the part of bestial apparition in the foreign snow?

Judging by what I read in the newspapers, it begins to look as if official Washington has nominated the American people as the enemy of first resort. I draw the inference from three pronouncements issued in different venues on or about the Fourth of July:

1. The Supreme Court decision (*Webster* v. *Reproductive Health Services*) restricting a woman's access to an abortion;

2. President George Bush's proposal for a Constitutional amendment that would make it a crime to harm the American flag;

3. The sentence (imposed by Judge Gerhard Gesell in federal district court) excusing Lieutenant Colonel Oliver North from a prison term on the grounds that the poor colonel didn't know enough about the art of government.

Taken together, and understood as expressions of the same habit of mind, the three pronouncements confirm what Justice Harry Blackmun, dissenting from the majority opinion in the Supreme Court's *Webster* decision, referred to as "the coercive and brooding influence of the State." The three bulletins also indicate an official preference for a government of men, not laws, as well as an intention to subvert the hope of a coherent or well-organized political opposition.

The Supreme Court decision asserts—arbitrarily, and without the courtesy or pretense of argument—the primacy of the state. Let no American woman make the presumptuous mistake of thinking that she retains, in her own hands, the care of her own destiny.

Foolish and misguided woman, says the Court, foolish and disloyal. It is the majesty and authority of the state that the law deems precious, not the life and liberty of the individual citizen.

The Court elaborated its ruling by saying, in effect, that the cost of providing poor women with abortions places on the state an intolerable and unseemly financial burden. The cost of all the abortions performed last year in public hospitals did not amount to even a fraction of the money stolen from HUD by the government's best-beloved clients and friends (to say nothing of the money deployed through the Pentagon in search of the perfect weapons system). But even so small a sum weighed more heavily in the Court's judgment than the lives of the women and children condemned to the misery of the slums.

As with the Court's ruling on abortion, President Bush's defense of the American flag assumes that the interest of the state precedes the right of the individual. The President doesn't condescend to argue. He merely asserts and declares. "Flag burning is wrong," he says. "Dead wrong." Or, more elliptically, "Burning the flag goes too far." Or, in a moment of pious devotion, "The flag is too sacred to be abused. If it is not defended, it is defamed."

None of these statements admits the possibility of error or a difference of opinion. Mr. Bush defines the flag as a sacred icon emblematic of the presumably sacred state. As president of that state he reserves to himself the right to draw the boundary between the orthodox near and the heretical far.

Never mind that the state repeatedly has proved itself ignoble and corrupt; never mind that the flag can be read as a symbol for the fatuous cruelty of the Vietnam War, or the systematic lying synonymous with a White House press release. Never mind that Mr. Bush, as a presidential candidate, trailed the flag through the mud of a notably vicious political campaign.

The President doesn't accept alternate readings of the symbol. Anybody who fails to agree with his interpretation commits the crime of blasphemy. By preferring idolatry to argument, Mr. Bush denies the principle, implicit in the First Amendment, that a republic always stands in need of as much disagreement and as many doubts as its citizens have the courage to muster, and that the most offensive forms of political speech (cf. the life and works of Samuel Adams and Thomas Paine) tend to be the ones most in need of protection. Freedom of thought brings societies the unwelcome news that they are in trouble, but because all societies, like all individuals, are almost always in trouble, the news doesn't cause them to perish. They die instead from the fear of thought and from the paralysis that accompanies the silencing of opinions that contradict the official wisdom.

The ritual almost certainly would be welcomed by Oliver North. Like Mr. Bush, the colonel assigns to the state the right to do as it pleases without reference to the rule of law, the will of Congress, or the objection of any common citizen uninitiated in the mysteries of the national security. During the entire seventy-three days of his trial, the colonel never wavered in his spaniel's devotion to whatever he could construe as a raison d'état. Assuming that the state was all-powerful, the colonel assumed that it was all-wise; because he had done what he had done in the service of so solemn an idol, he assumed that his actions were both good and just. Yes, he said, he had made mistakes, and yes, he was sorry about the trouble that he had brought upon his innocent wife and children. But he made the mistakes and brought the trouble because he believed that the state was "too sacred to be abused," and therefore he didn't deserve to be punished for anything other than an excess of patriotism. The colonel's earnest pleading, accompanied by his maudlin enumeration of the countless prayers that he had placed on the altar of his self-righteousness, wouldn't have convinced the judges at Nuremberg. But in Washington, D.C., on July 5, 1989, Judge Gesell found the defense persuasive. He didn't doubt that Colonel North, whom he defined as a "low-ranking subordinate," had obeyed the orders of "higher-ups" (among them President Reagan and the then vice president, George Bush), but because the colonel's superiors couldn't be punished (for fear of casting the shadow of impeachment on the smiling majesty of the presidency), the colonel could not be too severely reprimanded for doing what he was told to do. He was, after all, serving the national interest, and what merely secular court could interfere with the ecclesiastical imperatives of the state? Thus, the judge upheld the notion that the United States is governed by men, not laws, and he imposed on Colonel North a random and whimsical sentence—a $150,000 fine and 1,200 hours of work as a role model for inner-city youth—in keeping with the random and whimsical nature of both the *Webster* decision and President Bush's proposed Constitutional amendment.

Two centuries ago, the men who wrote the Bill of Rights would have regarded these three pronouncements as an assault on their liberties. They understood that their newly founded republic always would stand exposed to subversion and attack, not so much by foreign enemies but by those among their own number relentlessly pursuing their own interests—by the pride of the rich and the envy of the poor, by anybody and everybody (oligarch, bureaucrat, or demagogue) who could bribe a congressman, smudge a regulation, or incite a mob. Knowing that they had embarked on an enterprise committed to the ceaseless struggle between the wishes of the few (i.e., the permanent government and its allies) and the hopes of the many (i.e., everybody else), they took care to arm the many with the means to resist the depredations of the few.

The Bill of Rights still retains its force, most especially the Ninth Amendment ("The enumeration in the Constitution, of certain rights, shall not be construed to deny or disparage others retained by the people"). And so, as always, it is a question of whether enough people choose to exercise those rights. The government makes the choice more difficult by casting into the debate the emotional and divisive issues of abortion and the flag. If the two issues can inflame the passions of the moment, maybe everybody will forget to talk about anything else. The tactic is as familiar as it is cynical (cf. Bush's use of racial hatred and the Pledge of Allegiance in last year's presidential campaign), and the government has no reason to expect that it will fail. The American political conversation has been so moribund for so long that it is hard to imagine a revival of popular interest in any topic that cannot be resolved in fifteen minutes of discussion on *Nightline*. For eight years President Reagan comforted the television audience with his telling and retelling of America's best-loved myths and fables, and neither the media nor the voters raised much of an objection.

Still, with any luck and a few more displays of contempt on the part of the government that mocks the people in whose name it governs, American politics might recover a sense of urgency and meaning. It's even possible that the Democratic party might think of something to say other than "Please" and "Thank you" and "How much will you pay me for my vote?" Not likely, of course, but conceivable.

If a democracy is about people doing different things and a nation-state is about people doing the same thing, then somebody, usually somebody in uniform, has to align the priorities and reconcile the contradictions. With the Americans, this has never been easy to do. The Bill of Rights guarantees the freedom of expression and encourages behaviors that under a monarchy or a despot would be seen as dangerous, eccentric, selfish, or disloyal. The Americans sum up those attitudes under the rubric of individualism. Only in the twentieth century did the United States acquire a theory of national unity, but it has always been a grudging and synthetic thing, cutting against the American grain and constantly in need of being pasted together by wars and threats of war.

The American idea also expresses the will to organize the freedom of mind against the tyranny of privilege, superstition, wealth, and force. In Philadelphia in 1789, the framers of the Constitution understood that America was rising as a power in the world because it defined liberty not as the freedom to conquer and exploit but as the freedom to make and think and build.

HARPER'S MAGAZINE,
*September 1989*

# PART III

# STATES AND
# GOVERNMENTS

# GIFTS OF THE MAGI

BETWEEN THE ELECTION and the inauguration it is customary for the members of the permanent government to bestow upon the new President the precious gifts of their advice. The newspapers blossom with their warnings and recommendations—about the Russians (very dangerous), about the Congress and the press (jealous of their prerogatives), about seating arrangements in Georgetown (crucial to the success of any administration), and about the workings of the federal bureaucracies (infinitely more complex than might be apparent to a tourist). Departing Cabinet ministers submit their reflections to partisan journals; tax-exempt institutes issue reports and commentaries, and the Republican party, at a cost of $3 million, provides Mr. Reagan with "transition teams" composed of a thousand investigators who wander through the Departments of Defense and Agriculture making lists—of names, functions, titles, telephone numbers, and suspect ideologies.

The presentation of advice is as much a social as a political obligation. At Versailles during the reign of Louis XIV, the courtiers were required to play cards and scratch on doors with the little fingers of their left hands. Their knowledge in these matters proved their intimate acquaintance with affairs at court. In Washington the resident magi accomplish a similar purpose by writing texts for the op-ed pages of *The New York Times* and *The Washington Post* and by making politely wistful remarks about the passing of the imperial presidency. Most of the advice is useless, but it is expensive and ornamental, and it pays the new President the extravagant compliment of pretending that he is free to do with the government as he pleases.

The new President, of course, can do no such thing. The mandate that Mr. Reagan received from the voters in November vanishes, after his inauguration in January, into realms of theory and illusion. If he can put together a congressional majority, he achieves the freedom to decide a course of events; if not, he remains free to ride in limousines, wave at the crowds in the streets, and go to Kay Graham's dinner parties. No matter what his political origins, a new President takes the oath of office as an outlander, a representative of the American people (unknown and presumed hostile) in opposition to the permanent government. He can make a few thousand appointments at the higher levels, but he cannot shift the weight of the oxlike bureaucracy; a substantial percentage of the federal budget remains committed to the service of prior debt (i.e., prior intimations of freedom), and Poland cannot be moved to the safety of the Caribbean.

The Washington magi like to say that the United States is ungovernable, that no president or administration can impose a consensus on so many confused and popular definitions of freedom. By this they mean that between elections the American people resist the freedoms claimed by government.

The permanent government defines freedom not as intelligence or creativity, but as power. Given their institutional allegiances as well as the urgency of their own ambitions, the official classes identify the national interest with the several interests of the state, rather than with the multifarious interests of the individuals subsumed under the rubric of "the American people." The magi acquire their opinions for reasons of policy or preference, as if these were gilt swords or enameled snuffboxes, bought, at modish prices, from the artificers at the Hoover Institution or the Institute for Policy Studies. Different objects come into vogue with different seasons and administrations. The accomplished magi can make a successful appearance at court whether his thought is clothed in a Democratic or a Republican style.

The United States arose as a force in the world because it forced people to confront the power of their own intelligence. The American achievement can be described as the removal of obstacles from the dreaming mind, and its greatest resource has consisted not in its wheat fields or salmon fisheries but in the imagination and effort of its people. Even now the United States earns $5.5 billion a year in fees for the use of its patents, which are not of nobility but of invention. Talking about a government "of the people, by the people, and for the people," Lincoln defined liberty not as the freedom to exploit but as the freedom to make and think and build. Later in the nineteenth century Mark Twain described as "the makers of the earth after God" those people who discovered how to make grass grow where none had grown before, who invented steam engines, medical procedures, and electric light.

So humble a definition of freedom apparently has gone out of fashion. The Washington magi inevitably talk about number and weight—barrels of oil, the money supply—always about material and seldom about human resources; about things, not about people. The prevailing bias conforms to the national prejudice in favor of institutions rather than individuals, to the rule of money rather than the dominance of mind. To the extent that individuals come to depend upon institutions for their validity as human beings as well as their livelihood, so also do they measure the success of their existence by titles and badges of office. The advice published in newspapers always carries with it the testimonial of an official rank. Monsieur D. once served a deputy secretary of state; Professor N. teaches economics at Harvard; former minister C. has received a patent of nobility from the Ford Foundation. Without proof of an institutional affiliation, the advice would be judged worthless.

The perfect freedom claimed by the state gives rise to the dream of national sovereignty, which is the illusion of freedom extended into the arenas of foreign policy. In the name of this freedom the nations of the earth beggar themselves with the buying of weapons. In Sebastopol and West Virginia the people rot, their patchwork hopes of freedom sacrificed to the mud of ignorance and poverty in order that the magi in Moscow and Washington may enjoy the freedom of geopolitics. Perhaps this cannot be helped. The larger a nation's ambit in the world, the more likely it will be forced to abandon its principles. No American President takes pleasure in the burning to death of children, and yet Woodrow Wilson, as well as Franklin Roosevelt, Harry Truman, and Richard Nixon, found himself obliged to do so.

But in the absence of a moral explanation, which as yet the United States has been unable to phrase, the freedom of the state becomes confused with the freedom to exploit. When the late Shah of Iran was asked to leave the United States, Mr. David Rockefeller and Mr. Henry Kissinger spoke of his ill-treatment as a "moral outrage." This was perhaps true, but Messrs. Rockefeller and Kissinger neglected to express a similarly humanitarian feeling for the lesser clients of American policy. Neither of them said anything about the boat people floating off the coast of Vietnam, about the peasants left on the roof of the embassy in Saigon, about the guerrillas betrayed in Kurdistan. Of the four or five hundred members of the higher councils of the American foreign policy establishment, maybe a hundred had met, courted, or exchanged pleasantries with the Shah. It is doubtful that any of those same people had met a Vietnamese sergeant or a woman tortured by the government in Nicaragua.

Recognizing themselves as interchangeable and easily replaced, if not by this administration then by the next, the magi learn to do whatever is asked, and they take comfort only in their common cause against the heathen outside the gates. No matter what the election result in November, the interests of the American voters will give way to the wishes of the magi who come bearing gifts of napalm, sophism, and gold. The voters fight battles, not sieges, and the permanent government knows that given time enough and maybe another diversion in the Middle East, its collective interest will prevail.

HARPER'S MAGAZINE,
*February 1981*

# FEET OF CLAY

**D**URING THE WEEK of President Reagan's inauguration, in the midst of the parades and the days of national thanksgiving and the band music and the untying of yellow ribbons, I wondered why the country should want to celebrate a defeat as if it had been a victory. Perhaps it was because the return of the hostages from Iran coincided so closely with Mr. Reagan's remark in his inaugural address that "we are a nation under God, and I believe God intended for us to be free." A week later, welcoming the hostages on the White House lawn, Mr. Reagan rose to the occasion with the defiant rhetoric of what newspaper columnists were describing as a resurgent and assertive United States. "Let terrorists be aware," Mr. Reagan said, "that when the rules of international behavior are violated, our policy will be one of swift and effective retribution."

But the hostages had returned from Iran on terms as meager as a convict's hope, and as the celebration began to acquire the characteristics of a frenzied binge it became increasingly difficult to pretend that their homecoming had been a triumph. Like Mr. Reagan's speeches, the joyful noise had a hollow sound. People did what they could to hide the discovery of their weakness, concealing their fear behind the media's burbling about "heroes," behind the tax-deductible newspaper advertisements contributed by banks and department stores, behind the veils of ticker tape and the flights of balloons. As it was produced for television, the spectacle of American patriotism was not that of a nation assured of its strength. It looked more like the cheering of a mob shouting down a truth that it could not bear to hear. If only enough people would proclaim the defeat a victory, maybe the event could be magically transformed (if not by God, then by Alexander Haig or Frank Sinatra); maybe the world would go away again.

The hostages were let go when they no longer served the uses of extortion. The United States paid what amounted to a ransom of between $10 and $12 billion to a government doing business as a terrorist gang.

Arguing the case on its editorial page for what it called "a good deal for Americans," *The New York Times* refused to tolerate the use of the word *ransom*. "The money . . . is in no sense ransom," said the *Times*, protesting so loudly as to convince nobody but itself. The editorial went on to explain that the money belonged to Iran and that the Reagan Administration should not revoke the arrangement, because to do so would humiliate the Algerian intermediaries, risk the chance of reducing Iran to anarchy, and set a bad example for terrorists (as yet unknown), who might otherwise doubt the willingness of the United States to deliver suitcases filled with unmarked bills.

More rigorous students of the agreement pointed out (notably in *The New Republic*) that by giving up all claims arising from the seizure of the hostages and the embassy in Teheran, by vacating all existing claims and proceedings against Iranian interests in default of their contracts, and by agreeing to enforce in American courts the Iranian actions against the assets of the late Shah, the United States had not only paid a ransom but had also done serious harm to its constitutional principles.

The agreement signed in Algeria cast the United States, not the revolutionary regime in Iran, as the villain of the piece. The documents refer to "the 'detention' of fifty-two American 'nationals' " as if these were not individuals who enjoyed the international right to diplomatic immunity, and as if there might have been some legitimate pretext for their arrest. In its particulars as well as in its language, the agreement vindicated both the principle and practice of terrorism. How is it that so squalid a result comes by the name of victory?

In Wiesbaden, Jimmy Carter welcomed the hostages with a show of emotion and said that "terrorism has been proven not to pay." The lie was in character for Mr. Carter, as it was for the media that disguised the tragedy that had befallen the American republic with the melodrama of the hostages' escape from durance vile.

Of course terrorism had been made to pay, and pay very handsomely, even to the point of subverting the laws of the United States. An incident that began as a riot in an Iranian bazaar ended with American courts being asked to rearrange the principles of jurisprudence on behalf of a bankrupt foreign policy. Even as the deal was being closed, and as the hostages in Teheran ran the gauntlet of insult on their way to the airport, President Reagan in Washington was preaching the gospel of American exceptionalism, exhorting the faithful gathered to listen to his inaugural address to remember "how unique we really are." Later that evening, at one of the many dances held in Washington hotels, Andy Warhol said of Mr. Reagan's speech: "I loved it. It was just the way I feel."

During the 444 days that the hostages were held in captivity the American people behaved with exemplary restraint. The initial surge of anger, and the first demands for immediate action, subsided over a period of months into the patient hope that the Carter Administration could negotiate the return of the hostages. Even the failed commando raid in April of last year gave people reason to believe that the United States might be pursuing strategies other than those explained to the press. The national attitude of forbearance lasted through the entire term of the captivity, despite the news of Billy Carter's sleazy dealings with Libyan intermediaries and despite the imposition of the hostage question on the presidential campaign.

Unlike some of its figureheads, the American electorate had sense enough to acknowledge the limitations of power, to know that only a very strong or a very weak or a very foolish state can afford the luxury of cherishing unhealed wounds. Knowing that the United States bore some degree of responsibility for the despotism of the late Shah, and recognizing the country's dependence on foreign oil as well as the strategic ambitions of the Soviet Union in the Persian

Gulf, even the most belligerent of citizens could be persuaded to accede to the virtue of patience. It may have galled people to pay even a penny of tribute, but they understood that interests take precedence over feelings, that the conduct of foreign policy requires a talent for forgiving the unforgivable.

The hostages in Iran apparently endured their captivity with an equal measure of courage. Despite the sufferings inflicted on them, the hostages retained their sense of proportion as well as their strength of mind. Quoting a proverb told to him by the Spanish ambassador, Bruce Laingen said, "Patience is a bitter cup that only the strong can drink."

But when the hostages walked off the plane in Algeria, and later, when they walked off another plane in Newburgh, New York, they had become celebrities, and a celebrity, as everybody knows, is an immortal. For 444 days the American people had proved their collective steadiness of nerve. Within a matter of hours their good sense vanished in the smoke of red, white, and blue fireworks. In the confusion of camera angles the substance of republican virtue dissolved into magical incantation and desperate wish.

At their first press conference the hostages tried to distance themselves from the wish to make of them public statues, but their disclaimers couldn't prevail against the waving of flags. Jimmy Carter said that the United States would never do "any favors for the hoodlums who persecuted our innocent heroes." Vidal Sassoon announced that he was providing a year's free supply of beauty products for the hostages; the commissioner of baseball presented them with lifetime passes to Yankee Stadium; somebody else offered sides of beef, and the agents met the buses at West Point with the usual book and television deals.

Under the glare of the television lights, with the hometown politicians marching behind the color guard and the neighbors opening bottles of champagne, nobody thought to observe that if the hostages were heroes they were heroes in Woody Allen's sense of the word, that is, victims bedazzled by fate. Once the music stopped they would resemble the cast in one of Mr. Allen's comedies—a constellation of newly formed media stars wearing designer jeans and clutching tickets to the World Series, around their feet a policy in ruins, a principle obliterated, and the patriotic tinsel blowing away in the wind.

Nor did anybody want to say that the prisoners of war who had suffered far worse torture in North Vietnam returned, almost as anonymously as they had left, to a cheap Chinese banquet in San Francisco. Nor was there much mention of the eight airmen killed in last April's raid in the Iranian desert, who remained as obscure as the 50,000 American dead in Indochina.

In a week of dispatches from the nation's pulpits and editorial pages, few people counted the cost of making idols. In Washington, General Haig announced that the suppression of "international terrorism" had become a primary objective of American foreign policy, replacing "human rights" as a rallying cry for the proponents of justice and order. He failed to make the corollary point that by forging alliances with bloody-minded tyrants in the provinces of the Third World, the United States denied the moral principle supposedly at the root of its joyous thanksgiving.

Because their names had become known, because they had acquired faces and the bits and pieces of a life suitable for framing in *People* magazine, the fifty-two celebrities had become the nation's hostages to fortune. To the extent that popular feeling can outweigh strategic, economic, and political questions, so also has the United States no choice but to pay the next ransom asked for the next ambassador—or the next embassy chauffeur—taken prisoner on a road four miles east of the PX. How much of the future, belonging to how many people as yet unknown, does the United States thus mortgage to its passionate denial of time present? If the week's patriotic tableaux can be said to have been staged for the benefit of children, whose children will be asked to pay the price of admission in time future?

The effusion of patriotic sentiment was also a way of giving voice to the palpable relief from guilt. As a nation the United States has not yet had to acquire the fortitude exacted of Israel, and a majority of the American people remain unwilling to accept the price of liberty. The Israeli government long ago declared it a matter of policy to respond with military force to any taking of hostages. If an airliner is hijacked, a village captured, or a class of schoolchildren seized at gunpoint, the Israelis make the attempt at rescue. They do so automatically, without qualification and without placing a higher value on the lives of the hostages than on the principle of refusing to negotiate with terrorists. If the lives of the hostages can be saved, all well and good; if not, not.

American opinion cannot bear the weight of so terrible a necessity. Knowing this to be true (instinctively, not because anybody took a poll), most people in the country understood that the United States could have left the hostages in Iran for twenty years. Hence the collective feeling of guilt and hence the spasm of thanksgiving when the dilemma resolved itself. Given the chance to buy its comfort instead of being made to earn its freedom, the country lavished its rewards on people whom it knew it had failed.

The victory of the terrorists in Iran, as well as the denial of it in the United States, constitutes a giant step forward—not for the aspirations of mankind but for the regressive and criminal powers nudging the world, like a bear with a ball, into the pit of anarchy. But the United States doesn't want to recognize so melancholy a fact; doesn't want to know, in Winston Churchill's phrase, that the stones have begun to break beneath its feet; doesn't want to look the world in the face and see it for what it has become.

American foreign policy for the last thirty-five years has been dedicated to the pretense that everything has remained as it was in 1945, and certainly this was the spirit of the gala entertainment staged by Mr. Sinatra on the night before Mr. Reagan's inauguration. Aside from its vulgarity, the entertainment was notable for the performers' ages. The more prominent members of the troupe (among them Messrs. Hope and Carson, Charlton Heston, Ethel Merman, and Brigadier General James Stewart) belonged, like Mr. Reagan, to a generation that came of age before the Second World War, in a United States apparently as isolated from the rest of the world as the hero of an onanist's dream. The voices of the past sang of a world restored to the hygienic tidiness of an Eden on an MGM back lot. Seated in overstuffed armchairs, their demeanor vaguely reminiscent (in a comfortable, bourgeois way) of presiding royalty, Mr. and Mrs. Reagan smiled indulgently on the Step 'n' Fetchit routine of a black actor dressed up to look like a dim-witted Negro minstrel. They applauded the tasteless jokes of Bob Hope and Johnny Carson, and listened fondly to Mr. Sinatra singing, in a false and wheezing voice, "America the Beautiful."

The so-called new international order, about which a generation of statesmen issued complacent communiqués, was presumably to have transformed the dealings between nation-states into something comparable to a New England town meeting. Events unfortunately took a somewhat different course. Rather than confront a future in which the Iranian incident might prove to be merely one of a sequence of incidents, the United States consoles itself with increasingly romantic fairy tales. As the prospect grows bleaker, the lies attract more eloquent champions, most of them as eager to delude themselves as to calm the ladies and gentlemen in the $100 seats.

The Vietnam War was a defeat, but Henry Kissinger pronounced it a political victory and received, with Le Duc Tho, the Nobel Peace Prize. The policy of détente constituted a further defeat, a raffling off of American assets for whatever they would bring (in the way of time or comfort or illusion) in a thieves' market. For this Mr. Kissinger was proclaimed a man of genius. Even the emergence of the OPEC oil cartel was explained as a victory of sorts at first—a peaceful realignment of the world's wealth and a gesture of atonement toward the illiterate, the impoverished, and the dark-skinned peoples of the earth.

Each capitulation was supposedly to have made the world a safer and happier place; each resulted in the world becoming that much more dangerous. In the early 1960s the United States depended on volunteer heroes in the Peace Corps and the Green Berets. When heroism turned out to be too expensive, as it did in Vietnam, the United States resorted to the "brilliant diplomacy" of the Nixon-Kissinger regime. Not the least of the concerns that led to the entente with China was the apparent absence of any human or financial cost.

When brilliant diplomacy lost its breathless charm, the United States sought its salvation in alliances with the exploited nations of the "South," trying to prove its benevolence by the purity of its soul rather than by the caliber of its weapons. Now we make heroes of fumbling civil servants who, in imitation of Woody Allen's innocents, neglect to defend an embassy and forget to burn the files.

HARPER'S MAGAZINE,
*April 1981*

# ABDUCTION OF THE MAID OF WARSAW

**P**ROGRAM NOTES FOR *this evening's performance at the Kennedy Center.*

ACT 1: *Throne Room of the Imperial Palace.* The Tsar and Tsarina seated in state, attended by noble lords, ladies, military commanders, congressmen, professors of economics, oracles, jesters. A court ball is in progress. Brilliant costumes; glittering lights and movement; waltz music.

The corps de ballet dances Tableaux Vivants, representing happy scenes of American prosperity. Rubato, the Tsar's minstrel (Frank Sinatra), sings "La Via Mia," the famous ode to free enterprise.

Drums and alarms. A messenger enters and falls, dying, on a divan. The music drops into a tremulous minor. The messenger says that the Maid of Warsaw has been abducted by the infidel Turk. She was on her way to marry the Prince of Thuringia when she was seized in the forest by Janissaries. Animated consternation among the assembled notables; gentlemen make congressional gestures; ladies let fall their fans. Orlando Furiosio, captain of the guard (Alexander Haig), sings the famous aria "Dov'e Andata La Liberta?" He rushes offstage, followed by press agents.

The orchestra plays a fanfare for brass and percussion, and the corps de ballet assumes a set of military postures accompanied by a musical comedy arrangement of a Chopin polonaise. The Tsar and Tsarina descend from the throne and move gracefully among the guests, assuring them that all will be well. They sing the famous duet "Let Poland Be Poland." Nobody knows what this means. The dancers improvise a scene of drunken peasants carousing at the spring vodka festival. The act concludes with the famous march "Torn'alla Seconda Guerra Mondiale."

ACT 2: *A military camp in the Black Forest, six months later.* The Imperial expedition force has halted for consultations. Orlando, still dressed in resplendent court uniform, rushes on and off the stage, sword upraised, singing loudly in Italian. Everybody else sings in German. Confusion of voices takes the form of sixteenth-century church music, a sequence of fugues and canons sung in polyphonic combination by a chorus of statesmen, central bankers, weapons analysts, newspaper columnists, and credit managers. Rubato sings a reprise of "La Via Mia."

More messengers arrive and depart; soldiers carry guns from stage right to stage left; accountants carry ledgers from stage left to stage right; gypsies light campfires and buxom girls flirt outrageously with heavily mustached subalterns. The melancholy choral singing lasts for three hours, all of it devoted to the translation of the Polish debt into Swiss francs, Japanese yen, and Saudi Arabian riyals.

Suddenly the music swells to a crescendo; darkness descends; lightning glares in the forest, and Beglerbeg, who's escaped from the castle in California, appears in stage manager's smoke at the edge of the camp. Beglerbeg (Henry Kissinger) once befriended the Knights of the Third Crusade singing ponderously in rhymed hexameters. Beglerbeg offers to show the Imperial army the secret road to the castle in which the Maid of Warsaw lies captive. In return for this service, Beglerbeg demands a reward of 80,000 gold florin and the assurance that his image will be published in all the stained glassed windows in Christendom.

Appalled by Beglerbeg's cynicism and treachery, Orlando resigns his commission and tears his golden uniform into a thousand pieces.

He declares his love for Fatima, the gypsy princess (Jane Fonda), and together they sing the famous duet "Dov'e Andato L'Onore."

ACT 3: *The Imperial Palace, two years later.* The court ball continues as before, attended by the same suite of nobles. Beglerbeg has become captain of the guard. He wears black velvet tights, a turban, and an ermine cloak. The Maid of Warsaw has died and been transformed into a symbol of freedom. Nobody remembers what she looked like, but everybody knows that she was very, very beautiful and that her story was very, very sad. She appears— together with the lost maidens of Afghanistan, East Germany, Nicaragua, El Salvador, Angola, Cuba, Hungary, Czechoslovakia, and Lithuania—as one of the variations danced by the corps de ballet in the traditional hymn to democracy performed every night for three hundred nights during presidential election years. It is this dance that is in progress when another messenger enters and falls, dying, on the divan reserved for this purpose. He says the insolent Turk has taken the Maid of Panama. The opera ends as the court dissolves into its ceremonial alarm and as Rubato sings the second reprise of "La Via Mia."

*The funding for this evening's performance was provided by grants from Charlton Heston,* The New York Review of Books, *Lou Grant, and the American Heritage Foundation.*

THE WASHINGTON POST,
*February 1982*

# REALPOLITIK

$\mathbb{A}$FTER DINNER THE other night in the company of informed sources, most of them journalists or professors of political science, I heard a gentleman say patiently, as if to a backward child: "Come now, Howard, you don't seriously expect us to believe that you bleed for the cause of the peasants in El Salvador?"

Howard had been so gauche as to make a leftist argument denouncing American intervention on behalf of what he described as a murderous gang of thugs. Citing dispatches from the Catholic Church authorities, he had remarked on the way in which the Salvadoran treasury police routinely executed, without reason or provocation, innocent citizens standing quietly in city streets. His defense of "human rights" moved the notables seated around the table to a faint and scornful smiling. Most of them belonged to the neoconservative school of gunboat diplomacy. They had read Machiavelli, written briefing papers for President Reagan, endorsed the realpolitik of Ambassador Jeane J. Kirkpatrick at the United Nations and knew the difference between authoritarian and totalitarian states.

Intimidated by the weight of the opposition, Howard retired into a silence so sheepish that it would have done credit to one of the Democratic presidential candidates. For the next ten or fifteen minutes, I was free to imagine that I was in the presence of hard-eyed geopoliticians wise in the ways of empire, staunch advisers willing to send thousands to their deaths in pursuit of the national interest.

**264**

The illusion faded when they began to revile the Soviet Union for the shooting down of a South Korean airliner over the Sea of Japan.

The same professor who had been so disdainful of Howard's "naive romanticism" proved himself capable of equally romantic statements of faith. Banging his spoon on a plate, he demanded to know why the United States didn't take sterner measures against the Soviet ogres who so wantonly murdered 269 civilians in the midst of their innocent passage to Seoul. He was seconded in his outrage by most of the others present, many of them raising their voices to urge displays of military force and the breaking off of the Geneva talks, the expulsion of diplomats, the interdiction of the grain trade, and above all, the punishing of criminals who violated the norms of human decency.

Their indignation prompted me to wonder about the accuracy of their logic. By what measure of virtue did their definition of justice attain a higher rank than that of the doe-eyed Howard? If the destruction of a Korean plane and the deaths of 269 people could ignite in them the flame of moral passion, then why did the political killing of much larger numbers of people, not only in El Salvador, but also in Chile, Lebanon, Indonesia, and most of the other countries in the world, fail to excite in them so much as a spark of sympathy? How was it possible that they could bleed for Korean businessmen while Howard couldn't bleed for Salvadoran peasants?

None of them believed that the attack on the airliner was a deliberate act of policy. None believed that the incident signified the advent of World War III. Clearly it was a blunder—the result of Soviet clumsiness and stupidity combined with habitual Russian xenophobia and the characteristic Soviet talent for third-rate bureaucracy.

But if this was so, then why such an expanse of sentiment? Instead of being alarmed by the proof of Soviet incompetence, which, given the weapons available to pilots unable to distinguish between a 747 and an RC-145, seems to me a reasonable cause for concern, why would men who prided themselves on their tough-mindedness get so distraught over the loss of a few hundred people caught unaware in the machinery of the Cold War?

Their militant hyperbole reminded me of the different ways in which the polite newspapers report murders in Scarsdale and murders in Spanish Harlem. Assuming that the Scarsdale killing takes place at a good address and the victim, preferably female, belongs to a family socially prominent and decently rich, news of the crime remains on the front page for as long as the ingenuity of the press can contrive fresh speculation. News of an otherwise identical crime committed in economy class on East 134th Street seldom receives as much as two inches of type on page B-13 in an early edition.

When violent death comes to the prosperous suburbs, it comes clanking into the room dressed in Darth Vader's black armor, a terrible apparition born of trolls and risen from the abyss. Seen in the remote distance of the Third World, death loses its hideous visage and wears the livery of a meek and courteous statistic. The American papers didn't make much of a complaint about the 3 million Cambodians murdered by a regime that enjoyed the backing of the United States at the United Nations; nor was there much attention assigned to the killing of a few thousand Vietnamese boat people. On Sunday afternoons in Chile and Guatemala, law-abiding families vanish as abruptly from sight as did the law-abiding passengers en route to South Korea.

By thinking that the world should conform to their own moral specifications, a good many Americans confuse the rules of civilization with the laws of nature. Thus, as in Lebanon now, it is seldom clear whom the Americans mean to punish for what crime against which dream of human perfection. The failure to make distinctions allows the country to fight wars not against men but against devils.

LOS ANGELES TIMES,
*October 1983*

# DESERT SONG

SOONER OR LATER we may expect to see Yasir Arafat presented to American public opinion as The Desert Prince. Handsome Yasir Arafat, his beard trimmed in the Saudi manner and his photographs retouched to bring forward the likeness to King Hussein or Omar Sharif; heroic Yasir Arafat, his youth and early sorrow as a terrorist overlaid with the same romantic glaze that made of Menachem Begin's criminal escapades a proof of his patriotism; debonair Yasir Arafat, seen dancing at the Kennedy Center and gliding with other celebrities through the pages of *Vogue* and *Town and Country.*

American opinion insists on the fiction that relations between states belong to the same category of feeling and behavior that governs relations between individuals. It isn't that the United States won't do business with despots but rather that the United States first must persuade itself of the despot's innate goodness. The ally of a well-meaning democracy becomes overnight a well-meaning democrat.

In 1941 the United States allied itself with Stalinist Russia, as murderous a regime as has contributed its weight of crime to the sum of human suffering. But on the stage of American opinion, Josef Stalin appeared as good old Uncle Joe, the friend of small children, the savior of his country, the hero of the north, Harry Truman's "decent guy."

In 1972 President Nixon rediscovered China, declaring inoperative the official American truth that made the Chinese communists synonymous with the hounds of hell. Accompanied by a flourish of pageantry and seconded by the scholars of the press, Nixon in Beijing proclaimed the uncanny resemblance between the Chinese Revolution of 1949 and the American Revolution of 1776.

Because an ally must also be a friend, somebody with whom it is possible to talk about car pools and suburban lawns, the explication of American diplomacy is largely a matter of appraising the moral beauty of foreign political objects. The custodians of the national policy bear comparison to art dealers. They price the country's once and future friends in the market of ethical perfection. Instead of haggling about the relative values of Pissarro and Paul Klee, they ask whether Bokassa is more wicked than Amin, whether Pol Pot is as corrupt as Pinochet or Zia, whether the late Shah of Iran now commands a higher price than Ayatollah Khomeini.

These calculations provide steady employment for innumerable analysts, professors, and State Department spokesmen, but they ignore Charles de Gaulle's dictum that a "great nation has no friends." A sleepless, opportunistic, and necessarily ruthless entity, a state has neither a soul, a conscience, an enemy, nor a friend. It possesses only interests that, as Lord Palmerston once observed, are both eternal and perpetual.

Cavour made much the same point on behalf of the lesser nations (a point not lost on the current anarchs of the Third World) when, on being asked in 1859 to describe the diplomatic purpose of the newly unified Italy, he said: "It will be to astonish the world with our ingratitude."

The blood of the middle-class democracy isn't cold enough for such clarity, and so the state's appraisers continue to affix certificates of friendliness.

The Reagan Administration has deepened the amiable blush on the Chinese communists, entrusting them with weapons as well as compliments, and the generals in Argentina, Chile, and Brazil have been granted the benefit of a sentimental distinction between an authoritarian and a totalitarian regime.

But Arafat remains, at least officially, an unsalable commodity. President Anwar el Sadat did what he could for the fellow when he passed through Washington last week, but his suggestions were dismissed with indignation and contempt.

No, no, said Reagan and Haig, the United States cannot and will not speak with the PLO, not until the PLO recognizes Israel's right to exist and joins with America's many other friends in the Middle East in the wish to live in peace behind safe frontiers.

Not having frontiers behind which to enjoy the blessing of peace, the Palestinians make no secret of their preference for the simpler pleasures of conquest, subversion, and revenge. Nor do they want to give up their cherished hatred of the Jews.

It is this intransigence that disqualifies them as prospective guests at the White House—not because they couldn't make polite remarks about Jimmy Galanos or the second baseball season, but because they combine their fanaticism with weakness. A small-time despotism cannot set too high a price on its friendship.

Even so, it is conceivable that the nation's appraisers might yet discover beauty in the PLO's primitive chic. The newspapers these days show Arafat as a smiling and "moderate" figure.

Arafat may yet become, if not a friend, at least a close acquaintance. When it was more confident of its strength in the world, the United States took the trouble to befriend only those despots who did their killing on the scale of the baroque. To the extent that Arafat becomes more lovely, his rise in value will reflect the shift, both in American taste and power, toward an appreciation of minimalist art.

THE WASHINGTON POST,
*August 1981*

# REQUIEM

---

LAST WEEK'S STAGING of the apotheosis of Anwar Sadat did as little honor to the late President of Egypt as it did to the American promoters of the spectacle. The eulogists seemed to be speaking primarily about themselves, about the geopolitical fantasies dear to the self-esteem of the United States, rather than about the circumstances of a killing in a police state. The chorus of anguished voices acclaimed Sadat a prophet and a saint.

As might have been expected, it was left to Henry Kissinger, little friend to all the great ones of the earth, to bestow the most fulsome praise. Writing in *Time* magazine, Kissinger described Sadat as "a miracle of creation," "a very great man" as immortal as the pyramids, who "transformed the world by an act of will, shaping history according to his own vision."

In death as in life, Sadat suffered the weakness of his friends in Washington. As they had done with the Shah of Iran (also known to Kissinger, as well as to Presidents Ford, Carter, and Nixon, as a visionary, a man of peace, a great statesman, and a champion of civilization, etc., etc.), Sadat's American mourners strewed his coffin with flowers of ignorance and fear. Despite geopolitical braggadocio and loud talk about getting tough with the Russians, the makers of American foreign policy wish to be cared for, to be told, again and again, that the United States is the most wonderful, the bravest, the happiest nation ever blessed by the light of the sun. In return for such reassurances, the United States rewards its suite of flatterers with gifts of wheat, flour, AWACS, F14s, and little boxes of Henry Kissinger's scented prose.

**270**

The record suggests that Sadat was a competent despot, a military dictator less bloodthirsty than the Shah or Ayatollah Khomeini, not as cruel or as sybaritic as the Saudis, not as much of a fanatic as the rulers of Syria, Libya, and Iraq. All in all, as satisfactory an Arab client as the United States is likely to find.

He was a brave man with a talent for political intrigue and the courage to carry out his stratagems while balancing, like a circus artist, over the anger of the Egyptian mob. He was charming, intelligent, subtle, and resolute. Softly and with a courtier's smile, he persuaded four American presidents that he represented their last best hope against whatever it was they most feared in the Middle East.

He was also an ambitious and practical-minded despot who presided over a docile legislature and arrested as many of his enemies as he thought convenient. During World War II he collaborated with the Nazis against the British. His eulogists remarked on his admiration for Mahatma Gandhi, but they neglected to mention his equally fervent regard for Adolf Hitler. Twice arrested by the British on suspicion of murder and terrorism, Sadat served four years in jail, then in 1952 joined with Gamal Abdel Nasser in the overthrow of King Farouk. When it suited the romance of Egyptian nationalism, Sadat allied himself with the Soviet Union; when this line of policy was played out, he turned toward the Americans. He took up the cause of peace when he knew himself ill-equipped for war.

In the four years since Sadat went to Jerusalem, the voices of intransigence have been strengthened in Israel and in the Arab states; Lebanon has been destroyed; the Palestinian question has not been resolved; the United States has increased its shipments of arms to all the region's generals; and the American presence in Egypt (complete with five hundred diplomats, several dozen military advisers, and a heavily fortified embassy) has come to resemble the former imperial strongholds in Teheran and Saigon. By making the gestures of peace, Sadat earned for Egypt almost $7 billion in economic assistance since 1975, as well as $2 billion in weapons.

In 1937 Franklin D. Roosevelt could say of a murderous Latin American dictator that, yes, the fellow was a son of a bitch, but at least he was our son of a bitch. In the intervening forty-four years, the United States has lost the confidence necessary to so aristocratic a statement of policy. Instead of patronizing dictators, the United States looks to them as a child would look to its nurse—for protection, admiration, and love. The figure of the generalissimo stands on watch against the darkness at the head of the stairs.

THE WASHINGTON POST,
*October 1981*

# THE LOST
# AMERICAN EMPIRE

WRITING LAST MONTH in *The Atlantic* on what has become the ubiquitous topic of American economic decline, James Fallows tells a story about Senator John Danforth of Missouri, who went to Paris with his wife in the summer of 1977 and discovered, to his wonder and surprise, that the Japanese had money.

"It was unbelievable," Fallows quotes the senator as saying. "We went into the Gucci shop. There were Japanese people buying Gucci suitcases to carry home their new Gucci bags. We saw one Japanese family that had bought a Gucci suitcase for each member of the family, to hold all the other items. One Japanese man was standing there with bags hanging all over his arms. I said to Sally, 'Something's going on!' "

The tone of injured innocence in the senator's voice epitomizes the nature of the present obsession with the national fall from grace. There was the senator, in Paris, a man of substance and reputation in what he had thought was the richest nation in the world, and here were these small and anonymous Japanese making him look cheap. How could such things be? Didn't the sales clerk know that in Washington the senator's merest word attracted a crowd of admiring lobbyists, that his vote on matters of tax and weapons policy might mean the difference between peace and war? What was the world coming to? Was there no end to the humiliations being inflicted on the United States by ungrateful foreigners? How could he explain it to Sally?

For the last three years it seems that everybody with access to a microphone or the print media has been trying to explain it to Sally. In New York and Washington, it is all but impossible to avoid a conversation about the decline and fall of empire. The literary classes have been dwelling on themes of decay for at least a decade, but in the presidential campaign of 1980 even the politicians mourn the passing of the American dream. None of the candidates likes to use the word *empire*—possibly because it has an undemocratic sound to it, or maybe because their advisers don't want them to lose more than 20,000 votes a day—but they talk as if such a thing once existed, a broad expanse of lawns and mutual defense treaties that, through a sequence of accidents and apostasies, has been allowed to grow rank with weeds. The press magnifies the image of despair and babbles about lost American supremacy in both the temporal and spiritual realms of being—about failures of American arms (in Indochina and Iran), about the foreign occupation of domestic consumer markets, about the defeat of capitalism (in Guatemala and Detroit), about the collapse of the moral scaffolding on which their forebears erected the monuments of freedom.

Everybody has a different proof for the theorem of decline; they employ different euphemisms for empire and offer different sets of statistics in substantiation of what public opinion polls reflect as a consensus of disappointment. Military officers dispatch urgent letters to the newspapers, measuring the size and superiority of the Soviet arsenal, worrying about the insufficiency of American missiles and the illiteracy of American troops. Admiral Thomas Moorer (Ret.), formerly the Chairman of the Joint Chiefs of Staff, recently characterized the United States Army as "the largest grammar school in the world." Evangelists decry the "secular humanism" infecting the body politic, and they attribute the sorrows of the Republic to homosexuals and to the absence of the Bible from the curricula in the public schools. Economists and corporation presidents talk about the rate of inflation and the ransom paid for foreign oil (a sum now estimated at $90 billion a year). As might be expected in a presidential year, the candidates accept the verdicts of the polls, blame one another for the godless state of affairs, and campaign on a promise of empire regained.

Americans have a talent for self-dramatization, and they like to think that the United States belongs at the center of the world's discussion. If the country cannot play the part of the world's hero, then it will make do with the part of the world's victim or the world's fool. The most eloquent disquisitions on the decline of empire take place at the luxurious resort hotels in which universities, charitable foundations, and various agencies of the federal government sponsor a never-ending festival of seminars, symposia, and five-day conferences addressed to the solemn questions of the age. Few of the participants doubt that the United States should be deferred to by the lesser nations of the earth, that it deserves to be, as the sports-writers like to say, number one. The confusion descends on the conversation when people try to define the basis of the American preeminence. Should the United States be compared to Rome under the medieval popes, or does it more properly bear comparison to England in the nineteenth century? Was the lost empire temporal or spiritual? Is America a religion or a state?

Not that the answers to any of these questions would help explain it to Sally, but the belief in a lost empire (or in something very much like an empire) pervades so much of public conversation that it gets in the way of thinking about what else might be said. The record suggests that there never was an American empire, at least not in the conventional sense of the word as it pertains to the Roman, Byzantine, British, Ottoman, Spanish, French, and Russian empires. Americans do not possess the imperial habit of mind, and they never have developed an exalted doctrine of the state that would allow them to govern, with an easy conscience, conquered peoples and nations. The conquest of the frontier required the clearing of an empty and abundant wilderness in which the settlers could project, and perhaps construct, their individual dreams of Eden. The military academy at West Point was established in 1802 as an engineering school because the Army was expected to build roads and bridges rather than to administer provinces and fight foreign wars. When the United States bought the Louisiana territories from the French, I doubt whether many people in Washington thought to ask about the people already resident on the property. On their way west the Americans killed Indians, or buffalo, or passenger pigeons, or anything else that stood in the way of their interest or ambition, but they seldom killed for reasons of state. They found their empire in the continental United States, crossing the succession of frontiers as nomadic bands, not as conquering legions.

Toward the end of the nineteenth century, the United States entertained briefly the imperial pretensions attendant upon the Spanish-American War, but mostly these consisted of florid speeches and not very strenuous campaigns against the weakest of the old European empires. Within ten years of acquiring the Philippines, Americans found that imperialism wasn't as much fun as Teddy Roosevelt foretold, and they began to think of a decent way to grant the natives their independence. At the Treaty of Versailles in 1919 the United States, in the person of Woodrow Wilson, gave nobody the impression that it wanted to rule the world, which was perhaps a foolish thing to have done but not an act of empire. During the years between the wars American interest remained firmly fixed on things American, and if the United States intervened at will in Caribbean or Latin American politics, that was because the Western Hemisphere so clearly belonged within the sphere of its commercial interest that nobody thought to raise the questions of policy with the household servants. George F. Babbitt knew little and thought less about the world beyond the oceans, and among the privileged and educated classes only a few eccentrics took up careers in the Navy or the State Department. In his memoirs George F. Kennan describes a man who joined the foreign service in order that his mother need not suffer the indignity of a baggage search when passing through customs.

The Second World War put an end to the American wish to be left alone, and within a matter of six years the United States had acquired, largely by invitation and default, the semblance of empire. Japan was in ruins, and so was Germany; China was in the midst of civil war; France had disintegrated, both as a nation and as the embodiment of an idea, and the British were so exhausted with the effort of imperial ambition that they voted Churchill out of office within two months of the German surrender. If in 1941 the American presence outside the Western Hemisphere consisted only of a few islands in the Pacific, by 1945 it bestrode the narrow world like a colossus, presiding over an arc of territories and client states that extended from Japan to the North Sea. Apologetic and polite, in most instances not knowing how to speak the language, the American proconsuls, most of whom had expected to become Wall Street lawyers and bond salesmen, found themselves commanding the Japanese emperor to forswear his deity, taking over the British oil concessions in Persia, supplying arms to Greece and grain to India, reorganizing the international monetary system, consenting to the establishment of the State of Israel, posting garrisons on the Danube and the Rhine.

Everywhere they went Americans were received by crowds of smiling people who welcomed them with flowers. Amidst the applause of Japanese militarists as well as Italian oligarchs, Americans had become masters of the earth. The trouble was that they didn't know quite what to do with it. Nor were they sure why they had been vouchsafed so magnificent a victory. Was it testimony to their military genius or was it a proof of divine favor? Americans get easily confused by the different orders of things, and their civil religion holds that God manifests Himself by bestowing success on those found worthy of His grace. Not being a historically minded people, Americans assumed that if there had been empires before the war, so also must there be empires after the war. It was somebody else's turn to run the world, and who was better qualified than the amiable and good-natured Americans? Their military triumph proved the moral superiority inherent in the idea of democracy. Who could not fail to turn away in disgust from the competing model of imperialism offered in the world's show windows by the Soviet Union?

In the beginning the United States was ripe with good intentions, and for a few years Americans worked at the improvement of the earth with the enthusiasm of college students painting tenements in the slums. They thought they could inspire the world by their generosity and virtuous example, and if they displayed a somewhat careless attitude toward the uses of power, perhaps that was because the victory had cost them so little. The Union armies in the American Civil War sustained heavier casualties than were sustained by all the combatants in all wars fought in Europe between 1815 and 1914, but the memory of suffering seldom lasts longer than a generation, and the United States lost fewer lives in the Second World War than the Union lost in the war against the Confederacy. To the extent that the American empire was an immaculate conception, the accident of a moment rather than the labor of centuries, it had the character of an inherited fortune.

What was remarkable about American supremacy was the speed with which the inheritance was squandered. Henry Luce's "American Century" lasted about as long as Hitler's 1,000-year Reich, and by the middle 1950s Americans already had begun to show signs of inattentiveness and ennui. The nearest they ever got to an imperial tone of voice was expressed in the phrase, "How much does it cost in real money?"

As early as 1953 President Eisenhower could say that the detonation of a single artillery shell took bread out of the mouths of starving children, which is both an admirable and accurate statement but not one that would have occurred to Napoleon. An authentically civilian nation had acceded reluctantly to military power, and as the exercise of that power proved to be an increasingly difficult and unpleasant task, the United States began to repudiate the temporal definitions of empire.

The tenuousness of the Pax Americana can be deduced from the hesitant efforts exerted to preserve it. An empire was all well and good as long as it didn't cost too much, and as long as too many people didn't get killed. In 1952 President Eisenhower was elected on the promise to break off the engagement in Korea, and by the end of the decade the merchant fleets had been sold to the Norwegians and the Greeks. The CIA managed successful subversions in Iran and Guatemala, but against Sukarno in Indonesia (surely one of the weakest despots of the age) the agency could do nothing. Most of its exploits had the character of a comedy of errors. Nor was the United States much good at cultivating client states or waging wars of ideology. By 1970 the monetary system had collapsed, and General Charles de Gaulle, who knew the difference between a real and an illusory empire, had withdrawn French troops from the NATO alliance and sold American currency for gold.

Mostly it was the war in Vietnam that convinced Americans that empire was a bad bargain. The war might have been begun for noble and humanitarian reasons, but it couldn't be supported with a doctrine of state; once it became apparent that the war was going to cost too much, both in money and blood, enthusiasm for it disappeared as quickly as the memory of last year's social injustice. If the Viet Cong could fight as well as American troops, then what happened to the belief in American prowess as a proof of American virtue? Surely if the American cause had been just, God would not have withheld His favor. Nobody regarded the defeat as an imperial humiliation, and by the middle 1970s the trappings of a world state had largely been torn away from the more fundamental idea of America as a religion and an attitude of mind.

President Nixon's attempts to extricate the United States from Indochina coincided with the enthusiasms of environmentalism and with the impulse toward federal regulation of the commercial interests supposedly pillaging the innocent earth. Small was beautiful (an aesthetic that doesn't fit very well with the idea of empire), and the avatars of all the world's evil shifted from their encampment abroad (among the Russians in the 1950s and the Chinese in the 1960s) to a testing ground within what David Riesman once called "the great American parish"—in corporations, the political system, the FBI. The spasm of guilt and recrimination that followed the Watergate inquiries made possible the election of Jimmy Carter, who promised to redeem the country, not to govern it. His pious evangelism embraced a foreign policy committed to raising the world's consciousness, and his ministers went to Africa and the United Nations to ask forgiveness and to explain to people that American military power was the cause of the world's tensions and instabilities.

I don't know what Senator Danforth said to Sally, but I hope he didn't give her the impression that there once was such a thing as an American empire. Even now, after forty years at the center of the world's stage, the United States has not acquired either the taste or the stomach for imperialism.

Conceivably this is a flaw in the national character. The British could hold together an empire for nearly two hundred years because they accepted their racial supremacy as a matter of doctrine. Like the British gentleman, the British soldier could think of the natives as "wogs," but in so motley a nation as the United States, who is not a wog? Under one or another of the prevailing definitions, one's neighbor is likely to be a wog. So also is one's congressman, partner, teammate, husband or wife.

Although not a warlike people, the Americans can be aroused to battle by a sense of alarm, outrage, or moral fervor. But the martial impulse is difficult to sustain and soon fades in the absence of an obvious and dramatic enemy. They prefer to be seen not as bullies but as pals—large and friendly people who subdue their enemies not with firing squads but with cigarettes and smiles and chocolate bars.

HARPER'S MAGAZINE,
*November 1980*

# PICTURES AT AN
# EXHIBITION

---

As RECENTLY AS two years ago, the wisest magi in Washington were saying that gunboat diplomacy was a thing of the past, that no matter how convenient to the national interest, or how flattering to the national honor, it was no longer practical to sail the imperial squadron into the heathen bay to force the recalcitrant sultan back to his duty of purveying ivory, gold, or slaves. What they seemed to have left out of their advice was the effect of modern communication. Given the technologies of the media, the recalcitrant sultan stands to gain almost as much from an exchange of images as the imperial admiral.

This would explain the theatrical nature of last week's aerial combat over the Libyan coast. When it is judged on its merits as dramatic presentation rather than as military exploit, President Reagan and Colonel Muammar Qaddafi appear as co-producers.

Because Libya and the United States have been engaged for some years in an undeclared conflict, the incident in the Gulf of Sidra clearly wasn't meant to alter the relations between the two states. Libya presumably will continue to sell to the United States 40 percent of its oil (worth $3.3 billion per annum) and to devote the revenues to jihads of international terrorism. The United States presumably will continue to buy the oil and denounce Libya as, in the words Secretary Haig is reported to have used, "a cancer that has to be removed."

Both countries, therefore, must have been playing to secondary audiences. Reagan wished to "make American power impressive to the enemies of freedom" and to set an example not so much before the Libyans (already deemed Barbary pirates) as before the Cubans, the Soviets, the Europeans, the Africans, and any of his own countrymen still suffering doubt and embarrassment as a result of the failures in Vietnam and Iran.

Qaddafi wished to rally Arab opinion to the standard of anti-imperialism. Libya also has suffered reverses in recent years, and the colonel needs to restore his image as an innocent victim deserving of sympathy and allies. Within Arab spheres of influence, the colonel has few friends and an unfortunate reputation as a zealous employer of assassins.

The Libyans have been molesting American aircraft for several years, and Reagan could count upon them to continue the practice if he sent a task force into the Gulf of Sidra. Naval intelligence undoubtedly assured Reagan of the inferiority of the Libyan aircraft as well as the Libyan incapacity to attack the Sixth Fleet. All in all, an eminently safe enemy—sufficiently villainous to deserve the wrath of eagles but sufficiently weak to be estimated by the Navy as a "low-risk operation."

From Qaddafi's point of view the United States presented itself as an equally desirable enemy. Here was a chance sent by a merciful Allah to remind the faithful that the embodiment of the world's evil had come to darken an Arab shore. His pilots had to make at least forty-five passes at the F14s before two of them managed to get shot down.

The combat lasted roughly sixty seconds, avoided the loss of a single life, and destroyed military property valued at less than a day's expenditure for the forty-three private armies now campaigning in Lebanon.

For so small a cost how large and dramatic an effect: by means of vivid imagery, Reagan and Qaddafi succeeded in arranging what in the old diplomatic parlance used to be described as "a full and frank exchange of views."

Given the competition for space and time in the international media, the staging of a border incident requires the talents of an impresario. Gunboat diplomacy can no longer be left to chance, to kings or desperate men. The event needs to be staged publicly, as an expression of symbolic feeling and not as the pursuit of mere interest. If this means that fewer incidents would demand the world's attention, it also means that the world's peace now rests with poets and actors, not with statesmen or admirals.

As an illustration of the point, I can see in my mind's eye an American naval officer somewhere in Washington standing in front of a large and handsome map of the eastern Mediterranean. His uniform is as impeccably starched as his self-assurance. In his hand he holds an elongated baton with which, tapping lightly, he points out fleets, distances, force levels, cities, troop and helicopter landings, roads, estimated times of arrival and departure. He speaks in a calm but rapid voice to an audience of senior officials seated in comfortable leather chairs. The few reporters present take elaborately polite notes. Every now and then the briefing officer pauses to accept questions from anybody to whom his portrait of Operation Eagle Feather might lack a subtlety of nuance, color, or perspective. A lieutenant commander suggests a touch of aircraft in the upper left-hand corner; a captain thinks the composition might be improved by the addition of two or three squares of Israeli armor.

For about twenty minutes it is almost possible to believe that the diagrams being deployed and redeployed across the unresisting surface of the map have something to do with reality. The trace elements of belief vanish when it becomes apparent that the briefing officer, a man in his early thirties, probably never has suffered the indignity of combat. Nor is it likely that he has met a terrorist, watched a child bleed to death, or seen any of the terrain that he so artfully describes. The reflection prompts me to remember President Carter's bungled expedition into the Iranian desert, President Reagan's mismanaged invasion of Grenada, the long list of expensive American weapons that don't work, the shambles of the military communications system through which it can take five hours for a message marked "urgent" to travel forty miles.

Before the briefing comes to its triumphant end—the operation a success, Qaddafi dead, America unbound, etc.—I know that I have been looking at another exhibition in the Pentagon's Gallery of Abstract Expressionism. The resident academicians talk about "American credibility in the world," about pride, symbolism, and the sending of signals; about perceptions, analogies, and the effects on Arab or Guatemalan opinion. Sometimes the conversation can get pretty refined. Early in January I heard a government official say of the Libyan state that he was depressed by "the quality of the regime." Listening only to the tone of his voice, it would have been possible to assume that he was talking about a second-rate wine or a Hyatt hotel gone to seed in a town no longer attractive to conventions of art dealers. The official wasn't concerned about Libya's capacity to harm the United States; its army was small and ill-equipped, its mineral assets not worth the cost of a first-class embassy. What troubled him was the squalor of Colonel Qaddafi's aesthetic.

The practitioners of the old gunboat diplomacy usually had a palpable object in view—oil, slaves, tin, bananas, the safety of the British consul, the amputation of the insolent pasha's right hand. The new forms of gunboat diplomacy have to do with words instead of things, with the symbol of power rather than its practical applications. Like the ancient Chinese diplomatists, the adepts in Washington mean to give rather than to take, to project images of their own magnificence rather than to seize the spoils of war.

Anybody still in doubt on this point can refer to the collected works of Admiral James D. Watkins, the Chief of Naval Operations and the author of the nation's maritime strategy, published by the U.S. Naval Institute. The admiral suggested that in the event of a conventional war between the United States and the Soviet Union, the American Navy might decide to eliminate the Russian submarine fleet. He presented a list of things to be done during the opening phases of the hostilities, among them: "Destroy the Soviet Navy; both important in itself and a necessary step for us to realize our objectives."

The statement is so patently and gloriously abstract that it might as easily have been entitled "Ink on Paper, No. 5." Given the proven incompetence of American military services, the Navy has about as much chance of destroying the Soviet Navy as it has of winning the Battle of Trafalgar. But this, of course, isn't the point, and to say something stupidly literal-minded about the admiral's maritime strategy would be like looking at one of Picasso's horses and asking why it has a blue head.

The admiral's gift for images brings to mind the story, preserved within the oral tradition of the British Foreign Office, of Captain Hornsby and his gunboat.

In the 1880s, when England was still an empire and Lord Salisbury the Prime Minister, a sultan somewhere in Africa committed an unspeakable offense against the canons of civilized behavior and the sovereignty of the British crown. Summoning Captain Hornsby of the Royal Navy, Lord Salisbury instructed him to sail up the heathen river and deliver to the sultan a stern remonstrance. The captain asked what he was to do if the sultan refused to accede to the ultimatum. After a long and ponderous silence Lord Salisbury, mumbling in the approved diplomatic manner, said: "Well, yes, I see . . . well, you'll just have to steam away, won't you."

The captain took his gunboat to Africa and proceeded upriver to the sultan's compound. Knowing that if the sultan resorted to a test of arms he had no hope of victory, the captain made a brave show of noisily running out his guns. He went ashore with as much pomp as he could muster, attended by flags, drums, and smartly dressed marines. The sultan listened grudgingly to the news from London.

"And what happens, Captain," he asked, "if I reject this singularly insulting communication?"

The captain bowed and unobtrusively placed his hand on the hilt of his sword.

"Although I assure your highness that I would do so with profound regret, I would have no choice but to carry out the second part of my instructions."

The sultan went as pale as it was possible for him to do and promptly capitulated to the British demand. Upon his return to London, Captain Hornsby was promoted to the rank of admiral.

That was long ago and in another country, but the illusions of power still govern the world, possibly more so than in the reign of Queen Victoria. In the arenas of foreign policy the substitution of words for things blurs the distinction between the reasons of state and the uses of publicity. The distinction was never particularly clear, but the speed of modern communications makes it increasingly difficult to tell the difference between gesture and event.

The sophisticated act of terrorism is a form of high technology. The terrorist who fires a machine gun into a crowd at an airport counts on the complicity of network television; within an hour of committing the atrocity, he holds as hostage the rage and despair of an audience large enough to wreck a government. The band of guerrillas hiding out in the mountains bears comparison with the research team housed in a module six miles south of San Jose, California. In both instances the smaller cadres of energy and purpose enjoy a tactical advantage over the vulnerable complexities of the larger economic or political structures.

The apostles of the new information order have been making this point for twenty years, but their teaching hasn't yet been adequately impressed upon the public understanding. If American foreign policy comes down to a matter of delivering images instead of air strikes and artillery shells, then the current means don't correspond to the current ends. The old gunboats have become too dangerous and too expensive. The cost-benefit ratios make as little sense as the tortuous explanations subsequently offered to Congress. If the United States must send the Navy against every thug clever enough to play an anarchist music with the orchestra of the media, then the country must bankrupt itself with continuous performances in the theaters of the news. Not only must American Marines defend the principles of nineteenth-century democratic capitalism; they must also employ a nineteenth-century military technology better suited to a world that still was protected by the filtering agents of distance and time. The problem is less political than aesthetic. No matter how heavily armed, the gunboats cannot match the firepower of the television cameras.

Better a series of stately exhibitions at the Pentagon. The current show of conceptual art appearing under the rubric of "Star Wars," and representative of the California school of nuclear abstraction, offers as fanciful a display of omnipotence as has been seen in Washington in many years. The better critics understand the work as a set of contemporary images that depend for their effects on exquisite juxtapositions of space and line.

THE WASHINGTON POST,
*August 1981*

# IMPERIAL MASQUERADE

*How is the world ruled and how do wars start?*
*Diplomats tell lies to journalists and then believe what*
*they read.*

—Karl Kraus

**I**F IT WASN'T sentimental melodrama, and if it didn't hold so heavy a promise of tragedy, the Reagan Administration's war on terrorism would play as farce. All too easily I can imagine the President and his principal officers—most notably Secretary of State George Shultz and Secretary of Defense Caspar Weinberger—dressed in the uniforms of a Gilbert and Sullivan operetta. The curtain rises on Act 1 to discover the gentlemen admiring their medals and singing an idiot song about the glories of the military life. By the end of Act 3 the army has been lost and the lord mayor's daughter has run off with the pirate from Tangier.

Fortunately for the owners of vacation resorts in Florida and California, the Administration's spring offensive produced its most frightening effects among the Americans. In April President Reagan loosed a bombing raid against Libya, ostensibly to make the world safe for democracy and American innocents abroad. As might have been expected—certainly by Messrs. Gilbert and Sullivan—the raid achieved precisely the opposite result.

Wary of retaliatory gestures on the part of terrorists lying in wait behind every frontier, hundreds of thousands of Americans canceled their tours to Europe and the Middle East; athletes elected not to play on foreign grass; movie actors declined their invitations to the festival at Cannes. Instead of swaggering triumphantly through a world amazed by their courage and resolve, American tourists retreated to the safe corners of the nearest Disneyland. By the

**288**

middle of May, Secretary Shultz had begun to show signs of hysteria. Alarmed by the apparitions of his own devising, Shultz frantically beseeched the Congress for more money to fortify American embassies overseas.

"One of these days, there'll be another tragedy at some embassy," he said. "Then they'll come around and say you're derelict in your duty because all these people got killed, and I'm going to say I'm not derelict in my duty, because you wouldn't appropriate the money. . . ."

Shultz's voice had risen perceptibly toward the octave of a whine since the euphoric evening of April 14, when, together with Weinberger, he had convened a press conference to answer questions about President Reagan's improvisation on the theme of realpolitik. Both gentlemen seemed wonderfully pleased with themselves. The Air Force and the Navy had won a championship game in the Mediterranean, and they were happy to report that America was no wimp.

Although he accepted questions from the reporters in the room, Shultz addressed his remarks to the larger audience of delinquent children in Europe and the Third World. The United States, he said, had established the principle of just punishment. Colonel Qaddafi had sorely tried America's patience. Despite repeated warnings, economic sanctions, and the Sixth Fleet's staging of a bellicose regatta in the Gulf of Sidra, Qaddafi had persisted in his wickedness. His insolence no longer could be tolerated, and the United States had to teach a moral lesson.

Without any audible exception, the reporters present murmured their patriotic assent. Together with the American public—the polls showed 77 percent in favor of the bombings—nobody questioned the text implicit in Shultz's little sermon. Henceforth, the United States would use force to make sure the world behaved itself. If the world didn't behave itself, certainly that wouldn't be Shultz's fault, and the world could expect to suffer the consequences of its mischief. If any nasty terrorists anywhere in the world still had it in their heads to put bombs in cars or suitcases, they could damn well expect another visit from American bombers—presumably at night, without warning, and with a modest penalty of civilian casualties.

During the following weeks only a few voices in the American media expressed doubts or reservations. Apparently it didn't matter that eight years of lessons in Vietnam proved the futility of bombing missions against guerrilla targets; that President Reagan acted without consent of Congress and in violation of what remains of international law; that the Israelis give continual demonstrations in Lebanon showing that the motive of revenge leads only to more killing and the inevitable militarization of the state; that the United States appropriated, as gleefully as if it were a new toy, the ethic as well as the tactic of its enemies.

To people wishing to prove that they aren't wimps, such objections amount to little more than leftist sophistry. The Reagan Administration faithfully reflects the attitudes of a well-to-do American plutocracy enchanted by images of Teddy Roosevelt and John Wayne standing on the battlements of freedom. Caught up in the excitements of their adventures and crusades, the makers of American foreign policy—together with their liege men in the media—haven't got a very clear idea of the world in which they imagine themselves holding season tickets in the box seats. They neglect to make distinctions between kinds and degrees of violence.

A good many more Americans drown in bathtubs every year than die from the ill effects of terrorism; of the 3,010 terrorist attacks that took place across the world in 1985, only ninety-nine involved Americans. Although I haven't got the precise statistics, I suspect that the number of Americans murdered every month in Miami and New York exceeds the sum of Americans murdered during the last three years by Libyan, Iranian, and Syrian terrorists. A citizen walking alone after dark in the bleaker districts of most American cities stands a far greater chance of falling prey to terrorism (i.e., mugging) than do the passengers on any of the world's airlines or cruise ships. The criminal syndicates doing business with impunity throughout the United States earn roughly $150 billion a year by practicing the acts of terrorism under the homely rubrics of extortion, loan-sharking, and contract killing.

The polemicists who stage terrorist acts like to dress up their crimes in the gaudy slogans of political fantasy. Rather than think themselves engaged in the slaughter of defenseless people, they prefer to pose as idealists dedicated to the moral beauty of a noble cause.

This is nonsense, but it is nonsense accepted at par value by the nervous plutocrats who occupy the higher ranks of the Reagan Administration. Whenever I listen to the chorus of their outraged voices I think of portly gentlemen seated on the terrace of an expensive golf club, furiously stirring the ice in their gin and telling one another tales of monstrous crimes loose in the streets of Beverly Hills.

By casting Libya in the role of sovereign enemy (comparable, say, to Nazi Germany or the horsemen of Genghis Khan), the Administration assigns to Colonel Qaddafi powers that he doesn't possess. The American government might as well declare war on Fort Lee, New Jersey, because an appreciable number of Mafiosi happen to live in that town. If the President felt the need for a patriotic headline in an otherwise unheroic week, he could send the USS *Coral Sea* up the Hudson River and launch an air strike against every Italian restaurant within twenty miles of the George Washington Bridge.

Secretary Shultz's fulminations about terrorism as a threat to Western civilization (like the mumbling on the editorial page of *The Washington Post*) invariably remind me of the story of the princess and the pea. A young woman dressed in rags arrives one evening at a castle in the forest and asks for a night's lodging. The resident prince invites the young woman to sleep on a pile of soft mattresses under which he has placed a tiny pea. The next morning the young woman complains of a sore back, and because she complains, because of her exquisite sensitivity to what Californians would call her "personal space," the prince recognizes her as a true princess.

So also the complacent trustees of the American plutocracy. Because they are rich men who believe that their wealth should damn well preserve them from discomfort, they assume that first-class accommodations on anybody's airline ought to exempt them from the rude intrusions of death and time. Accustomed to the adoration of the media and the fawning deference of locker room attendants, President Reagan and his friends look upon any expression of hostility not only as crime but also as blasphemy.

It is a matter of indifference to them if less fortunate people must live with terrorism as if it were as unremarkable as the rain. If the criminal syndicates proliferate, if gunmen murder a few grocers in Brooklyn or a few FBI agents in Miami, if a few thousand peasants sicken and die because of Union Carbide's negligence in Bhopal, if thugs occasionally have to be hired to make sure that democracy works in Chicago and Nicaragua, well, that is the way of the world and easily explained under the headings of free enterprise.

But let their own comfort be placed at risk, and the outraged club members suspect the wine steward of fomenting Marxism. Let the stain of the world's unhappiness make a mess on the new carpet in the dining room, and they imagine that the day of judgment is at hand. Lacking the imagination to conceive of a universe that doesn't resemble Orange County, they can think of nothing else to do except to send the fleet.

HARPER'S MAGAZINE,
*July 1986*

# THE LAST HOHENZOLLERN

> *If we would please in society, we must be prepared to be taught many things we know already by people who do not know them.*
>
> —Chamfort

FOR ANOTHER SEASON at least, possibly through the whole of the summer and maybe into the fall, it apparently will remain obligatory at the better parties in Washington and New York to say something intelligible about the hydrogen bomb. As a topic of required conversation the bomb has had an eccentric history, and it is not always easy to know how to conduct oneself in its sullen presence.

During the late 1950s the bomb was very much in vogue and often in the news. Everybody who was anybody wanted to be seen thinking or talking about it. But then, soon after Richard Nixon was elected President, and for reasons never satisfactorily explained, the bomb dropped from sight, and nobody thought to ask where it went. Presumably it had taken an extended leave of absence. Maybe it had been granted tenure at one of those strategic institutes in California; possibly it had gone off with the last hippies on the gypsy wagons of the counterculture. For ten years everybody who was anybody forgot what it looked like and why it was so important.

With the advent of the Reagan Administration the topic staged a triumphant return. As ugly and unthinkable as always, but dressed in a wardrobe of modish abstraction, it was at first seen mostly in the company of the left. The apostles of peace and disarmament, deeply embarrassed by the Republican Risorgimento, once again had a heroic friend that could rescue them from obscurity and anomie.

**293**

Jonathan Schell wrote a hymn to the bomb's omnipotence entitled *The Fate of the Earth,* and Carl Sagan assembled a triptych, not unlike those painted by Hieronymus Bosch, entitled "Nuclear Winter." The journals of advanced literary opinion presented shows of pious alarm. The popular media took the topic around to folk festivals and rallies in Central Park, introducing it to Baryshnikov, Barbara Walters, and Sam Shepard. Among its admirers on the left, the bomb invariably attains the status of celebrity, a romantic persona comparable to that of a French film director who requires a limousine and flowers in his suite at the St. Regis.

The fierce professors on the militant right prefer to think of the bomb as German royalty, perhaps the last of the Hohenzollerns, but in any event an extremely austere personage wearing a high starched collar and not amused by small talk. By the autumn of 1983 they had managed to shift the conversation from disarmament to the Strategic Defense Initiative (a.k.a. "Star Wars"), substituting magical promises of an invincible shield for gloomy presentiments of the apocalypse. At an arms control conference some months ago in Washington a woman made the mistake of asking a question about certain technical aspects of nuclear strategy. Her impertinence annoyed Donald Regan, the President's chief of staff. Rising to the defense of the bomb's dignity, Regan said, testily: "Women don't know anything about throw-weights."

The subtleties of nuclear etiquette—obviously more complicated than they might seem—cannot be acquired as readily as a new dress or a New York City politician. As has been said, the proper attitude toward the topic varies with the company it keeps. Because it is sometimes difficult to think of a suitable phrase or inflection of the voice, and because the topic might remain current until Christmas, I have made a few notes about the protocols likely to be deemed both safe and socially correct:

1. On being seated next to the topic at dinner, refrain from making jokes. Whether approached from the left or the right, the nuclear holocaust is a very serious and very ponderous guest. It doesn't speak English. The tone of address should be respectful, as

if you were conversing with Alexander Haig or a large sum of money. Laughter and rude remarks will mark you as a person of low birth.

2. The topic is always in impeccable taste. Mention your acquaintance with it at every possible opportunity, and nobody can find fault with the interior decoration of your soul. You have chosen the best. What can be more important than the end of the world?

3. Sign all petitions circulated by the appropriate authorities. If you believe in a nuclear freeze, you can join committees of concerned authors, artists, and Nobel laureates. Your name might appear in a newspaper advertisement with the names of Barbra Streisand and Kurt Vonnegut. The billing can't do you any harm with the Internal Revenue Service, and it might get you invited to a party in East Hampton. If the committee asks for money, calculate the sum of your contribution by counting the number of celebrities listed on the letterhead and multiplying the result by $20.

If you believe in the miracle of "Star Wars," sign any piece of paper submitted by a quorum of retired Air Force generals. Your name will appear on a White House mailing list, and you might be invited to subscribe to *Commentary* or *National Review.*

4. Because of its ecumenical nature, the topic of the bomb absorbs and nullifies all the moral passion previously invested in the issues of civil rights, women's rights, Vietnam, Watergate, the deficit, affirmative action, government regulation, pornography, and the environment.

5. A noble preoccupation with the nuclear holocaust excuses your ignorance of lesser evils and explains your indifference to death caused by conventional weapons. The Soviet Union routinely sponsors the murder of unruly citizens, and the Israeli government, while "mopping up" Palestinian strongholds in Tunisia or Lebanon, sometimes has occasion to kill an impressive number of civilians. The victims die without benefit of radiation and thus do not merit much notice in the press.

6. If the conversation takes a nasty turn in the direction of the host's thievery in the stock market, you can interrupt and say, "Yes,

of course, but when one thinks of it in terms of 10 million deaths
. . ." The same strategy can be employed to divert the small talk
away from the sexual chicanery taking place among the guests at the
other end of the table.

7. The topic allows you to think only about important people—
generals, best-selling prophets, national security advisers, film
stars, television broadcasters, heads of state. You needn't give much
thought to the teeming mob of the world's poor. They, too, will be
consumed in the nuclear fire, but they can't do anything about it,
and their departure will be met with as little interest as their arrival.

8. The topic is restful. It stimulates anxiety about a catastrophe
that has yet to happen. This is the most comfortable form of despair,
far more convenient than trying to deal with a catastrophe already in
progress (e.g., the public schools).

9. If somebody asks you to recommend a course of action, you
need not worry about your lack of suggestion. None of the best
people know what to do. It is no disgrace to confess your helplessness, but you must do so with an air of profound regret, which, if
managed correctly, signifies your appreciation of modernism.

10. On weekends in the country the topic likes to read the Sunday
papers and go for long walks. It doesn't play tennis.

HARPER'S MAGAZINE,
*May 1986*

# THE RED QUEEN

*What matters most about political ideas is the underlying emotions, the music, to which ideas are a mere libretto, often of very inferior quality.*

—Sir Lewis Namier

**I**N JOHN LE CARRÉ'S novel *Tinker, Tailor, Soldier, Spy,* an old connoisseur of the world's secrets tells an apprentice espionage agent that what they had thought was their best information—acquired at large expense and with heavy loss of human life—is probably false. He phrases his judgment as a question: "Ever bought a fake picture, Toby? The more you pay for it, the less inclined you are to doubt its authenticity."

The same question might be asked of the American statesmen engaged in the current round of arms control talks with the Soviet Union. Over the years they and their predecessors have paid a fortune for a collection of portraits of the malevolent Russian empire, and they find it all but impossible to imagine a world in which the Cold War turns out to be a forgery. Whenever they return from another conference—in Reykjavik, in Geneva—they look like mourners returning from the funeral of a lost friend.

The expression of bewildered melancholy shows most plainly in the face of George Shultz. Earlier this spring in Moscow, Mikhail Gorbachev suggested to the secretary of state that their respective governments remove their inventories of nuclear missiles from Europe. *All* the missiles—short-range, medium-range, and maybe also tactical weapons outfitted with nuclear warheads. The idea was originally an American one, the "zero option" proposed by President Reagan in 1981, but Shultz looked glum, as if he'd been asked to shoot his dog.

**297**

Gorbachev reportedly laughed and said, "What are you afraid of?"

It's a fair question, and one to which few American public officials can afford to give an honest answer. I doubt that Shultz is afraid of a nuclear war. At innumerable briefings and conferences over the past fifteen years I've listened to innumerable authorities—weapons analysts, secretaries of state, congressmen, deputy secretaries of defense, military historians, generals—talk about the precarious weight of the strategic balance. Not once have I heard in their voices even the trace elements of fear. No matter how hard they try, and no matter how bold their display of maps and statistics, they cannot bring themselves to believe in the likelihood of a nuclear war. Their lack of anxiety is proved by the chronic ineptitude of the American military forces and by the ease with which equally inept military contractors can defraud the Pentagon of $30 billion a year. If the authorities were genuinely alarmed (i.e., if they thought their collections of weapons intended for actual use), I think it's fair to assume that they would pay closer attention to the worth and condition of their armaments.

Presumably they know, or at least strongly suspect, that the weapons race ended in 1968. In that year the Soviet Union placed nuclear missiles in submarines at sea; the United States had done so in 1960. The deployments imposed on each nation the condition of unacceptable risk. Because neither nation can avoid a nuclear riposte to a sudden attack, no attack can lead to anything but disastrous results.

Defined as unacceptable risk, deterrence is a condition as absolute as the law of gravity. It remains constant no matter what the variable numbers of missiles or submarines or cities destroyed. Four submarines armed with twenty missiles correspond to a hundred submarines armed with a thousand missiles.

If it isn't nuclear war that worries Shultz, possibly it's the safety of the American economy. The United States over the past forty years has founded much of its industry on a premise of permanent war. Our defense expenditures account for 29 percent of our federal spending, and the nation's military enterprises consume the energy and intelligence of many of our most talented countrymen. If we quit making weapons, the country might go broke. I don't think so, but the sorts of people who manage the nation's affairs tend to equate prosperity with the profits earned on government contracts. In order to justify the always rising cost of their martial pretensions, they conjure up the images of catastrophe. President Kennedy presented a "missile gap"; his successors discovered a "bomber gap," a "window of vulnerability," innumerable "arcs of crisis," and miscellaneous "years of maximum danger." After the election is won or the budget approved, the monstrous chimeras vanish as mysteriously as they came.

The trick with the missiles is getting harder to perform. At least some people in the audience can find the pea under the walnut shell, and if Gorbachev continues to press his proposals for ridding Europe of its superfluous megatonnage, the simplicity of the logic of deterrence will become increasingly difficult to hide. The shills for the defense industries clearly need a new fairy tale. Now that the Strategic Defense Initiative has been exposed as an astrophysical hoax, the prompters of the public alarm have begun to talk about the supposed magnificence of the Red Army. Informed sources already mention "the superiority of the Soviet Union's conventional forces" as if such superiority were a well-established fact, as solid as granite or as obvious as the sea. They speak of immense armies which, if given a moment's notice and a decent road map, could swarm across the Rhine in a matter of hours and stand at the gates of Paris within a matter of days.

This invincible host is, of course, another fiction, as remote in space and time as the Golden Horde that followed Genghis Khan out of the mists of the Asian steppe. As measured by the International Institute for Strategic Studies, and as enumerated by Tom Gervasi in *The Myth of Soviet Military Supremacy* (a book to which I'm indebted for other aspects of this argument), the full complement of NATO ground forces in Europe (8.2 million) outnumbers those of the Warsaw Pact (5 million). The NATO armies also hold the advantage in most categories of weapons. The numerical comparisons shift even more favorably toward the NATO alliance when the interested parties remember to take into account the character and nationality of the troops. The myth of the inexorable Russian advance presumes that East and West Germans will happily murder one another and that the Czechs, the Poles, the Latvians, and the Ukrainians will gladly sacrifice themselves to the Soviet cause. Just as improbably, the myth assigns to the Russian soldier an active and energetic nature that nobody has ever known him to possess.

Traveling in Moscow and St. Petersburg in the summer of 1901, Henry Adams remarked on the passivity of the Russian temperament and thought Russia at least a hundred years behind the United States in all sectors of civilization. In letters home he speaks of the "wonderful tenth-century people" and of a country that he saw as "metaphysical, religious, military, Byzantine."

The fear of Russia is as traditional in the West as the belief in witches and alchemy. During the eighteenth and nineteenth centuries the European nations repeatedly persuaded themselves that the "Colossus of the North" was just about to do something truly frightful. At the Congress of Verona in 1822 the Russian ambassador stepped out of his carriage one afternoon and abruptly died. Talleyrand assumed a maneuver of impenetrable guile. On being informed of the event, he said, "I wonder why he did that."

The fantasies persist despite the frequent and convincing testimonies to Russian military incompetence. As individuals or sovereign despots, the Russians might display an impressive genius for cruelty, but Russian armies only show to good advantage when directed against their fellow countrymen. In combat with more advanced nations—in the Crimean War in 1854, the Russo-Japanese War in 1905, World War I—Russian armies tend to parade their talent for defeat. Lord Palmerston, the British Prime Minister in the middle passages of the nineteenth century, thought Russia "a great humbug," and the historian Philip Guedalla, writing in 1936 after patient study of the relevant dispatches and casualty lists, concluded that "nothing is more undeserved than the respectful apprehension with which the world has long consented to regard the Russians as a military menace." Referring to a Russian cruiser that shelled the Winter Palace at St. Petersburg in 1917, Guedalla described the exploit as "almost the sole recorded victory of the Russian Navy, which had managed to defeat an admirable specimen of eighteenth-century architecture." The Soviet misadventure in Afghanistan sustains his irony.

Guedalla also noticed an "unhappy and recurrent rhythm in Soviet affairs" in which military defeat abroad was invariably followed by revolution at home. The rhythm presumably is apparent to Russian heads of state, whether communist or tsar, and if the makers of American policy choose to regard the Soviet Union with unduly respectful apprehension, it's for reasons of their own. The federal budget for 1986 invests $111 billion in American conventional weapons, which (*mirabile dictu* and most profitably for all concerned) cost even more to deploy and maintain than their nuclear associates.

The current round of arms talks holds the promise of a hope that hasn't been present in a conference room for many years. The obstacle in the way of even a modest agreement (the only kind of agreement worth having) is the exhibition of paintings on the walls. Gorbachev at least has the wit to know that he's engaged in a labor of the aesthetic as well as the moral imagination. He invites us to conceive of a world not quite so crowded with vicious images, and we would be foolish to insist on the authenticity of our priceless forgeries.

HARPER'S MAGAZINE,
*July 1987*

# SPOILS OF WAR

*But what good came of it at last?*
*Quoth little Peterkin.*
*Why, that I cannot tell, said he,*
*But 'twas a famous victory.*
                    —Robert Southey,
                    "The Battle of Blenheim"

FOR THE BETTER part of forty years I have been listening to people talk about the chance of war with the Soviet Union, but I have yet to hear anybody say anything about what might be gained from such a war. What would be its objectives, and what spoils would belong to the victor?

The ancient Romans at least had it in mind to loot the tents of their enemies. Their legions marched east and south in the hope of stealing somebody else's grain or elephants or gold. The British empire in the eighteenth century employed its armies to protect its trade in molasses or slaves or tea. Napoleon sacked Europe in the early years of the nineteenth century to pay off the debts of the French Revolution.

But what profit could the United States or the Soviet Union discover in the other's defeat? Suppose that both nations avoided the stupidity of nuclear self-annihilation. Suppose further that one of the two nations managed to win World War III—either by means of conventional arms (Soviet tanks rolling unhindered across the plain of northern Europe or American troops marching triumphantly north from the Black Sea) or because one of the two nations simply got tired of paying the bills for next year's collection of new weapons. On the American side, the second eventuality assumes that during one of Senator Jesse Helms's brief absences from Washington a consortium of frightened liberal politicians surrendered the United States without firing so much as a single naval salute.

Say, for whatever reason, that the war ends in a flutter of parades and that a chorus of new voices, slightly accented, begins telling the story of the evening news. What then? Who distributes the prize money, and how does the conquering host preserve the innocence of its ideological faith?

Consider first the consequences of a Soviet triumph. Imagine a Soviet fleet at anchor in New York harbor and the White House occupied by the proconsuls of the Soviet empire. Among the official classes of Washington the transition probably could be accomplished in a matter of days. Certainly the federal bureaucracy would welcome the expansion of its powers and dominions. Because so much of the nation's nominally private industry feeds—even now, at the zenith of the conservative ascendancy—on the milk of government charity, none of the city's accomplished lobbyists would have any trouble grasping the principles of socialist enterprise.

The directives handed down by the Politburo presumably would do little more than magnify the frown of paranoid suspicion already implicit in the Reagan Administration's insistence on loyalty oaths, electronic surveillance, urine testing, and censorship. In return for the trifling gestures that accompany any change of political venue— replacing the portraits on the walls, learning a few words of a new flattery—the government ministries would receive the gifts of suzerainty over the whole disorderly mess of American democracy. After so many years of writing so many querulous memoranda and bearing the insults of so many ungrateful journalists, the government would be free at last—free to meddle in everybody's business, free to indulge its passion for rules and its habit of sloth, free to tap all the telephones in all the discotheques in west Los Angeles.

The intellectual classes would go even more quietly into the totalitarian night. The American intelligentsia never has been notable for its courage or the tenacity of its convictions. If the Soviets took the trouble to shoot three or four television anchormen, the rest of the class would quickly learn the difference between a right and a wrong answer. The big media inevitably applaud the wisdom in office (whether announced by Gerald Ford or Jimmy Carter) and the universities teach the great American lesson of going along to get along. Many of the most vehement apostles of the Reagan revolution (among them Norman Podhoretz and Michael Novak) once professed themselves loyal to the liberal, even the radical, left. Given their talent for conversion, I expect that they wouldn't have much trouble working out the dialectics of a safe return to the winning side. Literary bureaucrats—in the United States as in the Soviet Union and whether construed as priests or commissars or English professors—prefer the kind of world in which words take precedence over things and statements of theory overrule the insolence of facts.

Nor would the monied classes offer much of an objection to a Soviet victory. The financial magnates who weren't traveling in Europe at the time and who even bothered to notice that the war had come and gone almost certainly would make some sort of deal with the new owners of the American franchise. Over the last seven years Americans have sold off (to the Japanese, the French, the British, the Saudis) $1 trillion in assets (land, bank debt, manufacturing capacity, real estate, office buildings), and we have gotten into the habit of deferring to the whims of a foreign buyer.

Again, as with the unoffending anchormen, the Soviets might make a halfhearted show of ideological seriousness. The communist state certainly would confiscate a fair number of yachts and racing stables, and it might subject a few conspicuous slumlords and investment bankers to the formalities of a trial for crimes against the working poor. But too zealous a schedule of punishments would violate the spirit of *glasnost*, and I expect that most of the native oligarchy would be allowed to keep as much of its property as it could decently hide.

People might have to reduce their standards of extravagance and forgo the comfort of the fourth Mercedes or the convenience of a choice between forty-seven Italian white wines, but within a matter of weeks the opulent magazines would reflect the craze for wood carvings, caftans, and oriental colors. The fashionable people in New York and Los Angeles soon would discover a remarkable similarity between the Marxist aesthetic ("so simple, so pure") and the Puritan charm of seventeenth-century New England. Ted Koppel could be relied upon to teach the television audience about the greatness of Peter the Great.

So far, so good, but not quite good enough. Among the privileged classes in the larger cities the Soviets might discover a crowd of new and eager friends, but in the *terra incognita* beyond the lights of New York, Washington, and Beverly Hills, I'm afraid that they wouldn't have such an easy time of it. The country is too big, and too many citizens like to carry guns. The Russians have trouble enough with the illiterate and poorly armed Afghans. What would they do with the subscribers to *Soldier of Fortune* magazine, with hundreds of thousands of restless adolescents looking for a reason (any reason) to dynamite a train, with bands of guerrillas trained at MIT and capable of reading the instruction manuals for automatic weapons, with the regiments of elderly duck hunters in Florida and Texas who have been waiting patiently ever since 1945 for the chance to blast the communist birds of prey? Lacking the sophistication of the New York police, how could the Soviets contain a crowd at a Bruce Springsteen concert, or suppress the computer networking in the San Fernando Valley? Where would the Politburo recruit the army of censors necessary to silence all the CB radios, raid all the pornographic newsstands, shut down all the telephone lines, and foreclose all the means of free and seditious expression?

Even with the enthusiastic help of Pat Robertson and William Bennett, the secretary of education, it is unlikely that the Soviet Union could accomplish so herculean a labor of purification. But unless the Russians operated the United States as a labor camp, how could they preserve the belief in the Marxist fairy tale? Let too many Russians loose in the streets of Orlando or Kansas City and they might succumb to the heresy of supermarkets or fall into the temptation of department stores. Within a generation communism would be as dead as the last tsar.

Nor would the Americans fare much better if we were unlucky enough to win the war. We are a people who lack both the talent and stomach for empire. Shooting partisans on sight doesn't sit well with what remains of the American conscience, and we complain bitterly (Mr. Reagan's Orange County friends foremost among the complainants) about the cost of keeping a military garrison in a terrain as comfortable as Western Europe. Where would we find the troops to stand guard on the marches of Uzbekistan? How could we administer the 8.6 million square miles of the Union of Soviet Socialist Republics? We can't provide enough of our own citizens with decent housing, fair employment, or a fifth-grade education. What empty political promises could George Bush or Michael Dukakis offer 283.5 million people speaking a hundred and thirty languages who expect to be fed and clothed by the state? Do we imagine that we can staff Siberia with graduates of the Harvard Business School, that we can teach the hard lessons of independence to a people used to the comforts of despotism?

If we cannot do for the vast expanse of the Soviet Union what we cannot do for downtown Detroit, then either we operate the country as a penal institution or, as with Germany and Japan in the aftermath of World War II, we lend money, provide technical assistance, and instruct our wards in the perfections of capitalism. By choosing the first option we transform the American republic into a police state. The second option probably dooms America to economic ruin. To our sorrow we have seen what wonders can be worked by people released from the sterile task of making the toys of war. Within a generation we would be importing Russian cars, wearing Russian silk, borrowing Russian currency to finance the miraculous debt incurred by our military triumph.

No, I'm afraid that World War III lacks the motive of enlightened self-interest. No matter whose troops march through which capital city, the conquerors become the conquered, their systems of political and economic thought changed into their dreaded opposites.

The certain defeat implicit in anybody's victory seems to me worth bearing firmly in mind. Yet, in all the official gabbling about missiles and tanks and the fierce portrait of "American credibility" in the Persian Gulf, I never hear anybody asking the questions "Why?" and "What for?"

HARPER'S MAGAZINE,
*December 1987*

# AGENTS PROVOCATEURS

*Nowhere more naively than in banknotes does capitalism
display itself in solemn earnest. The innocent cupids
frolicking about numbers, the goddesses holding tablets
of the law, the stalwart heroes sheathing their swords
before monetary units are a world of their own:
ornamenting the facade of hell.*

—Walter Benjamin

IN WASHINGTON AS well as Hollywood, it has long been an article
of faith that "communist subversion" is one of the most certain of the
world's evils. Secretary of Defense Caspar Weinberger offers it as
justification for any sudden or belligerent movement of the American fleet. His companions on the militant right, among them Secretary of State George Shultz and the theorists at the Heritage
Foundation, speak of it as if it were a pesticide guaranteed by the
manufacturer to do its awful work within seventy-two hours of being
sprayed on a free and democratic society. Chuck Norris and Sylvester Stallone decorate the movie screen with images of Soviet malevolence. Whether cast as military advisers in Angola, terrorists in
Rome, propagandists in Berlin, the agents of the Evil Empire never
rest from their labors; their victory is always imminent, their monstrous armament and seductive polemic never more than a few miles
over the innocent horizon.

Like Shultz and Weinberger, the producers of front-line espionage dramas have a pressing need for cash. Obliged to solicit
weapons appropriations or draw a crowd of paying customers, they
must invent frightful apparitions. I'm sure that some of their advertising has some basis in fact, and I don't doubt that the world is filled
with people who would like nothing better than to wreck the Ameri-

can bandwagon and break the American promise. What I question is the effectiveness of communist subversion as a means of destruction. Without intending any slight on the prowess of the KGB, it strikes me that the agents of capitalist subversion can do a good deal more damage to free and democratic societies than all the villains in all the Russias.

If I were the president of a Third World nation still prosperous enough to keep the airport open, I would be far more frightened by a well-dressed gentleman bringing loans from the IMF or Citibank than by a bearded guerrilla muttering threats of revolution. Even if the guerrilla commanded 2,000 followers in the mountains, all of them familiar with bad translations of *Das Kapital*, he could do little more than loot a provincial town or blow up an occasional train.

But the banker—the smiling, soft-spoken, impeccably reasonable banker drinking iced gin on the veranda—that fine gentleman might furnish me with a line of credit on laughably easy terms. Were I foolish enough or desperate enough to accept his deal—and if I weren't foolish or desperate he probably wouldn't have taken the trouble to stop by—within five years, or maybe six or eight, I could expect to see the country in ruins.

Compare the effects of communist and capitalist subversion over the last quarter of a century, and I think the record will show that the instruments of debt have proved far more harmful to the hope of human freedom than Kalashnikov rifles.

On his accession to the White House in the winter of 1961, John F. Kennedy confronted a world in which most of the obvious evidence favored the cause of a communist triumph. The Communist parties in Italy and France had a chance of acquiring their respective governments by popular vote. The nations of Eastern Europe, still referred to as "captive nations," were muffled in the silence that followed the suppression of Hungary. Egypt had strayed into the shadow of communist dread. China and the Soviet Union were suspected of forming an ideological hegemony across the whole of Asia. The newly independent states of western Africa looked as if they might choose communist ways of government as proof of their emancipation from the chains of the old colonialism.

Twenty years later, on President Reagan's arrival in the White

House, the specter of communist subversion was visible only to those people paid to make the ritual gestures of dismay. The Communist parties in Western Europe have fallen into the categories of irrelevance occupied by obscure religious sects. In the French elections of 1984, the Communist party attracted only 11 percent of the vote for the European Parliament, and in Italy the political conversation turns not on the questions of ideology but on the pleasures of conspicuous consumption known as *edonismo reaganiano*. Most of Africa remains free of communist regimes. In Eastern Europe, the Marxist-Leninist dogma has been so weakened since the early 1960s as to have become the stuff of satirical songs. China has drifted out of the Soviet field of gravity; so have India and Egypt.

But over the span of the same twenty-five years, the agents of capitalist subversion—that is, the moneylenders supplying cheap credit to the poorer nations of the earth—have done the work of invading armies. The burden of debt now weighs so heavily on so many countries that collectively they owe well over $1 trillion to the systems of international finance. Their governments must borrow ever more money merely to pay the interest on their loans. Nobody even speaks of repaying the principal.

Consider the catastrophes in progress in, among other places, Mexico, Argentina, Bolivia, Venezuela, Zambia, Zaire, Niger, Chad, Ghana, Jamaica, and Trinidad—all beneficiaries of munificent credit from their bountiful friends in London and New York. I don't question the motives of the gentlemen providing the loans. I'm sure they meant well; maybe they were thoughtless or greedy or vain. Their intentions matter less than the consequences of their charity.

After fifteen years on credit, the debtor nation as likely as not found itself in a condition appreciably worse than anybody had expected. As likely as not the country's well-being had depended on the export of a single commodity—sugar, copper, oil, grain, silver, coffee, rice, tin—that lost half its price on the world markets. As much as a third of the country's dwindling income must be paid in interest to foreign banks, and the rest distributed as ransom to a domestic population educated to the technologies of consumption but not to the means of production. The government maintains artificially low prices as a defense against riots in the overcrowded slums, and the ruling oligarchy exports its profits to Switzerland or Miami. Inflation gives rise to unemployment, and the debtor nation, condemned by its overborrowing to the poverty of its past, cannot afford to buy the machinery necessary to its transformation into an economy based on a new and competitive premise. The telephones stop working; the roads fall into disrepair; at the airport the landing lights go out. Large numbers of people wander back to the countryside and revert to the primitive forms of commerce—barter, smuggling, banditry—that sustained their ancestors in the sixteenth century.

All in all, a result that conforms in almost every particular to the textbook portrait of social disorder so dutifully but fruitlessly studied by the agents of communist subversion.

HARPER'S MAGAZINE,
*April 1986*

# GLASS HOUSES

*A girl of fifteen generally has a greater number of secrets
than an old man, and a woman of thirty more arcana
than a chief of state.*

—Ortega y Gasset

O N RECEIPT OF the news that an American family of espionage
agents had been routinely selling secrets to the Soviet Union for
eighteen years, almost everybody in Washington with claims to
being anybody released solemn statements to the press about the
need to get a firmer grip on the national security. Caspar Weinberger, the secretary of defense, declared himself in favor of execut-
ing traitors, even in peacetime, and said he would reduce the
number of people (4.3 million at present count) granted access to
sensitive information. A chorus of admirals seconded the motion for
silence; both the House and the Senate announced hearings; important columnists demanded to know how it was possible that a former
and low-ranking officer named John Walker, together with his
equally obscure and low-ranking brother and son, could do so much
damage to the American fleet.

The official alarm strikes me as excessive, and I suspect that
the military secret has become as obsolete a weapon of war as the
crossbow, the battering ram, or the cavalry regiment. Consider
the tonnage of secrets lugged across international frontiers during
the last forty years. Legions of agents working two or three sides of
every rumor have copied, transcribed, edited, collated, and sold
enough information to take up all the space on all the shelves in the
Library of Congress.

And what has been the result of this immense labor? How has the
exchange of classified news impinged, even slightly, on the course

**311**

of events? The knowledge of what secret could have prevented the United States from blundering into Vietnam? The makers of policy for both the Kennedy and Johnson Administrations already knew what they thought (not only about Southeast Asia but also about communism), and no amount of contrary evidence could have dissuaded them from embracing the beauty of their geopolitical romance.

The acquisition or loss of what secret could prevent the United States from building an arsenal of nuclear weapons as necessary to the American economy as to the American theory of reality? What seven perfect secrets could have rescued the Shah of Iran or changed Managua into a democratic suburb of Los Angeles? Assume that the Soviet Union could track every American submarine, or that the United States could decipher the launch codes of every missile on the Siberian steppe. What then? Somebody still has to decide to touch a match to the nuclear fire.

The history of the world's wars suggests that the fateful decisions have little or nothing to do with facts, whether overt or covert. They arise instead from passionately held beliefs, from dreams and songs and the fear of the dark.

When presented with a discovery of spies, the national media (as enthralled by their love of secrets as any secretary of defense) broadcast melodramatic reports of their exploits, outfitting even the least among them with vast and mysterious powers.

Together with Ian Fleming and John le Carré, the news media like to say that governments without perfect knowledge of other governments take actions that otherwise they might not have taken—with grave, far-reaching, and ironic consequences. Precisely the same observation holds true for any government or individual under any set of circumstances. The available evidence is never sufficient, the current information always sketchy or compromised.

Only people frightened enough to play at being gods imagine that they can attain an impregnable state of omniscience. Malcolm Muggeridge once made the point with reference to his employment during World War II in the British Secret Service.

"Secrecy," Muggeridge observed, "is as essential to Intelligence as vestments and incense to a Mass, or darkness to a Spiritualist seance, and must at all costs be maintained . . . whether or not it serves any purpose."

Muggeridge remembered that Kim Philby, the notorious double agent, sent his wife love notes on tiny fragments of tissue paper that could be easily swallowed in the interests of security. John Walker appears to have operated under the cover of an analogous fantasy. He was fond of disguises, carried a sword-cane, styled himself with the code name "Jaws," and thought himself engaged in a romantic line of work. At least one of his associates regarded him as a deluded fool, almost as inept in his paranoid cleverness as the antic Inspector Clouseau.

During the period of his service for the KGB Walker also belonged to the John Birch Society and the Ku Klux Klan. All three organizations place as much value on secrecy as do Secretary Weinberger and the curators at the Pentagon who believe that by administering lie-detector tests and limiting security clearances to a mere 2 million people they can lock the vagaries of human nature safely in a file cabinet.

Of the 19.6 million documents that the federal government last year classified as secret, the majority presumably were granted their honorary status for one of two reasons: to conceal the government's stupidity and guile from the American public; or to make the documents more precious, thus adding to the store of sacred amulets with which to ward off the corruption of the unclassified world and the malevolence of the evil eye set in the head of an evil empire.

Given the sophistication of current surveillance technologies, the condition of privacy has come to resemble the state of Christian grace. Nobody knows for certain where, or at what moment in time, it can be said to exist. Assume that a careful man takes expensive precautions, that he attaches encryption devices to his telephones, speaks in whispers to well-known associates while walking on a beach, allows himself to be photographed only by a butler who is both mute and deaf. True, he presents a more elusive target than Billy Martin or Lee Iacocca, but if somebody were to be seriously interested in his eyebrows or his conversation, it is likely that he could be watched or overheard.

Various government agencies, American as well as Soviet, routinely intercept much of the daily microwave traffic passing in and out of New York, Washington, Moscow, Paris, Los Angeles, Amsterdam, and any other points of origin deemed worthy of notice. The signals can be gathered into computer discs, and if anybody wishes to go to the trouble of searching the babel of data for a particular voice or bank statement, the technicians can produce either a tape recording or a transcript. Probably it is fair to assume that commercial institutions as well as nation-states now employ regiments of clerks who perform the task of priests hearing confession. I like to think of earnest bureaucrats sitting in long rows, slumped under the existential weight of their headsets, taking notes on the intrigues of fifteen-year-old girls.

When Secretary of State George Shultz picks up the telephone in his car, he can expect that whatever he says will be heard by an appreciative and knowledgeable audience in the Kremlin; Andrei Gromyko, the Soviet foreign minister, can count on an equally close reading of his text in Langley, Virginia, if he speaks into any telephone circuit open to the electromagnetic spectrum.

A multinational corporation transferring credit from Stuttgart to Miami, a bank shifting its balances between Geneva and Hong Kong, a government relaying instructions from Rome to Madrid— all these communicants expose their nominally private remarks to the chance of public review.

Satellite cameras drifting in orbit at a height of 100,000 feet meanwhile take a continuous sequence of pictures—of harbors and military installations and crowds at soccer matches, of an elderly gentleman sitting in a Venetian café, of a child rolling a hoop on the Ringstrasse. The powers of amplification allow for a high degree of recognition, even to the point of identifying a gold tooth or reading the time on a woman's watch. The angels in G. K. Chesterton's heaven couldn't see as clearly.

The politics implicit in the technology have yet to be fully grasped by people who still worry about keeping secrets or who still place their faith in the fictions known as sovereign states. Because no nation can defend its borders against the movements of money or information, no nation can declare itself safe from hostile additions or subtractions. Let the Saudis and the Japanese decide to withdraw their bank deposits from the United States, and the resulting rise in the American interest rate would burst the bubbles of President Reagan's fragile prosperity; a Luxembourgian satellite broadcasting contraband television images to England and France puts at risk two government monopolies as well as the morals of two cultures.

If markets respond within the instant to an economic collapse taking place at a distance of 12,000 miles, if the least gesture made by a head of state (in Lebanon, say, or Bitburg) translates within the hour into the loss of an election in Lisbon or California, if a disease rising in Central Africa as a form of swine flue can be transposed within a matter of months to an epidemic of AIDS in New York, then the charade of independent states solemnly governing their own destinies begins to look more than a little preposterous. The admirals of navies might as well be commanding fleets of toy sailboats.

The dream of nationalism, like the value assigned to privacy, satisfied the imagination as well as the commercial interests of the nineteenth century. It was thought that the social realm could be divorced from the political realm, that behind closed doors the anarchist and the country squire were free to make variant formulations of a secret society. It would never have occurred to the aristocratic eighteenth century to distinguish between the public and private spheres of experience; nor would it have occurred to the equestrian classes of the Italian Renaissance or the citizens of Periclean Athens.

Like Bruce Springsteen and Mayor Koch, Louis XIV was accustomed to a retinue of gossips attending his every occasion. Prior to the invention of the steam engine and the flush toilet, everybody with claims to being anybody assumed that they lived their lives in front of everybody else; what mattered was what was done in full view of the court, the prince, or the agora. The private man was a man without a name.

Once again the world has become a glass house. To the extent that everybody knows everybody else, if not "live and in person" at least through the pages of *People* magazine or the windows of ABC News, then the public world (oddly enough, and contrary to the usual expectations) becomes a much more intimate place than could have been imagined by Sigmund Freud or Karl Marx.

The medieval schoolmen believed that in the eye of God the falling of the least sparrow in the farthest field was an event as duly noted as the murder of an archbishop or the sacking of a Christian town. Something of the same belief must stir the minds of the clerks seated in long rows in a government basement, following the narratives of otherwise obscure and minor lives, listening, hour after hour, to recorded time.

HARPER'S MAGAZINE,
*August 1985*

# THE GODS OF THE
# EMPTY HORIZON

*Religion consists in believing that everything which
happens is extraordinarily important. It can never
disappear from the world, precisely for this reason.*
                                        —Cesare Pavese

Aﬧﬢ WORLD WAR I it was generally assumed that all the gods
were dead. Most of them had been reported missing on the western
front; the few that survived the armistice of 1918 soon perished in a
succession of purges mounted by enemies as various as Marxism,
psychoanalysis, quantum mechanics, and Dadaist aesthetics. For
the next thirty years, professors of history as well as literature
informed their students that it was no good trying to find the lost
light in the well of metaphor or the wine of orgy.

The vogue for modernist cynicism dissolved in the explosion at
Hiroshima. At first, of course, not everybody understood what had
happened, and for another twenty years the professors continued to
teach the language of Joyce and the doctrines of Freud. As long as
the nuclear weapons were neither too numerous nor too available, it
was still possible to believe that they might not be divine, that
maybe they weren't too different from crossbows or howitzer shells.

But the equations of destruction now stored in the world's arse-
nals, together with the sophistication of the guidance systems that
can cast the fires of heaven as accurately as Capitoline Jupiter,
make it impossible for the secular authorities to pretend that the
miraculous birth at Los Alamos somehow failed to take place, that
the makers of modern physics hadn't also succeeded in making an
appropriately modern religion. In consecrated ground on three con-

tinents, as serene in their indifference as Aztec or Delphic stone, the gods of the empty horizon wait patiently for the end of the world. Their fierce silence has imposed on the world what can be fairly described as the forty years' peace.

Even the blasphemous heathen who never has seen a cruise missile or an ICBM can infer the divinity of the weapons from the nature of the discussion that attends their deployment and use. President Reagan speaks of the Strategic Defense Initiative (known to the vulgar as "Star Wars") as if it had been shown to him in a prophetic dream. The apologists for the more orthodox dogma (known as mutual assured destruction) rely on an equally inspired acquaintance with the truth.

Once recognized as theological discourse, the weapons debate takes its place among the gospels of Revelation. Knowing that it is by paradox that the gods declare themselves, the nuclear clergy has devised at least six proofs of their presence.

1. What was irrational becomes rational. The dogma of mutual assured destruction, which has governed American strategy for thirty years, implies a threat so monstrous, so beyond reason, that it offers, in the words of its proponents, the only benign and rational policy. The United States preserves civilization by promising to obliterate civilization.

The theory of the impregnable defense guarantees, in President Reagan's words, "security against all contingencies," which, in its divine presumption, is an assurance as monstrous and as beyond reason as the promise of utter annihilation.

2. What was real becomes magical. The analysts of all sects concede that nuclear weapons no longer retain a practical military use. They have become so frightful that nobody, not even Patrick Buchanan, conceives of sending them against either a strategic or a tactical objective; these lesser purposes give way to the higher purpose of sustaining the myth of omnipotence. The logic of deterrence, like that of the Strategic Defense Initiative, requires an arsenal that stands as both symbol and embodiment of absolute power.

3. What was static becomes dynamic. By increasing its store of weapons, the United States hopes to reduce the burden of arms. The doctrine assumes that the Soviet Union will negotiate disarmament only if it feels itself intimidated. The United States thus has no choice but to pile missile upon missile, laser beam upon laser beam, bomb upon bomb. The tower of hideous strength must always overreach the competitive icon raised up by the Soviet Union.

The impious ask, What is the point of building so many weapons when it needs no more than a few thermonuclear displays to poison the earth? As always, the impious fail to make the leap of faith. Deterrence is never constant and cannot be measured out in what the Pentagon calls "mere numbers" (either of warheads or of casualties); it resides in the always shifting "interaction of capabilities and vulnerabilities," that is, in an unutterable mystery.

In his speech announcing the advent of "Star Wars," President Reagan observed that "the defense debate is not about spending arithmetic." Not only is it mystery, but it exists in a realm beyond the tawdry stink of commerce.

4. What was human becomes divine. The construction of a nuclear weapon depends upon as brilliant a work of the human imagination as the world has ever seen. Over the course of centuries the collective genius of hundreds of thousands of mathematicians, physicists, and engineers has gathered the wonder of the universe in a space not much bigger than a hatbox.

But the nuclear religion transfers the qualities of human courage and resourcefulness to supernatural objects. The substitution diminishes the men who make the objects; having become pygmies, they find their response to emergent political occasions reduced to the primitive shout: "Our gods will destroy your gods."

5. The unknown takes precedence over the known. As the weapons become more dangerous and more complex, it becomes more impossible to predict what would happen if they were to escape and walk abroad among the nations of the earth. What savage race would rise from the ashes? What fish would still swim in the oceans?

Nobody can answer the questions, and so the preachers of descriptive sermons can find nobody to quarrel with their visions of hell. Carl Sagan's nuclear winter is as plausible as the day of judgment advertised on network television. The strategists in both the United States and the Soviet Union make pictures on computer screens, but their calculations bear comparison to the paintings of Hieronymous Bosch.

6. What was temporal becomes spiritual. Statesmen come and go, but the nuclear fires abide. The congregations worship the terrible magnificence of the idols at rest in their sanctuaries, adorning them, as if they were statues of Apollo, with the votive gifts of higher accuracies and greater quotients of power. Despite the immense sums of treasure and intelligence offered in rituals of sacrifice, nobody can expect to live to see the result of his handiwork.

Among people accustomed to a religious understanding of the world, this final paradox permits a measure of peace. In New York a few months ago to speak to a university audience about the landscape of Armageddon, a Jesuit priest dismissed as irrelevant a question about the extent of the nuclear inventory. "These things are not of this world, my son," he said. "They belong to the afterlife."

HARPER'S MAGAZINE,
*June 1985*

# THE NEW PATRIOTISM

Some months ago *The Washington Post* published an exceptionally fatuous article advertising "The New Patriotism" as if it were an after-shave lotion. The *Post*, of course, has an impressive talent for publishing trendy foolishness, but in this instance the writer came close to parody. Employing the language of television commercials, he announced the return of a martial spirit to a body politic gone prematurely slack and old. By way of product endorsements he listed the following:

- The record sales being reported by manufacturers of American flags.

- The eagerness with which 75,000 students last year seized upon 75,000 Army gym bags distributed, free of charge, at high school football games.

- The testimony of selected Radcliffe girls that Harvard boys enrolled in ROTC units were more attractive than their civilian peers.

Similar articles citing similar evidence have been bolstering the morale of the media for the last eighteen months. Every three or four days another columnist or broadcaster makes the amazing discovery that ordinary Americans living anonymous and poorly dressed lives find nothing disreputable about declaring their love of country. In addition to the evidence offered by the *Post*, I have noticed these further proofs of the new patriotism:

**321**

- The declining percentage of college freshmen admitting to a sympathy for the ideology of the left (21 percent in 1982, down from 52 percent in 1972).

- The conservative sentiments currently in fashion among the intellectual classes.

- The resurgence of "old-fashioned values," expressed in the lobbying for prayer in the nation's schools.

- The opulence of the weapons budget.

- The popular enthusiasm for the American invasion of Grenada.

- The politeness and intelligence of the young men enlisting in the armed services.

- A general warmth of feeling for men in uniform.

- The steady sales of hunting rifles and Ford pickup trucks.

- The wisdom of a high school student in California who, when asked for his opinion of nonconformists, referred to them as "trolls—longhairs, transient types, commies, and welfare recipients."

Almost without exception, the voices of optimism regained draw the moral that the United States has renounced the selfishness of the 1960s and recovered from the apathy of the 1970s.

It is the uniformity of these announcements that makes them so depressing. Whenever the instruments of the mass media combine in loud and joyful chorus it is pretty safe to assume that they have got the music wrong. Like many other universal truths revealed in the last two decades (e.g., the perfection of President Kennedy's Camelot and the omnipotence of the Arab oil cartel), the current discovery of patriotism has less to do with the attitudes of the American people as a whole than with the pressures of the market in images. The makers of news and slogans serve the whim of fashion, and because they seldom take the trouble to cast their adjectives in the perspective of time, their constructions bear a closer resemblance to fantasy than fact.

The advertisements for the new patriotism neglect to distinguish between the meanings of different words; as with *The Washington Post*, the copywriters confuse patriotism with nationalism, and both of these with jingoism. For the most part they celebrate the latter, as if love of country somehow implied reading *Soldier of Fortune* magazine and telling racial jokes. The politicians and the editorial writers talk about "standing tall" and "not bugging out," but the Marines leaving Lebanon talked about being scared and glad to get away. The show of rhetorical force by the editors of conservative and neoconservative journals sounds as empty as the prerecorded laughter on network situation comedies. It is as if the new patriots were hoping to persuade themselves that the world remains as it was in 1945, that the United States still calls the shots and sends in the plays.

But most Americans haven't got the taste for military adventure or the stomach for the defense of empire. No matter how resplendent the uniforms or how soft the glances of Radcliffe girls, I cannot imagine an appreciable number of college students wishing to stand guard for twenty years in Panama or the Khyber Pass.

In a good many movie theaters these days, management has adopted the policy of playing the national anthem prior to the showing of the main feature. The words to the song appear on the screen together with a sequence of symbolic images—the New York skyline, waving fields of Iowa grain, New England fishing boats, the Golden Gate bridge, the flag over the Capitol building—meant to represent the great, good, safe, and happy American place.

Although I have seen the same patriotic footage in New York City as well as in smaller towns to the northeast, I have yet to hear an audience sing. The management prints the lyrics on the film in very large letters. But even this educational device doesn't encourage anybody to join the voice on the sound track. The customers get dutifully to their feet; sometimes the teenagers in the crowd quit eating popcorn. But nobody ever sings.

Maybe the tune is pitched too high, or maybe the audience is embarrassed by the presence of noble sentiments in such close proximity to movies that so often define entertainment as more or less sensational displays of sex and violence. Whatever the reasons, the audience seldom even bothers to attempt a polite and indistinct mumbling. The customary silence struck me with particular force last weekend in Newport, Rhode Island, formerly the locus of an important naval base and still a town imbued, at least in its more populous districts, with the attitudes of mind that reflect the old-fashioned and all-American virtues. In Newport, nobody was singing the national anthem.

Americans have always had trouble reconciling their amiable and commercial temperament with the demands of a necessarily cruel and selfish state. It is the nature of the state, whether totalitarian or democratic in its pretensions, to wage ceaseless war not only against foreign states but also against those institutions within its own borders (family, school, voluntary association) that would challenge its monopoly of sovereign power.

The founders of the American republic attempted to establish a balance between the claims of the state and the interests of those lesser institutions that arouse in most Americans the genuine emotion of patriotism. Writing last month in this magazine about the hollowness of President Reagan's militarism, Henry Fairlie noted that it was the photographs in a soldier's wallet that bore witness to the allegiance of his feeling. Maybe an overly zealous major might carry postcards of the Washington Monument or the New York Stock Exchange; among the troops under his command the record would show the view looking west from a back porch, a wedding portrait, the snapshot of a parent or a child.

Given so homely a definition of patriotism, Americans over the last thirty years have been remarkably faithful to the premise on which the country was established. The merchants of the new patriotism still denounce the excesses of the lost counterculture and the opposition to the Vietnam War, but those events could as easily be construed as signs of strength, as proof of the idealistic purposes that Americans still feel called upon to make manifest to a cynical and indifferent world. Who among them ever stopped loving America? What other people ever did so much for the sake of an idea?

At the risk of bankrupting their economy, Americans have transferred vast sums to their less fortunate companions. They have insisted on the right of free speech (to the point of confusing it with pornography) and have elected (to their sorrow and eventual disillusion) politicians in whom they thought they could recognize even the dim and flickering light of an honest dream.

The new patriotism is also the old patriotism, which has been there all along, usually no more than a block away from the television studios and newspaper offices in which the ladies and gentlemen of the media tend the altars of the official conscience. Out of sight of the cameras the majority of Americans have been caring for the principles to which the nation was dedicated, living up to the promise of the American enterprise. Few of them would have the gall to preach the virtues that they so carelessly practice.

HARPER'S MAGAZINE,
*June 1984*

# MORAL DANDYISM

*In case of rain the revolution will take place in the auditorium.*

—Karl Kraus

WHAT IMPRESSES ME about the people urging disinvestment in South Africa is the stinginess of their demand. Given the presumably boundless reserves of virtue held in escrow by the crowds that occasionally demonstrate at one or another of the nation's leading universities, I wonder why they limit their demands to only one country and only one proof of man's inhumanity to man. Surely they could ask for more. Why not also denounce any government or commercial enterprise that has anything to do with munitions, poisonous chemicals, tobacco, the Soviet Union, distilled spirits, Chile, gambling casinos, India, prisons, pornography, or George Steinbrenner?

My questions follow from my inability to grasp the necessary connection between capitalism and Christianity. For thirty years I've listened to sermons preached on this most holy of American texts, but as yet I cannot understand why money has anything to do with morality. The two stores of value seem to me as different as symphony orchestras and old tennis sneakers. Like the rain, money confers its blessings on the just and the unjust, on the criminal and the saint; it can commission Michelangelo's Sistine ceiling or underwrite the architecture of Auschwitz. The genius of capitalism consists precisely in its lack of morality. Unless he is rich enough to hire his own choir, a capitalist is a fellow who, by definition, can ill afford to believe in anything other than the doctrine of the bottom line. Deprive a capitalist of his God-given right to lie and cheat and steal, and the poor sap stands a better than even chance of becoming one of the abominable wards of the state from whose grimy fingers the Reagan Administration hopes to snatch the ark of democracy.

The media bring almost hourly reports of capitalists who have become confused in their efforts to reconcile two sets of ethics. As of late April, forty-five of the nation's wealthiest military contractors were under some sort of criminal investigation. In May, General Electric pleaded guilty to charges of defrauding the Air Force, and E. F. Hutton, a New York stock-jobbing outfit, pleaded guilty to 2,000 counts of wire and mail fraud in connection with an $8 million check-kiting scheme.

Commerce isn't necessarily a synonym for crime, but both the merchant and the thief define their success in the language of the hunt: they speak of "targeting" the market or the mark, of "setting up the score" and "making a killing." Undoubtedly admirable sentiments, which I'm sure many of the better business schools preach to generations of apprentice profiteers, but they run counter to the spirit appropriate to a strict reading of the Christian revelation.

I know that a number of earnest stockbrokers have set themselves up as dealers in what they call socially responsible securities. I wish them well in their mission, but the search for the innocent investment seems to me comparable to the search for the Holy Grail. Conceivably they could find such a magical object if they didn't ask too many questions or pursue their puritan program to its logical conclusion. But if they insist on their scruples, what can they buy?

Certainly not gold or diamonds or stock in any of the larger corporations. The bulk of the world's gold comes from South Africa or the Soviet Union, which, as at least a few of the protesters know, is another godless state that employs slave labor and subverts the hope of human freedom. Assuming that the advocates of South African disinvestment were serious in their objections, they would be obliged to sell their jewelry, dig the gold out of their teeth, and drink only the domestic brands of vodka.

Nor could they permit themselves the use of automobiles, elevators, electric light bulbs, jet aircraft, television sets, refrigerators, copying machines, or Hellmann's mayonnaise. Almost all the products found in the drugstore or the supermarket bear the mark of their satanic origin in the factories of companies that trade with Capetown and Johannesburg. During the spring divertissement at Columbia, the Coalition for a Free South Africa published a partial list of offending exports, naming, among other items, Anacin, Preparation H, Gulden's mustard, Woolite, Borden dairy products, Cracker Jacks, Wise potato chips, Clairol hair products, Excedrin, Windex, Skippy peanut butter, Mighty Dog, Coca-Cola, Duracell batteries, Tretorn shoes, Gillette razor blades, Paper Mate pens, Kleenex, Beech-Nut gum, Thomas' English muffins, Aziza eye makeup, and Certs. The citizen who drives a Ford station wagon, even a secondhand Ford station wagon equipped with a tape deck and a collection of baroque harpsichord music, joins hands with the enemies of liberty.

The blameless investor couldn't lend money to a bank, own a government bond, or send his petitions through the United States mails. As was demonstrated by the collapse of the Penn Square Bank in Oklahoma City, all the banks in the country mingle the pure streams of rural capital in the sewers of metropolitan finance. The metropolitan character of money corrupts even the very small bank in the West Virginia mountains owned by an old and kindly gentleman who went blind before he had a chance to see Paris, a secular humanist, or network television.

Because the American government recognizes South Africa as both an ally and a business partner, any buying of Treasury notes can be defined by the scrupulous as an endorsement of apartheid. Similar charges of public indecency can be brought, again by the scrupulous, against any paying of taxes or buying of stamps.

As the editor of *Harper's Magazine* I occasionally receive letters from readers who impugn the magazine's character because it accepts advertisements encouraging travel to South Africa. At about the time of the Columbia demonstrations I received a letter from a woman who construed the printing of such an ad as an act of moral and political sloth. *Harper's Magazine* could have refused the ad, she said, and so proclaimed its sympathy for black people in South Africa. Instead, the magazine sold its conscience for money and tacitly approved the practice of apartheid. She ended her letter with a flourish of scorn: "What other enemies of human liberty will buy their way into the pages of your magazine?"

The short answer to the question, of course, is "as many as stand willing to pay the going rates." But it is impossible these days to say things like that without being accused of cynicism. Nor is it wise to mock any impulse of compassion or generosity of spirit. But if I were to take seriously the woman's objection, *Harper's Magazine* could publish travel posters from relatively few of the world's nations. India tolerates a caste system in some ways as cruel as the South African policy of apartheid. Variant forms of political or racial discrimination persist in, among other countries, Nigeria, Poland, the Soviet Union, Sri Lanka, Brazil, Iraq, Iran, Saudi Arabia, and the Sudan. Extending the principle of divestment to the representation of commercial objects (i.e., trafficking in profane images), *Harper's Magazine* obviously couldn't accept advertising from the manufacturers of cigarettes, French brandy, or cruise missiles. In its purified state the magazine could go virtuously into bankruptcy. Such an end might be desirable, even Christian, but it would impose on a good many decent voices a silence as certain as the silence in a South African jail.

For people unwilling to follow the proddings of their conscience all the way into the deserts of renunciation, the demands for divestment become gestures more or less exquisitely rendered. On reading the declarations of the concerned clergymen who wish to launder the stains out of a university's stock portfolio, I think of Beau Brummell taking a pinch of perfumed snuff as a protest against the stench of the streets of nineteenth-century London. Their displays of sentiment might seem a trifle more convincing if South Africa weren't quite so far away, if they actually had seen any of the people whom they condemn, if they didn't leave the excitement of the afternoon's rally with the diamonds still in their watches and the gold still in their teeth. Having cast themselves in the role of moral dandies and transformed their feeling into something noble and abstract, they can excuse themselves from addressing the tiresome and all too specific instances of injustice sitting on a Harlem stoop less than 3,000 yards from their parade of virtue.

HARPER'S MAGAZINE,
*July 1985*

# GOING SOUTH

*Refresh my memory. Is it Upper or Lower Silesia that we are giving away?*

—Lloyd George

O N JULY 11 of 1986 the Central Intelligence Agency was given command of the American military adventure in Nicaragua, and on reading the announcement in the paper I was reminded of the story about the cabinetmaker, the undercover agent, and the birch tree. The story appeared some years ago in congressional testimony, and I made a note of it at the time as one of those exemplary tales that cast a sudden light into the abyss of government.

The CIA apparently wished to upgrade its surveillance of Soviet telecommunications, and somebody at the agency's headquarters in Virginia hit upon the idea of concealing a listening device in a tree somewhere in the vicinity of Moscow. The agency commissioned a Washington cabinetmaker, a craftsman highly regarded for his reproductions of Chippendale tables and chairs, to make a hollow birch tree. The cabinetmaker worked for many months on the design, earning upwards of $100,000 for what his patrons pronounced a masterpiece, and when he was done the agency's technical fellowship filled the tree with the newest electronics that money could buy. The agency shipped the tree to Russia, presumably through one of its more sophisticated freight-forwarding companies on the Black Sea, and the master technologists in Virginia congratulated themselves on their triumph. Alas, the undercover agent in Moscow knew as little about botany as he knew about Chippendale chairs. He planted the birch tree in a pine forest, and within a matter of days the Russians discovered a gift of high technology that would have cost them a good deal of trouble to acquire from a debt-ridden American sailor in San Diego.

The July announcement of the agency's appointment to the Nicaraguan command was slightly marred by the release, on the same day, of a Defense Department report to the effect that the 1983 invasion of Grenada proceeded along the lines of bungling farce. The report made particular note of an almost total lack of intelligence data about the island. The CIA guessed wrong as to the whereabouts of the medical students whom the American troops were sent to evacuate, and it compounded the error by portraying the military units on Grenada as "poorly armed, low in morale," and provided with "only three or four [anti-aircraft] guns." All of that information proved incorrect.

In the event, the invasion succeeded only because the Joint Chiefs of Staff, well aware of the incompetence of American intelligence, dispatched twice the complement of forces (ships, troops, helicopters) requested by the commander of the expedition.

The CIA over the years has given many virtuoso performances in the theater of geopolitical romance. It employs a repertory company of mimes and fantasts capable of believing almost any nonsense told to them in a paranoid whisper by almost anybody with a conspiracy theory to sell. The chronicle of the agency's exploits reads like a series of comic improvisations on a text by Pirandello or Molière.

Begin, for instance, with Ngo Dinh Diem, the Catholic despot whom the CIA established as the bulwark of democracy in the Buddhist country of Vietnam. Go next to the Bay of Pigs, where the CIA expected—without the least hint of a plausible reason—a crowd of grateful peasants to rise from the sugarcane and march, gloriously and extemporaneously, to Havana. Dwell briefly on the theory of "counterinsurgency" that the CIA promoted, with disastrous effect, in the mountains north of Saigon. Consider the lost guerrilla wars in Laos, Indonesia, and Angola. Contemplate the agency's stupidity in Iran, where its agents neglected to learn the language and failed to suspect, much less anticipate, the defeat of the late Shah. Reflect on the ease with which foreign agents rummage through the sack of American intelligence secrets, or the aplomb with which the agency last year lost track of a Soviet defector in a French restaurant in downtown Washington. Most pertinent to the forthcoming debacle in Nicaragua, bear in mind the CIA's habit of falsifying information to meet the dreams and wishes of the White House—telling President Johnson what he wanted to hear about enemy troop strength in Vietnam, providing President Carter with statistical proofs of the nonexistent "energy crisis," assuring President Reagan that the Caribbean Sea swarms with Soviet ships bringing weapons and communist subversion to the innocent coasts of Central America.

Given such a troupe of credulous footpads, among whom E. Howard Hunt represents the norm rather than the exception, who would want to lead the CIA on a tour of Europe, much less into a clandestine war? I suspect that the answer to the question has to do with the characteristically American assumptions of unlimited virtue and power.

The recent dispatches from Washington mentioned the Army's reluctance to undertake the Nicaraguan adventure. Having been defeated in Vietnam by peasants on bicycles, the Army presumably has learned that what looks impressive on paper isn't always so convincing to the targets of opportunity who missed the briefing. Not so William J. Casey, retired stock speculator and current director of the CIA. The newspapers quoted a government official saying that Casey "is dying for" the chance to show what his boys can do with a budget of $100 million preproduction and a clear field of fire. "If we can win," the official said, "he can walk away with an agency that is rehabilitated to the best days of the Cold War."

"The best days of the Cold War" (a phrase worth remembering) describes a brief period in the late 1940s and early 1950s when the CIA enjoyed the benefits accruing to the American account in a world wrecked by war and poverty. Dictators traded at discount prices and double agents could be hired for the cost of a meal and a package of cigarettes. Casey has said that he wishes to restore the agency to its former, largely imaginary, splendor, endowing it with a "paramilitary capacity" equal to that of Sylvester Stallone, Arnold Schwarzenegger, and the A-Team. Other enthusiastic gentlemen of

Casey's age and character collect Civil War cannons or dress up in the costumes of Arizona sheriffs when riding palominos in the Rose Bowl parade. I'm told that when Casey plays golf at Palm Beach he is attended by bodyguards carrying machine guns, and although I can't imagine anybody wanting to assassinate the gentleman (for the good and sufficient reason that even the Reagan Administration would be hard put to replace him with a more preposterous Scaramouch), I expect that he finds the machine guns flattering—like a flourish of trumpets or a murmur of applause. His old friends on Wall Street might amuse themselves with art collections, but who among them can mount an armed escort on the perimeter of a sand trap?

I don't doubt Casey's patriotism and zeal, but, like the other rich businessmen in the senior ranks of the Reagan Administration—not only the President but also Messrs. Weinberger, Shultz, Regan, Baker, Buchanan, and Meese—Casey confuses the power of money with the powers of the human character and spirit. It is a common failing within the American plutocracy. Knowing nothing of foreign languages, nothing of history or literature or any society other than their own, the members of the greens committee rely on the professional advice of sophists as accommodating as Henry Kissinger. It isn't fair to place too much emphasis on Kissinger, a man neither more nor less honest than most of his colleagues in the policy institutes, but he has an exceptional talent for composing idiot obiter dicta likely to meet with the approval of his clientele; and in 1974, in a handbook entitled *American Foreign Policy*, he set forth the rule of omnipotence: "A scientific revolution has, for all practical purposes, removed technical limits from the exercise of power in foreign policy."

An audience willing to believe that sort of drivel sooner or later comes to imagine that diplomacy is a form of screenwriting in which the producers in Washington assign all the parts and write all the dialogue. Other nations come and go like movie sets, their national identities nothing more than picturesque backgrounds for a trendy film complete with social statement. Given the dreaming somnambulism implicit in such an attitude, it wouldn't surprise me if the

CIA, on packing up its lights and costume trunks for the Nicaraguan tour, remembered to take not only mines and flares and plastic explosives but also one or two birch trees.

HARPER'S MAGAZINE,
*September 1986*

# OPÉRA BOUFFE

*It was not exactly a proper empire, but we did have a
damn good time.*

—Colonel Emile Fleury

$A$s with so much else about the Reagan Administration, the
misadventure in the international arms trade plays as opéra bouffe.
It isn't hard to imagine President Reagan's privy councillors dressed
up in preposterous military uniforms, wielding papier-mâché
swords and singing the music of Offenbach. Whatever they thought
they were doing—in Iran, Switzerland, Virginia, Israel, Nicaragua,
Brunei, and Saudi Arabia—probably never will be fully understood
or explained. After two months of earnest questions in the media
and the Congress, nobody can say with any degree of certainty what
happened to the money, the hostages, the weapons, or the President's senses. What was clear was the comic tawdriness of the
dramatis personae. The President of the United States stood revealed as an amiable dotard and his principal confederates as a
claque of self-regarding and not so amiable mediocrities. A play-
wright with a fondness for melodrama might set the characterizations as follows:

PRESIDENT RONALD REAGAN—an aging matinee idol, as well informed about history and geography as any other aging matinee idol.

VICE ADMIRAL JOHN POINDEXTER (formerly director of the National
Security Council)—a sycophant. Resentful of the law and suspicious of any view of the world that doesn't confirm his own
memorandums on the subject.

ROBERT McFARLANE (another former director of the NSC)—an

**335**

envious careerist. Persuaded that the media cheated him of his deserved applause.

WILLIAM CASEY (director of the Central Intelligence Agency)—a venal autocrat.

DONALD REGAN (White House chief of staff)—a bully. Notable for his arrogance and stupidity.

LIEUTENANT COLONEL OLIVER NORTH —a zealous fantast. The kind of man apt to believe fervently in UFOs and the lost Charles Manson treasure. Had he been available to the German army in the winter of 1944 he undoubtedly would have commanded a battalion of Hitler youth.

Given such a troupe of road-show Machiavellians, it's a wonder the NSC hasn't invaded Angola or set up naval blockades off both coasts of Panama. Certainly the council possesses the requisite spirit of presumption, and its games of imperial "let's pretend" in many ways resembled the toy realpolitik popular in France during the Second Empire of Napoleon III. That dreaming prince, comforted by romantic oversimplifications and long afternoon naps, also surrounded himself with courtiers (among them the chattering Colonel Fleury) remarkable for their vanity and gall. The court was as vulgar as it was fraudulent, delighting in gossip, fashion, and shows of military splendor. In the end Louis Napoleon took seriously his own nonsense and lost, over an unpleasant shooting weekend at Sedan, both the army and the empire.

Mercifully for the peace of nations, the quotients of intelligence within the NSC appear to be as minimal as the talent for geopolitics. Maybe the would-be saviors of the free world were in the habit of watching too much television. They devised a story line for an episode of "The A-Team."

Preening themselves on their righteousness, they allied the purity of their cause with a Middle Eastern consortium of thugs, sharpers, bankrupts, arms smugglers, cutthroats, swindlers, and disbanded soldiers. Congratulating themselves on their shrewdness, they bargained in languages that none of them understood, traded the diplomatic currencies of the United States for worthless promises, and discredited the government they hoped to defend. On being discovered in their criminal charades, all present conducted themselves in the manner traditional among thieves: everybody professed his own innocence and assigned the fault to a friend. Secretary of State George Shultz and Vice President George Bush moved fastidiously upwind from President Reagan; President Reagan blamed Israel or some other "unknown third country"; those who could do so (among them Poindexter and North) offered to incriminate one or more of their companions in return for immunity and safe passage into the nearest book deal.

Although not especially edifying for the nation's schoolchildren, the example set by President Reagan's counselors teaches a few unhappy lessons about the current state of American politics.

1. *The wish for kings.* Ever since its arrival in Washington in the winter of 1981, the Reagan Administration has made no secret of its contempt for anything so chickenhearted and un-American as the due process of law. Its characteristic tone of voice has been that of the adventurer and the zealot: Attorney General Edwin Meese saying he didn't think the Constitution relevant to the expediencies of the state; White House communications director Patrick Buchanan proclaiming the President and Colonel North heroes because they had the guts to do what they damned well knew was right; the CIA justifying its invasions of Central American as works of noble conscience; the Justice Department subverting the law in order to eliminate any impurities likely to appear in the citizenry's urine or speech.

Instead of advocating conservative habits of thought, which imply a decent regard for the established rights of individuals as well as institutions, President Reagan's companions construed the victory at the polls as a coup d'état. They seized the spoils of government with the swagger of brigands, as secure as Clint Eastwood in their knowledge of the good, the true, and the beautiful. The crooked dealing in the arms trade fits the moral specifications of an administration that delights in the simplicities of autocracy. As of the present writing, more than a hundred officials appointed to the government have suffered criminal indictment, resigned for reasons of ethical misconduct, or come under the suspicion of graft.

The dissension among President Reagan's subordinates also has been characteristic of the Administration since its earliest days in office. When not quarreling with one another about the sanctity of their prejudices or the favors owed their friends, the President's diplomatic advisers have distinguished themselves by their talent for betrayal. The President apparently maintains only a dim and tenuous grasp on the affairs of state, and over the last six years it has become embarrassingly obvious that his subordinates regard him as the prize in a game of capture the flag. The disposition of the nation's foreign policy belongs to the faction that can prevail upon the President (at least until the end of the week) to read the newest slogan.

2. *The polite silence.* Neither the Congress nor the media wish to draw all the conclusions implicit in the reports of the Iranian arms transfers. Suppose it turns out that the President doesn't govern the country? Suppose he hasn't been governing the country for some time? What if he's an idiot or a bald-faced liar? What if the government of the United States has been left to the management of knaves and fools?

None of the questions ease the collective mind of a Congress and media that have accepted the Reagan Administration at its own inflated estimate, applauding the sweetness of the President's smile, gladly mistaking the pageants staged in Libya and Grenada for coherent foreign policy, overlooking the repeated abuses of the law, granting the measures of moral weight to the expressions of watery sentiment.

It is, of course, the media's business to pretend that all is well within the happy household of the American republic, to assure their audiences that—by and large and excepting only the few well-advertised exceptions that prove the rule—our armies are invincible, our politicians honest, our intentions honorable, our money safe, and our democracy the wonder of an admiring world. Too close an inquiry into the rabbit warrens of the Reagan Administration might make those precious and necessary truths too difficult to sustain. Rather than risk disquieting answers, the press for the last six years has asked as few questions as decently as possible. It was fitting that the news of the Iranian arms transfers first appeared in a magazine published in Beirut.

The autumn riot of unwelcome revelation prompted the media and the Congress to deny the rumors of clownish incompetence at levels of authority supposedly stable. The solemnity of the voices on television was meant not only to conceal the absurd humor of the proceedings but also to allay the fear that maybe something had gone very, very wrong. If too many people gave way to blunt statement or raucous laughter, what would become of the fiction of President Reagan's imperial masquerade?

Senator David Durenberger reluctantly convened hearings before the Senate Intelligence Committee with the assurance that "there's much less here than meets the eye." The nation's more prominent newspapers (i.e., *The New York Times, The Wall Street Journal, The Washington Post*) blossomed with editorials advising caution and restraint, explaining that nothing was amiss and that no harm had been done, pointing out that the nation could ill afford two years of drift, calling for the appointment of a bipartisan council of wise men and women, beseeching the President to please tell the country a plausible lie.

3. *The unbearable lightness of being.* It is a tribute to the country's wealth, as well as to its anxiety and sloth, that it so gratefully applauds the sham of the Reagan government. Happiness can be defined as the state of being well deceived, and for the last six years the President has done admirable service as a front man for the America seen in Miller beer commercials. As long as the banks remain sound and enough people have enough money to buy the goods and services available in the nation's better stores, as long as the NSC refrains (at least to the best of anyone's knowledge) from espousing the Moslem religion or declaring war on Australia, the fickle and indifferent electorate (together with its surrogates in the media and the Congress) stands willing to accept, at par value, the counterfeit wisdom in office. What difference does it make if the second-story men in the White House lack intelligence, character,

decency, or, as it turns out and despite their noisy patriotism, courage? Their mere presence allows people with better things to do to excuse themselves from the tedious chore of preserving their freedom. The children let out of school can go to Acapulco or Aspen to play sexual charades or practice aerobiotic breathing.

Maybe this is as much as can be expected in the currently reduced circumstances of the American republic. People remark on a feeling of weightlessness. We inhabit a world of images that float across the mirrors of the news. Apparitions come and go, seemingly without effort, bobbing up from the depths of the void and then vanishing, as mysteriously as they came, without a trace. One week we're at war with Iran; the next week we're at war with Iraq. The National Security Council is seized by soldiers of fortune, and the White House places its trust in gamblers and thieves. In October the columnists say that the Reagan era will last forever; in December they wonder if the Reagan era can last through the end of the month. Who else but an actor, himself as light as a waterfly, could preside over the kingdoms of dream and counter-dream?

HARPER'S MAGAZINE,
*February 1987*

# FADE TO BLACK

*The public good requires us to betray, and to lie, and to massacre: let us resign this commission to those who are more pliable, and more obedient.*

—Montaigne

As EXPECTED, THE Tower Commission's report depicted the President of the United States as a matinee idol held captive by his retinue of zealous, vain, and remarkably inept subalterns. Although muffled in the language of bureaucratic euphemism, the text makes it plain enough that President Reagan knew as much about the Iranian arms deals as he knows about the dark side of the moon. The National Security Council did as it pleased—trading weapons for hostages, ignoring whatever laws it didn't care to understand, furnishing the President with the lies that he obligingly and uncomprehendingly read into the television cameras.

If with regard to the habitual somnambulism of the Reagan Administration the report confirmed what had been obvious for some years, it raised further and more difficult questions about the paranoid mechanics of any American presidency. Why is it that so many seemingly enlightened politicians (a.k.a. "the leaders of the free world") insist on making mockeries of their own dearest beliefs? How does it happen that they repeatedly entangle themselves in the coils of scandal and the nets of crime? How does it come to pass that President Kennedy approves the doomed invasion at the Bay of Pigs and sets in motion the idiot realpolitik of the Vietnam War, or that President Johnson sponsors the escalation of that war with the contrived incident in the Tonkin Gulf, or that President Nixon orders the secret bombing of Cambodia and entrusts his reputation to the incompetent thugs sent to rifle a desk at the Watergate?

At least some of the answers follow from two sets of fantastic expectations assigned to the office of the presidency.

## 1. THE TWO GOVERNMENTS

In response to the popular but utterly implausible belief that it can provide all things to all people, the American political system allows for the parallel sovereignty of both a permanent and a provisional government. The permanent government—the Congress, the civil and military services, the media, the legion of Washington lawyers and expensive lobbyists—occupies the anonymous hierarchies that remain safely in place no matter what the political truths voted in and out of the White House on the trend of a season. It is this government—sly and patient and slow—that writes the briefing papers and the laws, presides over the administrative routine, remembers who bribed whom in the election of 1968, and why President Carter thought it prudent to talk privately to God about the B-1 bomber.

Except in the rare moments of jointly opportune interest, the permanent government wages a ceaseless war of bureaucratic attrition against the provisional government that once every four or eight years accompanies a newly elected president to Washington. The amateur government consists of the cadre of ideologues, cronies, plutocrats, and academic theorists miraculously transformed into Cabinet officials and White House privy councillors. Endowed with the virtues of freebooting adventurers, the parvenu statesmen can be compared with reasonable accuracy either to a troupe of actors or to a swarm of thieves. They possess the talents and energies necessary to the winning of elections. Although admirable, these are not the talents and energies useful to the conduct of international diplomacy.

An American presidential campaign resembles a forced march through enemy country, and the President's companions-in-arms—whether Robert Kennedy, John Mitchell, Hamilton Jordan, or William Casey—inevitably prove to be the sort of people who know how to set up advance publicity in a shopping mall, how to counterfeit a political image or bully a congressman, how to buy a vote or rig a stock price. They seldom know anything of history, of languages, of literature, of political economy, and they lack the imaginative intelligence that might allow them to understand any system of value that can't be learned in a football stadium or a used-car lot.

The President and his confederates inherit a suite of empty rooms. The media like to pretend that the White House is an august and stately institution, the point at which all the lines of power converge, the still center of the still American universe. The people who occupy the place discover that the White House bears a more credible resemblance to a bare stage or an abandoned cruise ship. The previous tenants have removed everything of value—the files, the correspondence, the telephone numbers, the memorabilia on the walls. The new repertory company begins at the beginning, setting up its own props and lights, arranging its own systems of communications and theory of command, hoping to sustain, at least long enough for everybody to profit from the effect, the illusion of coherent power.

All other American institutions of any consequence (the Chase Manhattan Bank, say, or the Pentagon) rely on the presence of senior officials who remember what happened twenty years ago when somebody else—equally ambitious, equally new—proposed something equally foolish. But the White House is barren of institutional memory. Maybe an old butler remembers that President Eisenhower liked sugar in his tea, but nobody remembers the travel arrangements for the last American expedition to Iran.

Because everybody in the White House arrives at the same time (all of them contemporaries in their newfound authority), nobody, not even Nancy Reagan, can invent the pomp and majesty of a traditional protocol. The ancient Romans at least had the wit to provide their triumphant generals with a word of doubt. The general was allowed to ride through the streets of the capital at the head of a procession of captured slaves, but the Senate assigned a magistrate to stand behind him in the chariot, holding the wreath over his head and muttering into his ear the constant reminder that he was mortal. But who in the White House can teach the lessons of humility?

Within a week of its arrival in Washington, the provisional government learns that the world is a far more dangerous place than anybody had thought possible as recently as two months ago, when the candidate was reciting the familiar claptrap about the Russians to an airport crowd somewhere south of Atlanta. Alarmed by the introductory briefings at the Defense Department, the amateur statesmen feel impelled to take bold stands, to make good on their campaign promises, to act.

Being as impatient as they are vain, they know they have only a short period of time in which to set up their profitable passage back into the private sector (i.e., to make their deals with a book publisher, a consulting business, or a brokerage firm), and so they're in a hurry to make their fortunes and their names. Almost immediately they find themselves checked by the inertia of the permanent government, by the congressional committees, by the maze of prior agreements, by the bureaucrats who bring up the niggling reasons a thing can't be done.

Sooner or later, usually sooner, the sense of frustration incites the President's men to "take it inside" or "move it across the street," and so they make of the National Security Council or the White House basement the seat of "a loyal government" blessed with the will to dare and do. The decision inevitably entails the subversion of the law and excites the passion for secrecy. The technological possibilities presented by the available back channels, map overlays, and surveillance techniques tempt the would-be Metternichs to succumb to the dreams of omnipotence. Pretty soon they start speaking in code, and before long American infantrymen begin to turn up dead in the jungles of Vietnam or the streets of Beirut.

## 2. THE WILL TO INNOCENCE

Every administration has no choice but to confront the world's violence and disorder, but the doctrines of American grace oblige it to do so under the banners of righteousness and in the name of one or another of the fanciful pretexts ("democracy," "civilization," "humanity," "the people," etc.) that preserve the conscience of the American television audience. The electorate expects its presidential candidates to feign the clean-limbed idealism of college sophomores, to present themselves as honest and good-natured fellows who know nothing of murder, ambition, lust, selfishness, coward-ice, or greed. The pose of innocence is as mandatory as the ability to eat banquet food. Nobody can afford to say, with Talleyrand, that he's in it for the money, or, with Montaigne, that a statesman must deny himself, at least during business hours, the luxuries of con-science and sentiment.

After having been in office no more than a few months, the provisional government no longer knows when it's telling the truth. The need to preserve the illusion of innocence gets confused with the dream of power, and the resident fantasts come to believe their own invented reality—the one they made out of smoke and colored lights when they first arrived in Washington.

During the early years of the Reagan Administration, the Presi-dent's advisers were wise enough to remember that they had been hired to work on a theatrical production. They staged military pageants in the Caribbean, the eastern Mediterranean, and New York harbor, sustained the illusion of economic prosperity with money borrowed from the Japanese, dressed up the chicanery of their politics in the sentiment of Broadway musicals. They were as lucky as they were clever, and for a surprisingly long time their enemies in the permanent government stood willing to judge the show a success.

The media's applause prompted the President and his compan-ions to mistake the world behind the footlights for the world outside the theater. Flattered by a claque of increasingly belligerent and literal-minded ideologues (among them Vice Admiral John Poindex-ter, Lieutenant Colonel Oliver North, and Patrick Buchanan) and encouraged by the pretensions of his wife, Reagan came to imagine himself a real, not a make-believe, president. He took to wearing his costume in the street, delivering his lines to passing strangers (among them Mikhail Gorbachev and the Ayatollah Khomeini) with the fond expectation that they would respond with dialogue appro-priate to the scene. The most recent reports from Washington sug-gest that he apparently believed he was leading a Republican renaissance in America, that he had gathered around him not a gang of petty charlatans but a host of selfless idealists, and that in exchange for a Bible and a key-shaped cake, the Iranian despotism would abide by the rules of decorum in effect at the Los Angeles Country Club.

Despite having been repeatedly warned of his possible assassination that last weekend in November 1963, President Kennedy went to Dallas in the firm belief that he couldn't be killed. President Reagan invited the Tower Commission to examine his nonexistent foreign policy and his sentimental variations on the theme of America the Beautiful in the belief that his enemies would accept his ignorance as proof of his virtue.

HARPER'S MAGAZINE,
*May 1987*

# LANDSCAPE WITH TROLLS

*Youth is a fire, and the years are a pack of wolves who grow bolder as the fire dies down.*

—Anonymous

FOR SIX DAYS in July, Lieutenant Colonel Oliver North played so sweetly on the panpipes of the American dream that he allowed the television public to believe in any and all of its best-beloved fairy tales. The truth of what he was saying didn't matter as much as the timbre of his voice or the tears in his eyes. The audience could choose to see in his performance what it wished to see, and within a few hours of his appearance before the Iran-*contra* committee the opinion polls announced the birth of a star.

So much of the colonel's story made so little sense that it wasn't until the evening of the third day of his testimony—while watching Dan Aykroyd's comic variation of *Dragnet* in the company of several schoolchildren who had never heard of Fawn Hall or Manucher Ghorbanifar—that I finally understood the geopolitical theory at play in the wilderness of the colonel's mind. Some aspects of his confession had been easy enough to grasp. I could understand the colonel and his friends wanting to do brave and heroic deeds in distant lands across the sea; I could understand their bombast, their incompetence, even their belief in the magical properties of secret codes and passwords. What troubled me was the lack of plausible narrative and the absence of coherent motive. How in God's name did they form their impressions of reality? In what sort of world did they imagine themselves resident?

The movie—reported by *Variety* to be one of the season's leading

**347**

attractions at the box office—offered the beginning of an answer. About twenty minutes into the story, the principal villain entered the camera shot wearing the heavy mask of a horned goat, and even before he pushed the virgin from Anaheim into the pit with the giant snake, I knew I was looking at the geopolitics of Lieutenant Colonel Oliver North. Cast as clownish policemen, Aykroyd and his partner meet the villain in the goat's mask when they blunder into an orgiastic crowd scene in the Hollywood hills. The villain is the high priest of a pagan cult plotting to seize the municipal government of Los Angeles. The few thousand devotees assembled for the evening's ritual of human sacrifice, all of them wearing goatskins on their legs, dance frenzied dances in the light of a ribald moon.

The movie continues along similar lines for another ninety minutes, no more or less absurd in its plot devices than most of the movies that come and go every summer as quickly as mayflies. It was intended for what the producers of Hollywood phantasmagoria define as a "target audience" of citizens between the ages of eight and fourteen.

So was the testimony and derring-do of Colonel North. Eager and boyish in his adventurer's uniform of woodland green, the colonel sounded like Peter Pan telling Wendy and her little brothers about his marvelous exploits in Never-Never-Land. He didn't know what happened to Captain Hook and the pirates, but he told of how he challenged Abu Nidal, the terrible Arab terrorist, to a feat of arms "on equal terms, anywhere in the world." He told of wily arms merchants in far-off Persia and loyal mercenaries in the jungles of Honduras. He portrayed himself as the leader of a "handful" of brave companions holding at bay the princes of the world's darkness. By the end of his second day as a witness, it was clear that his covert operations took place in the kingdom of myth and fairy tale. Utterly lacking a sense of history or historical time, his mind wandering among fabulous beasts in a magical present, he sought to shape the world by the casting of spells. Together with his friends he invented a game of Dungeons and Dragons in which Israel was "banana," airports were "swimming pools," hostages were "zebras," and President Reagan was "Joshua." Apparently the colonel and his merry band of lost boys understood their gifts of cake and money as votive offerings placed on the altar of Moloch, their map coordinates as runes marking the approaches not to Nicaragua or Iran but to the land of trolls.

Grinning and earnest and young, always partial to "neat" ideas, the colonel spoke of himself as "this kid," so obedient and good that he would "go stand in the corner and sit on his head" if ordered to do so by his commander in chief. Anybody who opposed him, whether Iranian villain or congressional wimp, he identified as a dupe or a traitor, or, worst of all, as an adult. The colonel brooked no compromise with the "wicked world" of ambiguity and time.

The public, of course, adored the romantic colonel. He embodied all the myths and images of everybody's lost youth, and he reminded people of a time out of mind when all the animals were friendly and all the grass was green. The Style pages of *The Washington Post* welcomed the colonel into the lighted rooms of celebrity with exclamations of burbling delight: "Now we've got America's face. . . . The only good face the hearings have had . . . a face that is fierce, furrowed, boyish, angry, lachrymose, goofy, sly, handsome, smug, indignant, dissembling, wounded, gap-toothed, peeved, resolute, naive, contemptuous, resentful, bright, wary, cocky, and five-o'clock shadowed." In brief, a face with something for everybody and sure to sell a lot of tickets in Peoria.

Elsewhere in the media, the chorus of excited voices reiterated the theme of the colonel's boyishness. One critic spoke of the "last cavalier," another of "the little colonel who could." The editorial writers ransacked the archive of old movies in search of the sublime cliché and compared the colonel to Peck's bad boy, an eagle scout, Mickey Rooney, the young Jimmy Stewart, Clint Eastwood, Huck Finn, Errol Flynn, John Wayne, Tom Sawyer, and The Beaver.

Crowds gathered on Capitol Hill as early as 5 a.m., waiting patiently for a seat in the congressional theater and a glimpse of the colonel's performance. The nation's mothers sent flowers and telegrams. Thousands of citizens telephoned the White House to say they admired the colonel because he was "so American" or because he was "the boy next door" or because he so bravely defended the country against its host of enemies. A general quartered at the Marine barracks in Quantico, Virginia, said: "Setting aside his situational ethics, he adhered to the core values of the corps."

The tide of emotion running so strongly in the colonel's favor cowed the committee investigating his lies and evasions. Wary of the colonel's newly minted celebrity and mindful of the American axiom that celebrity in sufficient magnitude transmutes even the basest crimes into sympathy and gold, the politicians, at least for the first few days, refrained from asking rude questions. Joined with the media's delight in the colonel's ability to wear the multiple faces of the American dream, the committees' cowardice allowed the colonel to display the full range of his talent for greeting-card sentiment. He delivered little lectures on patriotism and offered homilies about the meaning of life, love, liberty, and the Constitution.

Because nobody wished to disturb the forces of elemental myth playing around the edges of the colonel's uniform, nobody insisted on too close an examination of the colonel's testimony. This was fortunate because the colonel's stories were as squalid as they were fantastic. What he was defending as proof of his strength and honor was the craven policy of paying ransom (arms for hostages) to the terrorists who had murdered his fellow Marines in Beirut. Seeking to impose his fictional reality on the texts of experience (i.e., applying the poetic rules of the world out of time to the world in time), he had betrayed the nation's noblest ideals and wreaked havoc among the people he had sworn to protect.

Throughout the hearings he presented himself as a humble patriot who never once disobeyed an order or did anything un-American. And yet, by his own repeated admission, he ignored the nation's laws whenever those laws stood in the way of what he regarded as a higher cause. In the interests of the national security state, he lied to the Congress as well as to American Cabinet officials and foreign intelligence agents; he wrote false chronologies and destroyed documents in order to prevent them from falling into the hands of his imagined enemies (i.e., the adults) in the Justice Department. Contrary to every impulse ingrained in the definition of what it means to be an American, the colonel portrayed himself as the faithful servant of a president whom he endowed with the powers of an oriental despot.

Presenting himself as a "can-do" sort of guy, the colonel said that he was proud of his success in the moral underworld. So loud was his self-praise that an inattentive member of the audience might have thought his zeal had resulted in triumph. But most of his efforts resulted in failure, betrayal, and death. During his tenure at the National Security Council the American government abandoned more hostages than it rescued. The inane and poorly executed policies that Colonel North advanced in Nicaragua and Iran weakened the cause of the *contras* and fouled the reputation of the Reagan Administration—that is, effects precisely opposite to those that the colonel intended.

The colonel's success as witness and celebrity testified to the ignorance of a credulous American public increasingly in thrall to the fairy tales told by the mass media. Like Oliver North, the big media stage their effects in the realm of myth and dream. Their audiences lose the habit of memory and let slip their hold on the ladders of history and geography. At last count, 50 percent of the American population believed an accused individual guilty until proved innocent; 50 percent didn't know which side the United States supports in Nicaragua; 42 percent couldn't name an Asian country "near the Pacific Ocean"; and 40 percent of the nation's high school seniors thought that Israel was an Arab country.

The mass media perform the function of pagan ritual. Archetypal figures come and go in the enchanted theaters of the news— weightless, without antecedents, dissolving like smoke on a neolithic horizon. For a few days or a few months, occasionally for a period of years, they give shape to the longing of the moment, and for six days in July it was the persona of Oliver North, inflated to the size of a float at the Rose Bowl parade, that comforted the American public with the promise of a world as simple as state fairs, quilting bees, and maple syrup. He offered proof and living witness to a world in which America remained safe from Bolivian drug smugglers and Soviet tank divisions, in which nothing had changed since the glorious victory at Iwo Jima, in which it was as easy to tell the good guys from the bad guys as it was to read the program at a Little League baseball game. Like President Reagan in the heyday of his popularity, Colonel North gave voice and expression to the wish to make time stand still. Defying the Congress, he defied the corruption of death and change and presented himself as the immortal boy in the heroic green uniform of Peter Pan.

HARPER'S MAGAZINE,
*September 1987*

# DERRING-DO

*Incompetent armies deify the commander.*
—Prussian maxim

WHILE WATCHING LAST summer's hearings before the Iran-*contra* committees, and again in the late autumn while reading the text of the congressional report, I kept expecting to hear somebody say something—not loudly, of course, and maybe only through a handkerchief, but at least something—about our slave's faith in secret wars. Surely, I thought, here was a chance to renounce both the theory and practice of covert action. About the practice, the politicians were often critical, a few of them permitting themselves an occasionally acerbic remark about the blundering dishonesty of Attorney General Edwin Meese and Vice Admiral John Poindexter. But on the point of doctrine the committees remained as silent as a colony of Christmas mice. Not once during the entire three months of testimony, or throughout the whole 690 pages of the published narrative, did anybody—not a single congressman, lawyer, or witness—utter so much as a single word against the fatuous and cynical belief that the cause of liberty can be made to stand on the pedestal of criminal violence.

A few members of the committees worried about what they called "the paradox" or "the contradictions" implicit in the waging of clandestine warfare under the jurisdiction of "a free, open, and democratic society." A few other members expressed the forlorn hope that covert actions might be limited in size and cost, or undertaken only with the written permission of the Congress. But in answer to any and all direct questions about the need to deal manfully with events not always to one's liking, all present bowed their heads and murmured in solemn unison, saying, in effect: "Yes, it is a very, very dangerous world, heavily populated with all sorts of dangerous enemies armed with all sorts of dangerous weapons, and in order to defend ourselves against threats of infinite number we have no choice but to resort—reluctantly, of course, and ever mindful of the temporary damage to our constitutional principles—to murder."

Nobody ever failed to reaffirm his faith in this doctrine despite its proven stupidity. Asked to swear fealty to what amounted to Clint Eastwood's theory of diplomacy, the committees knelt and prayed.

So did the chorus of attending journalists and the choir of once and future statesmen. The editorials in the larger papers regretted the loss of the nation's innocence, but they reminded their readers that it was no good pretending that the world is a big, blue sandbox. Two former secretaries of state—Henry Kissinger and General Alexander Haig—appeared on all three television networks to assure their audiences that secret operations were not only wonderfully effective but also, if properly conducted (i.e., by gentlemen as accomplished as themselves), entirely in keeping with the principles of Thomas Jefferson.

And yet, if somebody were to draw up a balance sheet reflecting the consequences of the covert actions we have let loose in the world over the last forty years, I expect that even a Pentagon accountant might concede the bankruptcy of the enterprise. Consistently and without noteworthy exception, the use of covert military action in support of American foreign policy has ended in failure or catastrophe. Whenever the United States embarks on one of those splendid little adventures so dear to the hearts of the would-be Machiavels in the White House or on the National Security Council, the patrol boats sink and the wrong tyrant seizes the palace and the radio station.

Unless the country stands willing to transform itself into a totalitarian state, even the theory of secret war is absurd. When mounted on any sort of large scale or extended over a period of more than two weeks, covert actions hide nothing from anybody except the people paying the bills. The Iran-*contra* hearings made it plain enough that the arms-for-hostages deals were known to several foreign governments (Israel, Iran, Saudi Arabia, Brunei, and Countries 8–16) as well as to an impressive crowd of Swiss bankers, Washington clerks, and Lebanese arms merchants.

Nor do the American operatives have much talent for covert action. The historical record is embarrassingly clear on the point. In the immediate aftermath of the Second World War, the earliest prototype of the CIA, under the direction of Allen Dulles (a.k.a. "The Great White Case Officer"), enjoyed a brief moment of triumph in a world still largely in ruins, at a time when the military and economic supremacy of the United States went unquestioned by German waiters, and when it was possible to hire native gun-bearers for the price of a bar of chocolate and a pair of nylon stockings. The American intelligence services placed a number of agents behind communist lines in Europe; recruited émigré armies to recapture the lost kingdoms of Poland, Bulgaria, and the Ukraine; and assisted with the removal of governments thought to be subversive in Iran (1953), Guatemala (1954), and the Philippines (1953).

Within a very few years the victories proved to be illusory or, at best, ambiguous. Advance scouts for the émigré armies parachuted into the Slavic darkness and were never seen or heard from again. By overthrowing a popular but socialist regime in Iran (at the behest of the Anglo-Iranian Oil Company), the United States opened the way to the vanity and ignorance of the Shah of Shahs (who had trouble speaking Farsi), to the quadrupling of the Arab oil price, the revolutionary zeal of the Ayatollah Khomeini, and the current impasse in the Persian Gulf.

The forced departure of Jacobo Arbenz from Guatemala (because his form of democratic socialism offended the United Fruit Company) allowed for the arrival of a notably vicious military junta, and in the Philippines the outfitting of Ramón Magsaysay with anticommunist propaganda served as prelude to the corrupt regime of Ferdinand Marcos.

By the end of the decade, the American variations on themes of subversion had acquired the character of grotesque farce. With the hope of eliminating Sukarno as the President of Indonesia (because he permitted communists to take their elected posts in his government), the CIA in 1957 armed a cadre of restless Sumatran colonels and engaged a Hollywood film crew to produce a pornographic film.

Entitled *Happy Days*, the film purportedly showed Sukarno (played by a Mexican actor wearing a mask) in bed with a Soviet agent (played by a California waitress wearing a wig). The coup d'état failed, and the film was understood as a joke.

In 1961 the bungled invasion at the Bay of Pigs (a.k.a. "the glorious march through Havana") ensured Fidel Castro's communist authority throughout Latin America. The subsequent attempts to assassinate him (at least five by the CIA's hired agents) quite possibly resulted in the assassination of John F. Kennedy.

By encouraging the assassination of Ngo Dinh Diem in Saigon in 1963, the United States allied itself with a policy of realpolitik no less cynical than the one against which it was supposedly defending the principles of justice. Four American presidents defined the expedition in Vietnam as a prolonged covert action and systematically lied to the American people as to the reason for our presence in a country with which we never declared ourselves at war. As a result of our effort to rid Indochina of Communism, Vietnam became a unified Communist state. As a result of our effort to teach the world the lessons of democracy, we taught a generation of American citizens to think of their own government as an oriental despotism.

The discovery of the CIA's mining of the Nicaraguan harbors in 1983 obliterated the precarious advantage that the *contras* (on whose behalf the mines were placed) so desperately needed in the American Congress. Similarly discordant effects have followed our interventions in Cambodia, Angola, and Laos.

So unequivocal a record of stupidity and failure begs the question as to why American officialdom persists in its idiot dream of invisible war. It isn't for lack of sound advice. The late Chip Bohlen, one of the wisest of American diplomats and once ambassador to Moscow, understood in the early 1950s that covert actions always take place at the not-very-important margins of not-very-important events. In 1961 President Dwight Eisenhower's Board of Consultants on Foreign Intelligence Activities reviewed the CIA's reputedly glorious record and was unable to conclude that "on balance, all of the covert action programs undertaken by the CIA up to this time have been worth the risk or the great expenditure of manpower, money, and other resources involved."

In the early years of the nineteenth century, John Quincy Adams took up the question of covert action and thought that America should send "her benedictions, and her prayers . . . wherever the standard of freedom and independence has been or shall be unfurled." But America doesn't send arms and munitions because "she goes not abroad in search of monsters to destroy."

Were America to embark on such a foolish adventure, Adams said, she would become entangled "beyond the power of extrication, in all the wars of interest and intrigue, of individual avarice, envy, and ambition, which assume the colors and usurp the standard of freedom. The fundamental maxim of [America's] policy would insensibly change from *liberty* to *force.* . . . She might become the dictatress of the world. She would no longer be the ruler of her own spirit."

Arthur Schlesinger, Jr., quotes Adams in the winter issue of *Foreign Affairs* and then goes on to quote John le Carré to the effect that covert actions recommend themselves to "declining powers," to men and institutions feeling the loss of their strength and becoming fearful of shadows. In le Carré's observation it is the timid and servile mind that places "ever greater trust in the magic formulae and hocus-pocus of the spy world. When the king is dying, the charlatans rush in."

Enter, to music for military band, General Haig, Admiral Poindexter, Colonel North, and the braided company of Washington mountebanks, sophists, and leaping acrobats that drags behind it the wagons of the national security state. In the American context, the king is the spirit of liberty, which frightened and cynical people no longer know how to rule, and which, gratefully, they exchange for what they imagine to be the shields of their enemies.

The theory and practice of covert military action inevitably subverts our own people as well as our institutions of government. The operatives in the employ of the White House or the intelligence agencies come to believe themselves surrounded by a host of evil spirits shrieking in a foreign wind. Paranoid and easily convinced of their virtue, they get in the habit of telling so many lies that they no longer know their friends from their enemies.

Hindsight, of course, is easier than foresight, but I wish that at least one member of the joint committees had taken the trouble to study the historical record and to raise his voice against the presiding superstition. I wish I wasn't so often reminded of a herd of docile cattle, lowing softly in a pasture, waiting for Clint Eastwood (or Admiral Poindexter or General Secord or Colonel North) to lead them safely to slaughter.

HARPER'S MAGAZINE,
*February 1988*

# THE ROAD TO
# SHAARAIM

*He who makes a beast of himself gets rid of the pain of
being a man.*

—Dr. Johnson

T HE NEWS FROM Israel this spring is about a rain of stones, and as
I read the reports about the suppression of the rioting in Nablus and
Gaza, I sometimes wonder how the story would be told in the
American press if Israel were a less favored state. Suppose that a
popular uprising were taking place in Panama or the Philippines or
Northern Ireland. Suppose that General Noriega's troops were kill-
ing sixteen-year-old boys at the rate of one or two a day, or that
Corazon Aquino's army was blowing up houses and imposing the
rule of an iron fist, or that Margaret Thatcher, borrowing a phrase
from Prime Minister Yitzhak Shamir, told a crowd of cheering
Englishmen on Christmas Eve that the Irish rebels must be crushed
"like grasshoppers" and their heads smashed against the walls of
Westminster Abbey.

It doesn't need much effort to imagine the outbursts of editorial
indignation, and the congressional fact-finding commissions leaving every Wednesday and Friday for the scenes of international
crime. If, God forbid, any of the events in question were to take
place in a socialist country, I assume that the best conservative
opinion (i.e., precisely some of the very same people who so furiously promote the cause of Israel) would demand ultimatums and a
show of gunboats. On "Nightline" most of the guests would be
wearing uniforms.

The Palestinian uprising at least has had the salutary effect of

**359**

making Israel more visible through the mists of wish and dream. As long as Israel could win its wars in the desert, the Israeli army could be seen as a company of heroes lately arrived from Camelot or Troy. The presumption of military grace gained wide currency in the United States during the years of its confusion and defeat in Vietnam. Fighting a war that they could neither win nor justify, the Americans envied the Israelis their freedom of maneuver in the tactical as well as the moral theaters of operation. But unless wars can be fought in the military equivalent of a football stadium (in the Sinai, say, or the Falkland Islands), they presuppose the random and indiscriminate killing of civilians. The Israeli army lost the aura of romance when, in the summer of 1982, its invasion of Lebanon ended with the killings at Sabra and Shatila.

Now that Israel has to fight its wars in town, under conditions likely to be imposed by any prolonged war in the late twentieth century, Israel has become a state like any other state, forced into complicity with the acts of barbarism. Attempting the hopeless task of conquering a peace, the Israeli army makes itself an accomplice to the murder of children.

The photographs in every morning's paper give to the Palestinian nemesis the sorrow of a human face. The Arab terrorist becomes the massacred innocent, and the Israeli soldier, once thought to be the paragon of chivalry, the cossack. The exchange of images poses questions that even as recently as six months ago would have been thought rude or anti-Semitic. Let too many corpses be seen on too many broken streets (one hundred and forty-nine Palestinians reported dead as of late April), and in another six months it might be possible to talk about Israel not as sacred mystery but as secular geography. I can imagine a fair number of well-meaning people, Jews as well as Christians, questioning the terms of the American alliance with Israel. What do we owe, and what do we expect in return for a subsidy of $3 billion a year?

As between the Israelis and the Palestinians, in which diaspora is justice to be found, and does the argument take place in the realm of existential absolutes (civilization and democracy pitted against chaos and pagan superstition), or is it a quarrel about real estate— the colonial settlers haggling with the native tribes about the ownership of the almond trees? Is the alliance with the United States founded on the reasons of state or the pangs of conscience? If the former, then how does it come to pass that Israel feels no compunction about ordering political assassinations or setting loose its spies in the corridors of the Pentagon? Why did Israel encourage the American sale of weapons to Iran, and from where, and for what purpose, did it acquire its nuclear arsenal? Against what enemy, and in what grandiose imperial design, does the United States seek to enlist the Israeli host?

If the alliance rests on compassion, does the terrible suffering visited upon the Jewish people by Nazi Germany invest them with the rights of the martyred and grant them a kind of moral *droit du seigneur*? If so, how long does the license last? Indefinitely? For forty years? Until the Holocaust has become a parable and all the Palestinians have been deported or lost at sea? Throughout the twelfth century, the Crusader Kingdom of Jerusalem exulted in its dominion over precisely the same landscape now known as Israel. Paid for with money extorted from the faithful in western Christendom, baptized in the name of a holy cause, governed by Norman knights as pitiless as the Stern Gang, the Kingdom of Jerusalem preserved its realm of make-believe for almost a hundred years.

Turn the questions the other way, and ask whether the United States wishes to exploit Israel's military ambition or protect its conscience. Do we ally ourselves with David or Goliath? On the latter question, opinion within Israel divides more fiercely than it does in the United States. The Israeli writers and politicians in what is now an eloquent minority argue that the iron masks of power ill-become a country whose founders conceived of it as a "light unto the nations." In 1948 the most devout of the Jewish surveyors in the Promised Land regarded even the suggestion of a nation-state as blasphemy. Defining the strength of Israel as the strength of a transcendent idea, they thought that the power of David resided not in the weight of his stone but in the luminousness of his spirit.

The Israeli heirs to this belief advised against holding the captured Arab territories after the 1967 war—not because of the harm that would befall the Palestinians but because of the corruption that would likely subvert the Jews. David Ben-Gurion insisted that all the occupied lands be given back, as quickly as possible, before the attitudes of mind habitual to prison guards could "distort, and [maybe] ultimately destroy, the Jewish state." The current members of what might be called the party of David (among them the writers Amos Oz and Amos Elon and former Israeli Foreign Minister Abba Eban) argue that the occupation already has become untenable, that time and demography favor the Palestinians, and that sooner or later the Kingdom of Jerusalem falls (as it did in 1187) and Saladin stables his horse in the tabernacle.

Writing in *The New York Times* this February, in support of the peace initiative put forward by Secretary of State George Shultz, Eban said: "The fact that Israeli military rule is rejected by the Palestinians does not mean that it is tolerable for Israel." He went on to ask whether a "nation-state can really exist in any degree of coherence and harmony if it exercises permanent rule over a foreign population that does not enjoy even the pretense of equal rights and that is not linked to Israel by any flag, tongue, faith, historic experience, national sentiment or common allegiance."

Eban's point seems to me irrefutable, but probably that is because I don't know what it means to live in Israel in the midst of resentful Arabs, some of whom might have killed my daughter or maimed my son. Certainly the Shamir government looks as contemptuously on parleys with the infidel as did Godfrey of Bouillon, Defender of the Holy Sepulcher. It places its trust in the force of arms and so must resort to tear gas and the vocabulary of a police state. As in South Africa or Algeria before the civil war, the subject peoples forfeit their definition as human beings. Menachem Begin in the late 1970s described the Palestinians as "two-legged beasts of prey thirsting for Jewish blood." His successor, Shamir, reduces them to the stature of insects. The children born within the walls of the Israeli garrison inherit the gifts of hatred and anger. They learn to tell the necessary lies, to one another as well as to foreign television crews, and they learn to see not with the eyes of the soul but with the propagandist's floodlights.

Just as it's hard to know why so many prominent Americans tacitly approve Shamir's impersonation of Goliath, so also it's hard to know why so many well-informed Israelis accept American assur-

ances of good faith. Surely everybody knows by now that the story of
Goliath ends unhappily for the Philistines—their camp plundered,
the road to Shaaraim strewn with the bodies of the slain, and their
champion from Gath dead on the ground under bronze-plated armor
weighing 5,000 shekels. The Americans left armament of commen-
surate value on the roads to Da Nang and Hue, and one might have
thought that the Washington geopoliticians might have learned, after
twenty years in the Asian wilderness, the old lesson that an army
can defeat another army but not a people.

Apparently not. Despite his hope of peace, Secretary Shultz
assures everybody in Jerusalem that he will do nothing to interfere
with the supplies of American weapons. By and large the American
media borrow the definitions of the Israeli government and refer to
the riots in Bethlehem as a cynical strategy in a long-standing war
rather than as a popular uprising born of desperation and genuine
national feeling. The presidential candidates say as little as possible about the riots, and Henry Kissinger advises the friends of Israel
to blind the television cameras in the occupied territories and
suppress the rioters as "rapidly" and as "brutally" as circumstances
permit. He suggests, as always, that the fault can be found not in the
deed but in the image, not in the policy but in how the policy looks
in print and on film. If only the Israelis could portray Goliath as a
victim, maybe the Palestinians would feel sorry for the fellow and
agree to go to Mecca.

Were I an Israeli politician, I think I would be wary of American
promises. The record of our dealings with client states, particularly
those client states in which we discover the military virtues, does
not inspire confidence. We feel drawn to dictators who we think
might stand between us and the fear of our own impotence, who
might hold back, if only for twenty minutes, the darkness of the
Third World. For a few years we pretend that our ally is democracy's
best friend in one or another of the poorer latitudes, and for however
long American public opinion (notoriously fickle) remains convinced of its moral beauty, we send F-16s and messages of humanitarian concern. But then something goes wrong with the slogans or
the band music. The despot's troops don't know how to fire the
machine guns, or the prime minister's brother annexes the traffic in

cocaine. For one reason or another, we decide we can't afford to sponsor any more parades, and we leave by helicopter from the roof of the embassy. By aligning Israel with the American dream of cut-rate empire, Shamir casts his lot with Diem, Somoza, Thieu, Marcos, Noriega, and the Shah of Shahs. It is a line of sterile and ignoble succession.

HARPER'S MAGAZINE,
*June 1988*

# THE ACCOUNTS OF
# DEMOCRACY

*He made Germany great and Germans small.*
—William Gladstone, of Bismarck

O<small>N</small> DECEMBER 7 of last year, the thirty-eighth anniversary of the Japanese bombing of Pearl Harbor coincided with what the television networks were calling "Day 34" of the crisis in Iran. Writing that morning in *The New York Times*, Mr. James Reston, eminent columnist and counselor to kings as well as presidents, reminded his readers that freedom could be too much of a good thing. He was worried about the rudeness of the press. Some of the more vulgar members of the profession had forgotten their place and were taking liberties with the privileges extended to them under the First Amendment. Here were these awful people, he said, asking Senator Edward Kennedy questions about his sexual appetites and the drowning of Mary Jo Kopechne. Other reporters, equally impious, were asking Governor John Connally about his indictment for bribery and his connections, possibly criminal, with the unlucky Nixon Administration. All this was bad enough, and surely a sign of the self-destructive rage run amok within the marble halls of the American ego, but what was even worse, and the occasion of Mr. Reston's admonition, was a newly published book, *The Brethren,* into which Bob Woodward and Scott Armstrong of *The Washington Post* had gathered a compendium of second-rate gossip about the Supreme Court. Mr. Reston mentioned the book as a deplorable example of what can happen in a democratic society to perfectly nice people (not to say worthy and dignified people doing their best to uphold the weight of important institutions), and he quoted with

**365**

approval a judge of his acquaintance who thought the book proved that "sometimes you can carry the truth too far."

This remark, together with Mr. Reston's endorsement of it, testifies to the present confusion about the nature and purpose of democracy. Like many other senior officials in the media, Mr. Reston conceives of the press as an office of government. More at ease with the prophetic than the analytic mode, he offers advice on matters of high policy instead of trying to figure out how A——'s tax payments came to be spent or how it was that B——'s son came to be killed. Earlier in the season he effusively praised Henry Kissinger's book *White House Years*, which seems to me curious, because I would guess that Mr. Kissinger's gossip is more calculated than Woodward and Armstrong's. Messrs. Woodward and Armstrong seem to have discovered that Supreme Court justices are men like other men—a revelation that caused them to avenge their disillusion with the kind of indignant self-righteousness that commends itself to the Book-of-the-Month Club. Presumably they thought that Supreme Court justices should attain to the perfection of gods. The authors had the misfortune to come of age in the 1960s, a decade during which the republican idea of government passed out of fashion and people began to pretend (for reasons of vanity as well as self-interest) that their magistrates should not be capable of doing anything venal or stupid.

Mr. Kissinger's book makes the more unpleasant mistake of presenting the author as a god and the other 4 billion inhabitants of the earth as marionettes waiting for Mr. Kissinger to endow them with the breath of life and assign them a role in the great puppet show of geopolitics. Relying on the logic of power rather than the logic of freedom, and by defining morality as anything that serves the ends of policy, Mr. Kissinger's gossip embodies the antithesis of democracy.

For as many days as Ayatollah Khomeini has been holding hostages in the embassy at Teheran, I have been entangled in what seems like a ceaseless round of arguments with people who conceive of democratic government as either a world state, a holy city, or a work of art.

On the same morning that Mr. Reston's counsel appeared in the paper I spoke to an army officer who had drawn up a list of a hundred targets on the Iranian plateau. "You know the sort of thing," he said. "Railheads, road crossings, airfields—the stuff we used to hit in Nam." No, he said, he didn't think that tactical air strikes would bring about the rescue of the hostages, but the hostages he had already discounted as casualties. "What the hell," he said, "the bastards declared war, and in war some of your own guys get hurt. The object of the exercise is to hurt the other guys worse." He pointed out that fifteen U.S. servicemen had been killed during the rescue of the *Mayaguez* in the Gulf of Siam in 1975 (not to mention the 360,706 Americans killed or wounded in Vietnam), and so he didn't think that the loss of fifty lives was too high a rate of exchange for what a generation of American statesmen had described as twenty-five years of tranquillity in the Persian Gulf. The gutlessness of President Carter he thought not so much Mr. Carter's fault ("What can you expect from a preacher?") as proof of a democracy's inability to defend its interests in a world of thieves.

A few hours later, over lunch with a celebrated novelist and his agent, I listened to the same complaint expressed in terms of aesthetics rather than military strategy. The novelist had spent a lot of time in the service of noble causes, and he spoke from what both he and his agent regarded as the moral height vouchsafed to the signers of petitions. Like Senator Kennedy and William Kunstler, the novelist blamed the United States for the Shah's despotism, and he thought that President Carter should have denied the Shah admittance into the sanctuary of New York Hospital. "We have no business funding evil," the novelist said (as if despotisms were somehow analogous to reactionary theater groups supported by the National Endowment for the Arts). "And we deserve to suffer the consequences of our crimes." The agent barely restrained himself from an outburst of applause, and for the next two hours the novelist discussed the failure of the American government to resemble Plato's Republic.

Still later in the day, I attended a dinner at which a number of militant social critics congratulated one another on their foresight and perspicacity. As long ago as 1968 they were writing articles about the weakening of American power and the slackness of American resolve. Now that events had proved them right, they were exultant. They quoted passages from their own texts with the glee of children shouting "I told you so" at the teacher who had said that it wasn't going to snow. As I listened to them count the many ways in which the United States most probably would suffer further defeats (the public hanging of the hostages, the extension of Soviet hegemony in the Persian Gulf, the collapse of the American economy, etc.) I understood that I was in the presence of people immensely relieved to know that they no longer had reason to envy the future. Obviously the future was going to be a lot worse than even their most doom-ridden companions had supposed, and this meant that the age of American triumph was safely in the past, and that they had enjoyed the best of it.

Not knowing how to answer so many people with so many complaints against democracy, but feeling that somehow they had misconstrued the promise of freedom, I spent several days reading Karl Popper's book *The Open Society and Its Enemies*. It is a book that I recommend to anyone who has grown sick of the pleasures of despair. Popper defines democracy as the ceaseless working out of the principle that nobody knows enough, that nothing is final, and that the faith in human reason promises neither comfort nor immortality. A democratic government doesn't ask the question "Who is the best ruler?" (on the ground that even despots have their benevolent afternoons); it asks, instead, "Which ruler can do the least harm?"

The mechanism of checks and balances places as many obstacles as possible in the way of the passions of the moment, and by so doing it preserves the principle of freedom against the desire for the security of a totalitarian state or the stateliness of oligarchy. Because a democracy protects freedom of thought, it proceeds by means of additions—of opportunities, knowledge, questions, factions, and wealth. These additions on what might be called the forward side of the ledger lead to equivalent additions of disorderliness, humiliation, uncertainty, and doubt. Every new good raises the possibility of a new evil, and the proliferation of knowledge imposes on the citizens of a democracy what Popper calls "the strain of civilization." This implies the perpetual expansion of the discovery that the world is not oneself, and most people feel uncomfortable with such unwelcome news. They would rather be doing something else, and so they confuse freedom with the possession of goods or with the self-destructive amusements advertised as self-fulfillment. The Shah of Iran amassed a collection of weapons and hired a secret police that carried out its interrogations in basements deep enough to muffle the screams of the witnesses. Perhaps it was this delicacy of feeling on the part of the Shah that prompted Mr. Kissinger to describe him as "a gentle and sentimental man." The so-called neoconservatives make a comparable mistake when, in their celebration of capitalism, they place the emphasis of their argument on the conservation of things (property, titles, land, privilege, etc.) instead of on the conservation of rational inquiry and the freedom of mind.

The army officer, the novelist, and the social critic all tend to think of freedom as a moment of transcendence (in battle, the act of composition, or on the receipt of an invitation to the White House), and so they confuse the highest good with a once or future golden age. The army officer wonders why it isn't still 1952 and the United States the only country in the world with a weapon that can destroy millions of people in a flash of radiant light; the novelist and the social critic lament the passing of 1946, when all the world was in ruins except the United States. Together with most other people they wish to make time stand still, to delay the evolution of society into a future likely to find them ridiculous or irrelevant. But this is precisely what a democracy cannot do and why its rules of government attempt to unite the necessity of self-sacrifice with the dignity of self-respect. The faith in reason insists that the poverty of democracy offers a greater hope for mankind than the prosperity that attaches itself to aristocracy or despotism.

By preferring the immortality of the whole to the immortality of the part, and by allowing for a multiplicity of forms and the probability that one's children will prove to be happier (or stronger or wiser or luckier) than oneself, democracy assumes a constant making and remaking—of laws and institutions as well as art forms and matinee idols. The other fellow always has something to say (without being prompted by the Shah's secret police), and maybe what he has to say will shake the earth or shift the angles of perception. Franklin Delano Roosevelt was one year out of Harvard when Albert Einstein, an amateur physicist employed by the Swiss Patent Office, formulated the theory of special relativity. Who could have known that within the space of forty years President Roosevelt would call into being the explosion at Los Alamos?

No matter how often it has been corrupted and abused (simply by reason of its being such a difficult feat to perform), the democratic government constitutes the only morality currently operative in the world. Now, as in Athens in the fifth century B.C., democracy represents the attempt to organize the freedom of mind against the tyranny of money, force, and superstition. I don't know how it is possible to read the newspapers without coming to something approximating this conclusion. In the midst of the Christmas advertisements, the papers offer a smudged portrait of a world not much advanced from the world of the Homeric poems. The nations of the earth tear at each other like dogs, fighting wars in the name of oil or nationalism. The ayatollahs in Iran and the clergy in Ireland set the faithful to killing one another over the question of whose god, among the 4,000 extant, is the true god. In the Straits of Malacca and off the Patagonian coast, oil tankers burn and sink, polluting the oceans with their cargo because the owners, usually Greek, find it profitable to sail the ships without adequate maintenance or competent crews. The arms merchants in France and Germany sell weapons to any dictator who can pay the going price for counterrevolution.

Within the United States the journals of respectable opinion do what they can to present a more flattering portrait, and so they don't dwell at length on the traffic in cocaine (selling last month in New York at $3,000 an ounce), the number of people left dead in the streets, or the criminal means by which Americans every year manage to defraud the IRS of the sum of about $500 billion. A few weeks ago in New York two young girls were found dead in a West Side motel room, their hands and heads severed from their mutilated bodies. The papers didn't give the crime the sensational attention it might have commanded prior to the difficulty in Iran, and I assume that their restraint had something to do with the intimations of what might happen in the event of a nuclear war. Why else do those missiles stand so quietly in their silos, all of them pointed at playgrounds in Moscow, Paris, London, and Washington? How many other children might be changed into objects beyond human recognition?

To the extent that democracy gives people the chance to come to their own conclusions and to develop opinions likely to subvert the established order, so also a democratic government stands the chance of surviving its mistakes. Unlike Henry Kissinger and his admirers, who, with Mr. Reston, accept the rule of force as the wisdom of experience, people who place their faith in reason assume that mankind has more to gain from the skepticism of individuals than it does from the orthodoxy of commissars and philosopher kings. Because democratic institutions do not renew themselves as effortlessly as flowering trees, they demand the ceaseless tinkering of people who possess both the courage and the honesty to admit their mistakes and accept responsibility for even their most inglorious acts. As has been said, this is not easy to do.

Freedom of thought brings societies the unwelcome news that they are in trouble, but because all societies, like all individuals, are always in trouble of one kind or another, the news doesn't cause them to perish. They die instead from the fear of thought and from the paralysis that accompanies the wish to forestall change. Even the neoconservatives choose to ignore this point. By accepting the Marxist formulation that the wealth of nations derives either from capital or labor, they forget that the greatest of all sources of wealth is intelligence. Perhaps they don't like to imagine the consequences of so clear a statement of the obvious. Consider that Athens in the fifth century B.C. was as small as Dayton, Ohio, and then consider what would happen if, by removing the burden of cant and superstition, the United States could release the immense reserves of thought and energy in a population of 220 million people.

# ELEGY FOR A
# LOST ENEMY

*The world of politics is always twenty years behind the
world of thought.*

—John Jay Chapman

IN PARIS LAST July the weekly newsmagazine *VSD* published on
its cover a cinnamon-sweet photograph of a Persian cat surmounted
by the headline: AIDS: CATS HAVE IT TOO.

The announcement caused a sensation. On the morning of the
next day thousands of Parisians showed up at the city's animal
shelters in the suddenly suspicious company of their pet cats.
Subsequent newspaper accounts described the scenes of tearful
farewell. Sometimes maudlin, but mostly laconic or brusque, the
owners of the cats filled out a form, looked for a last time on their
companions of the sofa and the windowsill—"Adieu, Fifi," "Au
revoir, Bidot"—and then adjourned with their sorrow to the nearest
café. Some of the city's less sentimental citizens simply dropped
their cats in the Seine.

By noon of the second day the alarm had been proved false. In
answer to hysterical questions from the health authorities as well as
the news media, the editor of *VSD*, Anne-Marie Cattelain,
shrugged, presumably with a gesture of Gallic contempt, and freely
admitted that she had invented the diagnosis of AIDS in cats. Her
magazine had received reports of a new and obscure disease afflicting some cats in some parts of France, but it was a slow week in a
slow season, and the magazine needed a *coup de théâtre*.

"If we use the real name of the disease," the editor said, "we sell
nothing. With the word AIDS, *ça marche.*"

Her cynicism prompted a second round of sensation. Speaking on behalf of all animals everywhere and their right to be protected from slander, Brigitte Bardot convened a press conference in Saint-Tropez. The president of the Union of French Veterinarians submitted a lawsuit. In the Parisian press the most prominent keepers of the nation's editorial conscience fulminated against *VSD*'s callow and outrageous disregard for the truth.

A few voices in the disreputable minority, however, expressed sympathy for Madame Cattelain's lack of a headline. The summer was indeed slow, and commercial alarms were in short supply. What was a newsmagazine for, if not to remind its readers of their imminent peril?

Several weeks later, at a Republican lawn party in Southampton, Long Island, I told the story of the maligned cats to a professor of American history whom I hadn't previously met but whom I knew from his writings in the political journals. He was a round and self-satisfied man, small, nattily groomed, dressed in a yachting blazer and a yellow bow tie. He looked depressed, which I thought out of character in a man who enjoyed a reputation for being infallible, and I had intended to lighten his spirit with news from the frontiers of liberal infamy. Under ordinary circumstances nothing so delights the defenders of the conservative faith than further proofs of the ways in which the media poison the wells of truth.

But the circumstances weren't ordinary, and the historian didn't think the story was funny. Abruptly, and with an air of annoyance, he said: "I don't think you appreciate the woman's courage."

It turned out that he was looking for work with the Bush campaign, and he knew that if only he could prove the continued existence of the Cold War, he was certain to be rewarded with an academic sinecure or an appointment to the State Department. He had been searching through his maps for the geopolitical equivalent of a cat with AIDS, but as yet he had found nothing suitable, which was embarrassing because Bush insisted on making speeches about the need to protect the American continent and the American people.

"Protect them from whom," he asked, "and against what?"

We stood on the veranda of a large, wooden house overlooking both an apple orchard and the sea. On the lawn in the foreground an orchestra played dance music under a striped tent. Upwards of two hundred people, many of them in evening dress, wandered between long white tables crowded with Russian vodka, Mexican tomatoes, and Japanese shrimp. The women's clothes had been made in Paris, and the men carried keys to German automobiles and code numbers for Swiss bank accounts. The world asked nothing better than to bend the back of its cheap labor to the whims of American luxury.

"It's awful," the historian said. "We're all dressed up for war on five continents and six oceans, but there isn't an enemy in sight."

Not only were the Russians gone from Afghanistan, the historian said, but even worse, they were beginning to dismantle their missiles on the Siberian steppe. Iran and Iraq had come to the end of their murderous war, and the U.S. Navy was hard-pressed to remember why its ships were sailing point-to-point courses in the Persian Gulf. The Cubans and the South Africans had agreed to a cease-fire in Angola. The North and South Koreans were talking about the chances of reunification. Even the Vietnamese (the sly, treacherous, alien Vietnamese) had expressed at least a preliminary wish to leave Cambodia.

"What's the world coming to?" the historian asked. "Where is the land of Mordor?"

He lapsed into a disconsolate silence, poking the ice in his drink with a plastic stick molded in the shape of an elephant. The orchestra was playing a Cole Porter tune, and the evening was bright with the glitter of laughter. The historian stared off into a gloomier distance, and when he again took up the thread of his thought, his voice had a wistful, almost elegiac sound.

"I don't think you realize," he said, "how much we owed the Russians. They were the enemy of first resort. As important to our economy as General Motors or Iowa corn. As fundamental to our freedoms as the First Amendment."

He wondered if I knew how much had been invested in the making of the Soviet icon—how much money, how many careers, how much poetic imagination. It wasn't only the weapons and the research laboratories. It was the books and the policy analysis and the headlines. During a span of more than forty years the study of the Cold War had become a theological discipline not unlike the study of God in a medieval monastery.

Absent the Russian beast, he said, what would become of the history and political science departments at the nation's better universities? Who would write the spy novels and preach the sermons on the texts of Armageddon?

Again he fell silent, and I remembered that recently I had tried to read a novel by John le Carré, but the intrigue had seemed irrelevant and the derring-do as behind the times as the adventures of Lancelot or Brigadier Gerard. The historian looked so troubled that I was moved to comfort him with villains.

"Surely," I said, "there must be somebody else . . . an African despot, maybe, or a Colombian drug king . . . the kind of a fellow who can order the execution of an entire regiment without a moment's thought or delay."

The historian smiled wanly.

"Good," he said, "but not good enough. None of them commands an evil empire."

"Slums, racial hatred, illiteracy, poverty, disease . . ."

He interrupted me with the impatient gesture of a teacher looking for a different answer.

"Too un-American, too close to home. Ask too many questions along those lines, and you come across somebody you know—a campaign contributor or your brother-in-law."

"The environment," I said, ". . . acid rain, toxic wastes, dead fish . . ."

"Too complicated, and too many unintended puns. Begin with something specific, like surgical needles on a beach or the lobsters sick with tumors in Narragansett Bay, and you end with the moral vacuum that floats the bubble of advanced capitalism. Remove the needle from the beach, and Aunt Mary, who does so much for charity, loses the fortune and the town house. Rescue the lobster, and Providence, Rhode Island, can't afford to pay its schoolteachers."

"But that's the point," I said. "Everybody learns that nobody's innocent."

The historian laughed and shook his head.

"You learn that from literature, not from politics."

The orchestra played a fanfare, and the owner of the house (a Wall Street bond salesman said to have earned $100 million from the destruction of companies) grasped a microphone and began his much-rehearsed introduction of the evening's politician. The American flags on the tent poles fluttered placidly in an offshore breeze.

"If I were managing Bush's campaign," the historian said, "I'd send him to study with George Steinbrenner."

Democracies, he explained, trade in two markets—the market in expectation and the market in blame. The collapse of prices in one market entails the rise of prices in the other. To watch the New York Yankees lose was to wonder what Steinbrenner, the team's principal owner, would say in the next day's papers. Which player or pitching coach would he name to the roster of villains plotting against the happiness of the American people?

"Like Steinbrenner," the historian said, "politicians need somebody to blame. Not an abstraction—not the chemical industry or the ozone layer, but somebody with a name and a face and a current address. Preferably somebody in uniform."

As well as supplying both the economic and iconographic staples of American life, he said, the belief in the lost Soviet empire provided the domestic excuse for collective and individual behaviors that otherwise might be seen as despotic or cruel.

Let a man ask why the government sets up surveillance of its own citizens, or why so many Americans must go hungry or live in poverty and despair or why American politics has become so mean-spirited and small, and invariably the answer turned on a variation of the nostrum, "Yes, but think how much worse it would be in Russia."

"But Bush," the historian said, "doesn't know who to blame for what. Anybody he names to the lineup is likely to be a friend of Oliver North or a business associate of Edwin Meese."

We walked to the other side of the house, away from the speeches and the torchlight. A light fog was lying along the beach, and the air was sweet with the scent of honeysuckle. In a well-ordered state, I thought, the people would elect a council of scapegoats and hags who would present themselves as villains for all occasions—in traffic court, at ball games, in corporate boardrooms, at Cabinet meetings. When things went wrong, as surely they must, the respectable people could point and jeer and know they had seen the goblin who had blown the deal, run the red light, or lost, by a score of 5–2, Southeast Asia and "the spirit that made this country great."

Pursuing his own lines of reflection, the historian said: "As enemies go, the Russians were better than most. They had the shambling and clumsy demeanor of familiar trolls—unspeakably sinister, of course, but so thoroughly incompetent as to allow for the hope of escape."

Raising his glass in a gesture of farewell, he offered a toast to the legion of lost enemies.

"They came, as all good villains should, from the land of ice and snow, and they never spoiled a good story by trying to make it come true. We'll be lucky to see their like again."

HARPER'S MAGAZINE,
*October 1988*

# FIN DE SIÈCLE

**I**N A LITERARY journal the other day I noticed that a woman with a sense of humor, the English novelist Angela Carter, already had become wary of end of the century sermons. "The *fin*," she noted, "is coming early this *siècle*." It's true that for the better part of the last two years none of us has been safe from the din of prophecy. The evil omens appear every week in the newspapers and public opinion polls, on the television networks and with every delivery of a newsletter forecasting depletion of the reserves of oil and deutsche marks and conscience. Almost without exception, the seers who look into the abyss of the millennium predict catastrophes appropriate to the fears of the audiences they have been paid to alarm. The season's political candidates talk about both the trade and the moral deficit; economists who compose statistics for banks announce the collapse of the international monetary system; environmentalists mention the loss of the Atlantic Ocean. Authorities less well-informed make do with polite and conversational remarks about the likelihood of plague, famine, revolution, and war.

On the assumption that at least some of these people know what they are talking about, I conclude that the 1990s will foster a boom in the markets of transcendence. Who will not want to escape from a world made hideous by anarchy and disease? If only half the prophesies come true, the final decade of the twentieth century should bring about an era of unparalleled prosperity for the dealers in miracles and redemptions.

In the Middle East, the dream of heaven already trades at inflated

**378**

prices. The Ayatollah Khomeini, having promised the faithful to cleanse the world of corruption, counts as a possible cost of this endeavor the death of the entire population of Iran. His pronouncement was received by crowds in Teheran with demonstrations of joy.

Given such an auspicious beginning, I expect that the misfortunes of the *fin de siècle* will satisfy the expectations of all but the most implacable prophets. Even so, against the pessimism implicit in the omens, I like to think that the millennium offers as much of an occasion for hope as for dread. I think it fair to assume that the undesired and unexpected events of the next ten years will revive in the United States, as well as elsewhere in the West, the use of both the political and the artistic imagination. With any luck, this revival might lead not only to a lessening of human misery in Des Moines and East Los Angeles but also to an improvement in the texture of the nation's literature. My optimism follows from the assumption that the United States will be forced to give up its dream of innocence as well as its dream of power. I expect that it no longer will be possible to preserve the illusion, so lovingly cherished for a period of forty years, that nothing has changed—at least not in any important or fundamental way—since the end of the Second World War. The immense discoveries of the twentieth century might themselves at long last impose on the attention of the American equestrian class, and this in turn might make it possible for a sufficient number of people to see and conceive of a world infinitely more beautiful, more creative and diverse than the one reflected in the mirrors of the self.

As I read the Ayatollah's program for spiritual purity, I cannot help hearing, as if in the fading echo of a Bob Dylan song, the voices of transcendence that have subjugated American art and politics ever since the first days of the Kennedy Administration. The Ayatollah desires to rid the world of "devils"—that is to say, of feminists, communists, imperialists, sodomites, journalists, profiteers, Israelis, merchants, lawyers, Americans, and anybody else who doesn't love him. To this end, his firing squads execute "God's enemies."*

---

* Before he died, the Ayatollah reduced the general categories of the world's enemies to the specific person of Salman Rushdie, the novelist on whose head he placed the sum of $1 million.

Unhappily, his egoism has a familiar sound. In the United States for the past twenty years, spokesmen for various agencies of the higher consciousness have located the world's wickedness in the personae of oil companies, media syndicates, big business, black men, white men, the federal government, homosexuals, and real estate developers. During the heyday of what was known as "The New Left," Susan Sontag identified the white race as the cause of the world's sorrow. The triumph of the neoconservative right shifted the blame to black welfare mothers and Colombian drug dealers. Attorney General Edwin Meese wishes to search the American electorate for impurities in its blood, its urine, and its speech. The Reverend Pat Robertson promises the voters in Iowa and New Hampshire that if elected President, he will purge the State Department of diplomats stained with the sins of the eastern establishment. As a defense against AIDS, Mayor Koch exhorts the people of New York to swear the vows of monastic celibacy, and the Reverend Jerry Falwell goes about the country accompanied by a choir and a battery of American flags, assuring the faithful that "Jesus was not a pacifist" and inciting them to rise up against "the infidels" in the public schools who teach Satan's doctrine of "secular humanism."

Whether employed in the service of religion or the service of the state, the transcendental voice shouts down the objections of the merely human. Who could dare defile the beauty of an ideological abstraction by something so contemptible as a specific case in point? For the sake of a social program, who would be so tasteless as to bring up this or that particular individual caught up in the confusion of suffering and desire? Abstractions prevent the servants of the id from seeing what they are doing, and this allows them to thrust weapons into the hands of Arab despots (in the name of preserving peace in the Middle East), or to place the economy in the safekeeping of speculators (in the name of Keynes or Adam Smith), or to kill as many people as might be required to purify the race (in the name of Allah or the thousand-year Reich).

During the decade of the 1960s the transcendent impulse in the United States allied itself with the parties of hope and optimism. All the authorities agreed that we had conquered the earth. If the country possessed unlimited wealth and power, then the inheritors of the American fortune saw no reason why they should not live forever. God had been made manifest in everybody under the age of thirty, the stock market boom assured the ceaseless renewal of temporal credit, and even seminary students believed in the capacity of government to reopen the gates of Eden. The Republican Risorgimento of the 1980s allied the transcendental impulse with the parties of memory and pessimism. The locus of moral purity shifted from time future to time past. President Reagan campaigned on the promise to restore the ease and innocence of an imaginary American Arcadia that combined the simplicity of poverty with the luxury of wealth.

As in the 1960s so also in the 1980s—the art and politics of the age provided a defense against the awareness of death and time; the imagination served as a means of escape from a reality suddenly become too ambiguous, too complex, too hard to express in the space of ninety seconds or at the length of fifty words. The fear of change encouraged the belief that the happy few were opposed by monsters and apparitions instead of by the ordinary human interests and desires of other human beings. This imparted a sense of moral significance to the lives of people who lacked occasions to read and think. The simplification sustained the illusion that nothing had occurred, either in Detroit or the Persian Gulf, that might make it necessary for the American self to concede the humiliation of its own mortality.*

Over the course of the next ten years the makers of American fables will be hard-pressed to make people believe that the world is so much painted scenery. To the extent that the reserves of money and light fail to magically replenish themselves, or that governments fail to work the secular miracle of the loaves and fishes, the United States might come to recognize itself as a nation among nations, and its citizens might come to think of themselves as mortal

---

* By the end of 1989 it was becoming increasingly difficult to pretend that the world was still more or less the way it was in 1945 or 1965. In Detroit the Japanese were making as many cars as the Americans, and in Moscow Mikhail S. Gorbachev was pressing for an end to the Cold War and a thorough reform of the Soviet political system; in Brussels an army of European bureaucrats was constructing (in nine official languages) the foundation of a newly united Europe; and in Beijing the Chinese were confronted with an urgent and rising trend toward free markets and free expression.

men among mortal men, who acquire strength and wisdom only by acknowledging their habitual stupidity and weakness.

Montaigne put the point as follows: "People try to get out of themselves and to escape from the man. This is folly. Instead of transforming themselves into angels they turn themselves into beasts; instead of lifting, they degrade themselves. These transcendental humours frighten me, like lofty and inaccessible heights."

Over against the parties of transcendence stand the parties of experience—the quack doctors and astrologers opposed by philosophers and physicians, the demagogues opposed by magistrates, the faith healers by parish priests. The parties of experience never enjoy much of a popular following. Their spokesmen speak the language of conjecture and speculation, which is dull and wearisome and muffled in doubt. To listen to the voices of experience is to condemn oneself to being proved always mistaken. The most beloved certainties last no longer than a few seasons and vanish as suddenly as an autumn frost. Neither intellect, nor courage, nor the best of intentions can protect a political policy, a scientific discovery, or a fashionable truth against the erosions of the weather.

Who can endure so terrible a blow to his self-esteem? No wonder so many people assign the blame for their damaged egoism to external events, and speak of humiliations in Nicaragua and Afghanistan. The very contingency of life is inflammatory, exciting people to frenzies of simplicity and rage. Who can deny the indescribable pleasures of abandoning oneself to the infantile wish for omnipotence? The Iranian crowd expresses its joy and enthusiasm on being informed of the Ayatollah's murderous jihad against the complexities of the ego. A comparable excitement animates the crowds pushing into the gambling casinos at Atlantic City seeking to lose themselves in the formlessness of orgy.

Even so, and much to everybody's annoyance, the party of experience constitutes the last, best, and only hope of mankind. This is a galling and bitter thing to acknowledge, but the artifact of civilization has been made by men willing to acknowledge not only Montaigne's point but also the observation of Edmund Burke, who said: "Society cannot exist unless a controlling power upon will and appetite be placed somewhere, and the less of it there is within, the more of it there must be without."

For the last three decades American opinion, like Molière's *Le Bourgeois Gentilhomme*, has been loath to admit that the world is not oneself. As this habit of mind becomes both more dangerous and more patently absurd, I expect the country to regain its characteristically sardonic humor and to value wisdom over sanctity. It might even be possible for the country to take as its motto the inscription with which the ancient Athenians welcomed the conquering armies of Pompey the Great: "You are a god only insofar as you recognize yourself as a man."

*Sermon at Grace Cathedral,*
*San Francisco, January 1988*

# INDEX

# ABOUT THE AUTHOR

Born in San Francisco, Lewis H. Lapham was educated at Yale and Cambridge universities. He is the author of numerous essays, articles, broadsides, reports, satires, and reviews for a wide variety of publications: *The Saturday Evening Post, National Review, Life, Forbes, The New York Times, Fortune, The Wall Street Journal, Vanity Fair,* and *The Observer.* In 1980 he published his first collection of essays, *Fortune's Child;* in 1988 he published *Money and Class in America.* He has been editor of *Harper's Magazine* twice (1976–1981 and from 1983) and writes a monthly essay for that magazine under the rubric *Notebook.* He appears as the host of the weekly PBS series "Bookmark" and is the writer and host of the PBS documentary series "America's Century." Mr. Lapham lives in New York City with his wife and three children.